JANE ROBI————————————————————in history
witnessed by ———————————————————— travellers
(*Wayward Women, Unsuitable for Ladies, Angels of Albion,* and *Parrot Pie for Breakfast*) have established her as a scholarly social historian with an appreciative eye for eccentricity. Visit www.jane-robinson.com to find out more about Jane and her work.

Mary Seacole

The Charismatic Black Nurse
Who Became a Heroine of the Crimea

JANE ROBINSON

ROBINSON
London

Constable & Robinson Ltd
3 The Lanchesters
162 Fulham Palace Road
London W6 9ER
www.constablerobinson.com

First published in the UK by Constable,
an imprint of Constable & Robinson Ltd 2005

This revised paperback edition published by Robinson,
an imprint of Constable & Robinson Ltd 2006

A copy of the British Library Cataloguing in
Publication Data is available from the British Library

ISBN-13: 978-1-84529-497-7 (pbk)
ISBN-10: 1-84529-497-1
ISBN-13: 978-1-84119-677-0 (hbk)
ISBN-10: 1-84119-677-0

Printed and bound in the EU

1 3 5 7 9 10 8 6 4 2

To Diana

Contents

List of Illustrations		ix
Introduction and Acknowledgements		xi
Maps		xv
1	A Female Ulysses	1
2	Daughter and Doctress	21
3	Up and Doing	39
4	An Inclination to Rove	57
5	Pomp, Pride and Circumstance	75
6	Enjoying it Amazingly	93
7	Comfort and Order	113
8	Proud and Unprotected	135
9	A Bold Front to Fortune	153
10	The Crimean Heroine	171
11	Age and Consequence	189
	Notes and References	203
	Bibliography	217
	Index	225

Illustrations

Mary Seacole's neighbourhood in downtown Kingston, Jamaica (*Courtesy of the National Library of Jamaica*)

Up-Park Camp, Kingston, where Mary and her mother nursed British servicemen (*Courtesy of the National Library of Jamaica*)

The earliest known likeness of Mary, in her mid-forties (*Courtesy of the National Library of Jamaica*)

The infamous Lola Montez (*Courtesy of Mary Evans Picture Library*)

The Dutch screw-steamer *Hollander*, which took Mary to Istanbul on its maiden voyage (*Courtesy of Collection Municipal Archives Rotterdam*)

Balaklava Harbour at the time of Mary's arrival in the Crimea, photographed by James Robertson (*Courtesy of the author*)

Mary's Crimean stamping ground, between Balaklava and Sevastopol (*Courtesy of the author*)

A powerfully eloquent portrait of Mary painted in 1869 by A.C. Challen (© Courtesy Helen Rappaport / National Portrait Gallery, London)

The original cover of Mary's autobiography, 1857 (*Courtesy of the Bodleian Library, University of Oxford*)

A sketch by Florence Nightingale's friend, Lady Alicia Blackwood, showing the position of the British Hotel (*Courtesy of the Florence Nightingale Museum Trust,* www.florence-nightingale.co.uk)

The site of the British Hotel as it looks today (*Courtesy of the author*)

Mary featured in *Punch*, 30 May 1857, dispensing copies of the magazine to cheer her patients at the Land Transport Corps Hospital.

The celebrated Chef Alexis Soyer visiting the British Hotel.

The Royal Surrey Gardens Music Hall on London's South Bank (*Courtesy of Mary Evans Picture Library*)

An announcement of Mary's benefit festival at the Royal Surrey Gardens in the summer of 1857.

A bust of Mary Seacole sculpted by her friend Count Gleichen (*Courtesy of Conway Library, Courtauld Institute of Art*)

The only known photograph of Mary Seacole, taken in about 1873, when Mary was nearing seventy (*Courtesy of the Amoret Tanner Collection*)

Introduction and Acknowledgements

Authors don't usually attempt an Introduction until the rest of the book is finished. That might sound perverse, but it's quite sensible. That final stage is when they should be at their most objective, best able to distil the essence of their work into a promising aperitif. So I find myself now, a week away from my publisher's deadline, in a room still musky with the scent of Mary Seacole's presence, trying to sum up in a few short paragraphs a woman to whom I've been closer during the past two years (in many ways) than any other.

It can't be done. I could tell myself that Mary's too large a person, and personality, to cope with in such a confined space, and that it would be doing her a disservice to attenuate her extraordinary achievements in any way. But really, it's because I lack the courage, and conviction, to try. No one shares a stage with Mary with any degree of comfort or success. No one ever did. What's more, précis leads too often to over-generalizing and pigeonholing, which are two of the cardinal sins of biography I'm anxious to avoid.

Mary Seacole's greatest qualities were her warmth and spontaneity, and her most precious possession was her own idiosyncrasy. All her life people responded to her instinctively, and rarely analysed her motivation or her rationale. Yet since her death in 1881, her reputation has suffered from being crammed into a series of narrow, politically correct boxes with regulation labels proclaiming her (depending on who's doing the cramming) to be either a black heroine or a Victorian feminist, a medical or literary pioneer, an alternative Florence Nightingale, a brave imperial victim, a champion of ethnic minority, a political subversive – even a complete charlatan. She was some of these things in part, no doubt, but none of the labels defines her.

I suppose it's Mary's versatility and charisma that prove her so irresistibly appealing to those in search of an icon, particularly given the unhelpful circumstances of her gender and colour, her time and place. She advanced no cause but her own, however, and never saw herself as a representative. Two things were pre-eminent in her life: the achievement of her personal aspirations, and due recognition for that achievement by those she respected. She had panache and integrity, but little missionary zeal, and no desire to be at the vanguard of anything.

Mary was a true eccentric, relying entirely on herself to make the decisions that shaped her life and guided her strange odyssey from the disadvantaged streets of Kingston, Jamaica, into the homes and hearts of the British Empire's finest. I don't want to dull any of her gaudy originality with earnest discussions of what being Mary Seacole meant, nor am I interested in painting a picture of her to look at. I'd rather try to illuminate the real thing: to clean the glass (that's all it is) that separates our world from hers, and look through. It's been obscured by the accumulated grime of a century's prejudice, forgetfulness, and ignorance; now it's time to let in some light.

A word about sources: Mary always insisted on speaking for herself. This biography owes much, therefore, to her own account, *Wonderful Adventures of Mrs Seacole in Many Lands*, published in 1857. The epigraphs at the beginning of each of my chapters are all taken from

Mary's book. The best modern reprint to date is Ziggi Alexander and Audrey Dewjee's lovingly researched edition of 1984 (published in Bristol by the Falling Wall Press). Since Mary never kept a diary, and none of her letters survives, her autobiography is (almost) our only means of hearing her voice. It's a loud voice, though, and carries far. I have also used contemporary newspaper accounts, official and unofficial records, assorted ephemera, a few portraits, and the memoirs of those who knew her, to reinvigorate this most improbable of Victorian celebrities.

It should be no surprise that Mary Seacole still has a large (and growing) number of friends and acquaintances around the world. After all, she was – and remains – an impressive woman. It's been an unexpected bonus, though, that so many of them have shown such generosity in sharing their knowledge and impressions of her character, her career and her background. I am grateful to them all, but some deserve a special mention for services well beyond the call of scholarly duty. In Jamaica, I couldn't have done without Patricia Jackson's assiduous research; Aleric Josephs of the University of the West Indies at Mona invited me into her home to talk of Mary; Eppie Edwards of the National Library of Jamaica and Lisa Whiteman of the Institute of Jamaica both helped point me in interesting directions; Christopher Thompson guided me through downtown Kingston with pride and great care, and everyone at Strawberry Hill was wonderful. My good friends Larissa Kazachenko and Professor Natalia Ischenko were responsible for the success of my visit to the Crimea, together with Ian Fletcher, Ludmilla Golikova, Simon Butt and Anna Rosikhina.

I'm indebted to Professor Elizabeth Anionwu CBE FRCN, Head of the Mary Seacole Centre for Nursing Practice, Thames Valley University, for her help, encouragement and inspiration; Jenny Lightstone of Minneapolis for information on the Seacoles; Charles and Veronica Bunbury and their family for access to the letters of their kinsman Colonel Henry Bunbury; Chris Willis for her open-handed expertise and support; Amoret Tanner of the Tanner Collection for allowing me to reproduce Mary's photograph; Major Brian Oldham

MBE and Helen Robinson for their advice on the typescript; my editor Carol O'Brien and agent Caroline Dawnay for their heartening enthusiasm, and to the following people for information or advice: John Barham, Nick Barratt, John Bilcliffe, Ron Brand of the Maritime Museum in Rotterdam, Frank Clement-Lorford, Revd Ian Dickie of the Westminster Roman Catholic Diocesan Archives, John Gilmore, Eddie Glynn, Norman Gooding, Jim Guerin of St Mary's Catholic Cemetery at Kensal Green, Tina Harrup, Pete Helmore, Paul Kerr, Ruth Kitchin at the National Museum of Photography, Film and Television, Ben Ledden at the BBC, Tony Margrave, Connie Mark, Col. I.H. McCausland, Polly Patullo, Susan Ranson of the Claydon House Trust, David Rogers, Sonja Royes-Willis, the Seacole family, Bruce Seymour, Fr Alexander Sherbrooke, Sr Monica Tywang, C.P.P. van Romburgh of the Netherlands Maritime Museum, Col. H.B.H. Waring OBE, J.V. Webb and Dinah Winch.

I'm very grateful to the curators and staff at these institutions for all their assistance: the Black Cultural Archives in Brixton, the British Library Newspaper Library, the Crimean Patriotic Fund archive at Essex County Record Office, the Florence Nightingale Museum, the Imperial War Museum, the Institute of Jamaica, the National Army Museum, the National Library of Jamaica, the National Maritime Museum, the News International Archive, the Public Record Office, Punch, Regimental archives throughout the UK, the Royal Archives at Windsor Castle, Sevastopol Museum of the Heroic Defence and Liberation, Southwark Local History Library, Suffolk County Record Office, the Thomas Cook Archives and the Victoria and Albert Museum.

Finally, special thanks to Edward James, my classroom consultant on Seacole matters; to Richard James, who, when I was fretting about exploring Kingston, advised me to relax and travel 'in the spirit of Mary'; and to Bruce, who shares that spirit too.

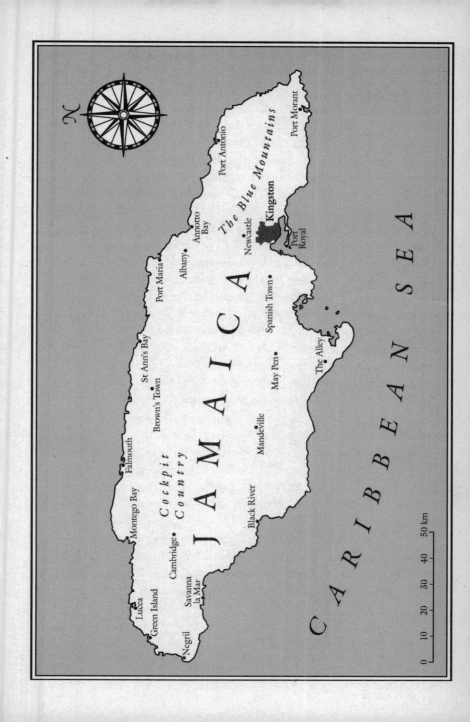

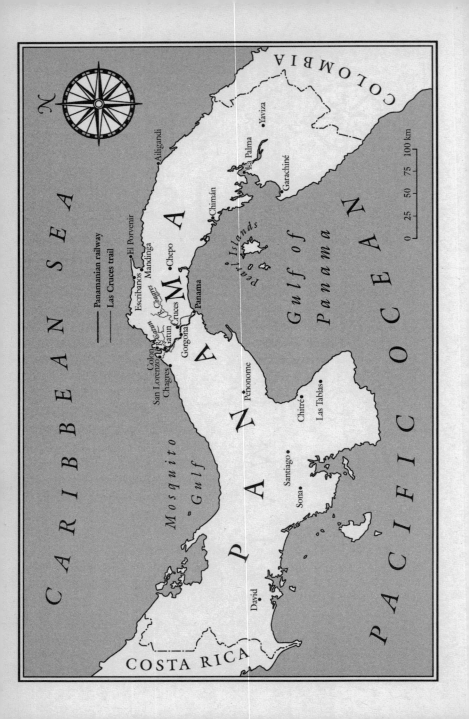

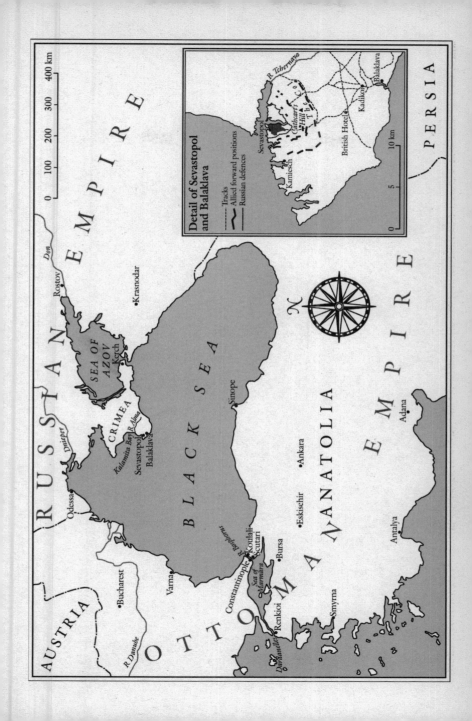

AUSTRIA

RUSSIAN EMPIRE

Don

Dnieper

Rostov

•Krasnodar

SEA OF
AZOV

Kerch

CRIMEA

Kalamita Bay

R. Alma

Sevastopol

Balaklava

BLACK SEA

Odessa

•Bucharest

R. Danube

Varna•

Bosphorus

Constantinople•Koulali
•Scutari

•Bursa

Sea of
Marmara

Dardanelles•Renkioi

Smyrna

OTTOMAN EMPIRE

ANATOLIA

Sinope

•Ankara

•Eskisehir

Antalya

Adana

PERSIA

0   100   200   300   400 km

N

Detail of Sevastopol and Balaklava

R Tchernaya

Sevastopol

Cathcart's Hill

British Hotel

Kamiesch

Kadikoi

Balaklava

Tracks
Allied forward positions
Russian defences

0   5   10 km

1

A Female Ulysses

Some people . . . have called me quite a female Ulysses. I believe that they intended it as a compliment.

Anyone studying the British history of the Crimean War soon becomes, by default, a connoisseur of the bizarre. All military campaigns have their moments of madness, but this one bordered at times on the surreal. Think of the Charge of the Light Brigade: why should a largely superfluous and suicidal episode – a disaster – remain the defining image of what was essentially a victorious campaign? How did Britain find itself allied to an Islamic Empire at war with fellow Christians? It's barely credible that the imperial administration, while busy enmeshing half the globe in a cloak of colonial officialdom, still struggled to organize enough food and clothing during the Crimean winter to keep its army alive, never mind fighting fit. And, on the face of it, it's absurd that when the war ended in 1856, two of its most celebrated veterans were women. One of them was a small, pale, thin-lipped spinster from the English shires with a rarefied upbringing and an urge for reform. The other was Mary Seacole.

Mary's unlikely odyssey from the place of her birth down by the docks in Kingston, Jamaica, to national heroism in the Crimea began in 1805. Then, her hometown appeared a pleasant place to be. One enthusiastic British visitor reckoned Kingston 'the largest, best-built, most opulent, and spacious town we have in the West Indies'.[1] It stretched for about a mile along the south-eastern coast of the island and half a mile inland towards a fine range of sheltering mountains. Its buildings were regularly organized in grid-patterned streets, the houses in single or double storeys with lacy 'gingerbread' carvings on the eaves and verandas, and roofed in silver cedar shingles or 'shakes'. The public buildings around the squares and parades up-town stood more proudly of brick or stone (often the ballast of incoming merchant ships). Its prosperous harbour was protected by a 10-mile spit of land, a protective, embracing arm with the former citadel of Port Royal like a clenched fist at the end.

Before the great earthquake of 1692 Port Royal had been huge both in size and importance. Founded by the British a year after their capture of Jamaica in 1655, it grew from a collection of forts to a city of some 8,000 souls. It was the base of the British navy, home to the island's British governor, and headquarters of the government-sponsored pirates who buccaneered about the Caribbean Sea disposing of the Spanish. In those days Port Royal was an opportunists' dream. Merchants, traders, buyers, sellers, parasites and criminals of every degree came to gorge on its free-flowing wealth and by the time the quake came, with a tidal wave to tidy up afterwards, it had earned a notorious reputation as 'the wickedest city on earth'.[2]

Only one tenth of Port Royal survived 1692. The rest still lurks nastily a few metres beneath the surface of the sea, as though intending to rear up from the underworld again when the time is right. Planning the replacement town of Kingston was a chance for the British to start again, and it was designed to be altogether more wholesome, orderly and attractive than Port Royal. No doubt many of its 11,000 residents in 1805 found it so, despite the temporary ravages of several further hurricanes and earthquakes in the years since its founding. A splendid aqueduct elegantly conducted fresh water from the Blue Mountains, lending an impression of salubrity; there were new, neat little churches, a theatre, a thriving (if somewhat profane) Sunday market and, visitors noted, an easy and cheerful tendency amongst its inhabitants to make music, dance and celebrate. Maria Nugent, the governor's wife, lived in Jamaica from 1801 to 1805, and described a typical Christmas carnival in the idiom of the time:

> 26th [December]. Nothing but bonjoes [sic], drums, and tom-toms, going all night, and dancing and singing and madness, all the morning . . . Some of our blackies were most superbly dressed, and so were several of their friends, who came to join in the masquerade; gold and silver fringe, spangles, beads, &c. &c. and really a most wonderful expense altogether . . .[3]

But, for all its supposed attractions, people like Maria, the white ruling class, rarely chose to inhabit Kingston themselves. The climate down by the coast was clammy and debilitating. It made the sequins on one's dresses dull and sticky, and dyes dissolved to stain the skin; multiple layers of stockings had to be worn to foil mosquitos, and books grew foxed and mouldy. There were more pests in the town than up in the hills, too – mostly of the insect variety, but not exclusively so. Maria continued her diary:

> 27th. Noise all night; and, if possible, to-day worse than ever . . . At 9, all was profoundly quiet throughout the town; for almost every woman as well as every man was so exceedingly tipsy, they could do nothing but sleep; and I may say, too, so thoroughly fatigued with their dancing and masquerading, poor things! Though people say, they are all really so drunk they are unable to move.[4]

Kingston was, and is, an edgy town. A town of facades. For those, including Mary Seacole in her 1857 autobiography, whose interests were best served by presenting it – even perceiving it – in terms of its success, or its Britishness, it might indeed have seemed an amusing and good-natured place. Exotic, given the almost overwhelming preponderance of black and coloured faces over white, but generally relaxed. It was a fact of life that the majority of Kingston's inhabitants, like the majority of the whole island's, were slaves, or slaves' descendants. But that was all part of the general orderliness of things. Edward Long, in his distasteful *History of Jamaica* (1774), composed a little ditty refuting any Rousseau-like ideas of savage Jamaican nobility:

> The general *order*, since the whole began,
> Is kept in *nature*, and is kept in *man*.
> *Order* is heaven's first law; and thus confest,
> Some *are*, and *must be*, *greater* than the rest.[5]

Anna Maria Falconbridge, a visitor to Jamaica in 1793, saw many pragmatic advantages in the British subjection of African negroes. She had sailed from Sierra Leone to Kingston aboard a transport ship (on which effigies of William Wilberforce and Tom Paine, both ardent abolitionists, were gleefully burned by the officers en route) and found conditions to be both sanitary and comfortable. 'All the slaves I had the opportunity of seeing in Jamaica seemed vastly well satisfied,' she wrote, 'and they discovered more cheerfulness than I ever observed the Blacks shew in Africa, unless raised by liquor.'[6]

Her optimism is misleading, but she neither sought nor found any reason to change her mind. She described her ship's arrival at the Kingston wharves, where its human cargo would be severally sold into bondage at one of the plantations; there it could expect to be housed, fed and given the freedom to garden a patch of land. The proceeds of this little allotment could be sold for personal profit at Sunday market. There were slave hospitals (probably next to the stinking punishment blocks) at many of the principal plantations to attend to bodily needs; Christian missionaries were spreading over the island to take care of underdeveloped souls (and conveniently quash any worldly ambition). To protect the good, or acquiescent, from the pernicious influence of discontents and malefactors, a local militia was stationed throughout the colony, with thousands of free men of almost every hue in its ranks, and white officers to keep control.[7] In fact the caption to an eighteenth-century print of a plump and beaming negro says it all:

> Me sing all day, me sleep all night;
> Me hab no care, my heart is light;
> Me tink not what tomorrow bring,
> Me happy so me sing.[8]

A slave 'free' of responsibilities was supposed to be a happy slave, and a happy slave was a productive one.

Of course, blithe Mrs Falconbridge, together with the bigoted Mr Long and thousands of other Jamaican observers, were unaware, often voluntarily so, of the foul and greasy machinery brutally grinding away behind this shining society. Britain had been helping itself to Africans for a century and a half to man the sugar and other plantations that spread brazenly up the leafy hills of Kingston and along the margins of Jamaica's dense interior. By 1805 there were over 280,000 slaves at the disposal of their planter landlords in Jamaica. At the same time there were only 28,000 whites.[9] Those negroes who had survived the manacled voyage from home, usually brokered by more opportunistic Africans than they, were first 'seasoned' for a while to acclimatize them to their new conditions (during which time one would reckon on a quarter 'wastage' from illness, exhaustion or suicide). Then they would work till they dropped.

The British plantocracy was naturally loath to reward its workforce with any political privilege: apart from the half-acre 'provision grounds' many were granted on which to grow their market goods (which was itself advantageous to the island's economy, saving others the bother and expense of providing food), they had negligible rights. Rumblings of insurrection in the past taught imperialist entrepreneurs the prudence of zero tolerance. Look what had happened to neighbouring Saint-Domingue (Haiti) when, inspired by the French Revolution in 1789, its black slaves had bloodily overthrown their French masters and declared their island a free state.[10] It was a frightening precedent, given the overwhelming disproportion of slaves to non-slaves on Jamaica. The abolition of the British slave trade was a concept busily being ruminated in the mother-country – it was legally declared in 1807 – but that didn't mean that slaves already in ownership were entitled to freedom. Emancipation was not to happen for a good quarter-century yet.

Meanwhile the crippling British blockade of trade links with North America during the wars of Independence (resulting in 15,000 slave deaths due to starvation),[11] together with growing competition from the cane-fields of the East Indies and European sugar-beet, and preparations in Britain to end its subsidy of Jamaican exports, all conspired against those with a financial interest in the colony. The pressure was on, and while the planters cast around for other crops to maintain income – coffee, cotton, soft fruit, spices – their slaves were forced to work harder, and in harsher conditions, than ever.

To keep the numbers up, and because it was impossible to prevent it anyway, negroes were allowed to mate with one another, but a planter's desires overrode anyone else's. So new generations were born with varying degrees of white blood. These not-quite-negroes were graded – like sugar or coffee – into different castes with an elaborate taxonomy. The coarsest was the sambo, born of a mulatto and a black. A mulatto had one white and one black parent; a quadroon one mulatto and one white; a mustee one quadroon and one white; a mustiphini one mustee and one white; a quintroon one mustiphini and one white, and an octoroon, the most refined, one quintroon and one white.[12] In almost all cases it might safely be assumed that the white parent was the father. And although it was against the law for coloured offspring of a white father to inherit or otherwise benefit legally from his estate, such mixed parentage could mean freedom. As it did in the case of Mary Seacole's mother.

Mary was always coy about her origins. Most of what we know about her first-hand is written in her 1857 autobiography, *Mrs*

Seacole's Wonderful Adventures in Many Lands, reported in transcripts of the odd comment she made during a court case, recorded in her will, and printed in letters published in *Punch* and *The Times.*[13] No manuscript material survives, and as all the above, except – arguably – the will, were designed for a middle- or upper-class British audience, amongst whom Mary would count herself, they only reveal (ostensibly) what she wants to be revealed. She claimed vaguely that the nineteenth century and she were 'both young together', and that she was born a Creole – that is, a native of Jamaica (usually of mixed race) rather than a 'salt-water negro' from Africa or an expatriate European – with a 'Scotch' father and a Creole mother. Given the time and place one would not expect to find a register of her birth; nor has a baptismal record emerged (implying that she wasn't baptized in Jamaica, or that the relevant archive is lost: either more than likely).[14] But according to her death certificate, which states her age in 1881 to be seventy-six, it appears that she was born in 1805. Her mother, being a free Creole with African blood, was probably a mulatto, which would make Mary, technically, a quadroon. Mary was always proud of a complexion tinted rather than tainted, considering herself more yellow than brown. Predictably, the fairer one's skin in Kingston then – as, to a certain extent, now – the better one's social prospects and expectations. No matter how essential her African heritage was to her, and how crass a boast it might appear today, it would have been important to Mary that she had more white ancestors than black: three sets of grandparents to one.

Her mother, by vocation and profession, was a well-established and respected member of Kingston society, being both 'doctress' and lodging-house keeper. Healers like her, fusing generations of African culture with local Caribbean herbal remedies, provided an alternative or even complementary service to the inexperienced European doctors sent out to supervise the colony's health. A wan-faced gentleman who had never met local maladies before, pontificating uncertainly from books and looking (probably feeling) half-dead himself, can hardly have been as comforting to Creole patients – if indeed available to them – as the strong and knowing hands of a natural doctress. And because of their native immunity to some of the tropical diseases (particularly yellow fever) that seemed to sniff and snuff out weakling whites almost as soon as they disembarked, Creole women were frequently called upon to tend visiting Europeans too. Where a more conventional doctor might carry his black bag full of pills and instruments, women like Mary's mother would take a collection of flowers, stems, leaves and roots in various degrees of preparation and carefully match each 'simple', or single remedy, with its corresponding symptom.

The English botanist Thomas Dancer, who produced a book on Jamaican remedies in 1801, enthusiastically encouraged traditional practices amongst the European residents of the island because – quite simply – they worked.

> The virtues of Officinal, or Shop Medicines, and the manner of administering them being, in general, better understood, they are, in most cases, preferred, but many of the Simples of [this] Country are endued with considerable efficacy, and may be substituted for the Officinal ones.[15]

He recognized good common sense in the nettle/dock-leaf philosophy Mary herself described: that what harms and what heals us are never far apart.[16] Britain's greatest contemporary hero, Admiral Lord Nelson, was consumed by dysentery off the Caribbean coast of Central America in 1780; he gladly succumbed to the homely ministrations of Couba Cornwallis, a Jamaican doctress in Port Royal, when sent there to recuperate (or, more likely, die). A brand new naval hospital had been founded in Kingston the previous year, but it was ill-ventilated and full of disease: a dangerous place for the sick. Couba boiled thistle-seeds to calm his diarrhoea, water-lily roots to quench his thirst, lemongrass for his fever and fig-tree sap to soothe and cleanse his stomach. He thrived, and always thought fondly of Mrs Cornwallis thereafter.[17]

Mary's mother was the same sort of practitioner as Couba. Like Couba, too, she kept a lodging-house which doubled, when necessary, as a convalescent home for British officers and their families. Mary remembered her home, Blundell Hall, with great affection. It stood at the bottom of East Street, within hearing of the waves slapping at the low sea wall down by the wharves. East Street had no pavement: its buildings opened straight onto the road outside, which was hard as limestone and heavily rutted when dry but like molasses in the rainy season. There was a magnificent date palm by the neighbouring house, and if she stood outside and looked south towards the sea, she might see the neon flash of a hummingbird or a pelican lumbering by, against a background tangle of ships' masts and topgallants gently creaking and flapping, rising and falling, against the horizon. In the distance, if there was rain in the air, there would be a glimpse of Port Royal across the harbour.

Looking the other way she could follow the line of East Street straight up to the forested slopes of the Liguanea hills and the beginnings of the Blue Mountains beyond. There would hardly ever be silence in Kingston, but she could imagine coolness and quiet by gazing north through the haze to the heights. Not that Mary was ever much of a one for coolness and quiet. She preferred the bustle of Blundell Hall, especially when her mother was nursing there, and her patients, or guests, were officers of the British Army.

Mary's mother has not been given a name yet. Perhaps she was Jane, Mary's second name. It is most unlikely that she was married. Traditionally she would, as an intelligent and enterprising mulatto woman, have been the mistress of a white man – planter, officer, administrator – and have given their children his surname. She would not necessarily have taken his name herself, however. She might instead have kept her (white) father's name, or simply be known as Miss Jane. There would be no shame implied locally by the arrangement: her lover's money and influence would support any business ambitions and add to her social credibility and standing.[18] Visiting Europeans, of course, were apt to consider this well-established colonial practice proof of a shocking and innate laxity of morals amongst the natives. Or visiting European ladies did, at least. Maria Nugent was not surprised to hear while visiting a penn, or country estate, in 1802 that the little mulatto girl brought in to entertain her – a 'sickly delicate child, with straight light-brown hair and very black eyes' – was the daughter of her host, a 'cross old bachelor' who detested the society of women. He had numerous progeny, apparently: 'some almost on every one of his estates'.[19] Mary's parents' morganatic relationship would not have embarrassed her at all at the time. She would have been content that her father had chosen her mother to bear (some of?) his children and to help provide for his Creole family. Which begs the question of who, exactly, Mary's father was.

It's best to work backwards. There is an entry in the Kingston Registers of the death of a spinster, Louisa Grant, on 21 July 1905.[20] She was 'formerly a Lodging-house Keeper' and was ninety when she died. Mary Jane Seacole's will, written in 1876, made her sister Louisa Grant her main beneficiary, and when the novelist Anthony Trollope visited Kingston in the 1850s he was amused to find that the landlady of his hotel, 'Blundle's Hall', was none other than 'a sister of good Mrs Seacole'.[21] So Mary Seacole's unmarried sister's father was surnamed Grant. But Louisa must have been born in 1815: a full ten years after Mary. There was a brother Edward, probably born in between (as Mary always gave the impression of being the head of the family once her mother died): he appears to have had a different father. Mary's nephew, named in her will, was one Edward Ambleton; his baptismal record suggests that his father was another Edward Ambleton, who must surely be the Edward Mary speaks of as her brother.[22]

Mary never mentioned her own maiden name in her autobiography, but her marriage certificate recorded it, like her sister's, as Grant. She claimed her father was a soldier, and contributed the 'good Scotch blood' coursing through her veins. I'm sure she felt that further details would only worry her British readers, given what to most of them would be an unorthodox and discreditable upbringing. It would not have been unusual, after all, if Mary's mother (whom I shall call Jane) had had her children by different men. But there *was* an officer of the 60th Regiment of Foot, called the 'Royal

American Regiment' at the time, named James Grant; he was a Captain from 1802 to 1809 and then a Major until 1815, during all of which time the 6th Battalion of his Regiment was based in Jamaica. As luck would have it, no muster papers, service details or personal records of the 60th survive, and all we have to prove James Grant's existence is the Army List – from which he disappears in the year Louisa was born, perhaps to retire to Kingston, to a home and family in Scotland or the Isle of Wight (the 60th HQ), or to die.[23] But it's a good Scots name, and he's the only possible Grant whose posting spans the dates of Mary's and Louisa's births. He may have been stationed away from the island at the time of Edward's birth. He probably met Jane at Blundell Hall: maybe he succumbed, as so many of his colleagues did, to fever on arrival in Kingston in 1802, and Jane was his nurse. As in so many areas of Mary's life, we are dealing with informed likelihood rather than certainty here, but likelihood is all we've got.

Grant doesn't feature at all in Mary's account of her childhood, even though he must have been a part of it until she was at least ten. She does mention a voyage to and stay in England, probably in her teens, in the company of relatives who have been assumed in the past to be her father's, but they might just as easily have been her mother's. Jane was related to the Henriques family, members of whom were West Indian merchants who later settled in London and Ireland.[24]

Jane, on the other hand, had enormous influence on her daughter. Mary remembered her as 'an admirable doctress',

. . . in high repute with the officers of both services, and their wives, who were from time to time stationed in Kingston. It was very natural that I should inherit her tastes; and so I had from early youth a yearning for medical knowledge which has never deserted me. [25]

Mary used to watch Jane with her patients and copy what she did, using her doll as the victim: 'whatever disease was most prevalent in

Kingston, be sure my poor doll soon contracted it'. When the doll was too heavily bandaged and clogged up with potions to respond satisfactorily, the dogs and cats of East Street stood in, and when they had had enough of Mary's medicines and run away to be sick, she turned to herself. She not only learned what herbs and roots to look for, where to find them, and how to prepare them for use, but also, with typical thoroughness, what they tasted like and what effect they had on the body. It was all part of the experience she was to rely on later, not only as a doctress herself in Kingston, but when treating cholera and yellow fever in the dank and stifling heat of Central America, or dressing the wounds of dying men, her fingers numb with cold, on some bleak Crimean battlefield.

There was another woman in Mary's life, almost as important to her as her own mother, who receives tantalizingly short shrift in the autobiography. There she is just described as a surrogate grand-mother, 'kind patroness', 'an old lady, who brought me up in her own household among her own grandchildren, and who could scarcely have shown me more kindness had I been one of them'. Mary lived with this lady until early womanhood, when, after nursing her patroness through a long final illness, she returned to her mother, brother Edward and little Louisa at Blundell Hall. It wasn't particularly unusual for daughters to be thus farmed out. If it were not that Mary claims she grew lazy in the lady's house, one might assume that young Miss Grant was sent as a servant or companion to the grandchildren. It's more likely, however, that Mary, obviously quick-witted and eager to learn, was carefully placed away from the distractions of home (which she frequently visited) in the care of someone who could adequately educate her. Her patroness may have been a connection of James Grant's, since schooling of their coloured children, if undertaken at all, was usually the father's responsibility – either locally, privately, or back home in Britain. But whoever she was, she must have been remarkably perceptive and inspiring. She helped instil in this bustling little child with the determined grey eyes, thick, wavy hair and tender heart, a sense of ambition, self-confidence and optimism which shaped Mary's life.

She taught her not only how to read and write, but how to appreciate good reading and writing, and – perhaps even more important – to ignore the labels white society liked so much to fix to its various subjects. With the help of her parents and her patroness Mary grew up believing herself utterly uncircumscribed, either as illegitimate, coloured or a woman. She was an unusually lucky girl.

Mary's social position as the educated daughter of an officer and a respectable, useful mulatto woman, was well-founded in Jamaica. It may have been received wisdom amongst whites that a coloured skin represented a sort of dilution of civilization, but in Mary's milieu she was either ignorant or dismissive of any sense of her own inferiority. She was unaware – for the moment – of the prejudice she would encounter in London, devoutly believing North America to be principally responsible for the slave trade and all the vulgar dis-crimination that went with it. She had ached to go 'home' for as long as she could remember. Never shy, she would have begged her mother's recuperating patients to tell her about Great Britain, to describe the vast and smoky grandeur of London, the pastures and meadows that rolled for miles and miles, the castles and cathedrals of its past and its inconceivable millions of people. Her Scottish father would tell stirring stories of clans and Culloden; her patron-ess, assuming her to be of European origin, would reminisce about the belligerent reign of George II. Mary would try to imagine what it felt like to sit, tingling, in front of a coal fire while snow clung to the windows outside. She'd dream of the delicious 'pomp, pride and circumstance of glorious war' that veterans of Trafalgar remem-bered so longingly, and choose the best bits of all the British history she knew to piece together a great shimmering quilt in her mind, studded with kings and queens, lords and ladies, to keep her imagination warm until she could see for herself. Mary was a determined woman all her life, confident of her own capabilities. In her youth it may have seemed 'improbable', as she put it, that she would ever manage to get to Britain, but until it proved impossible, she was not to be put off.

Quite rightly: Mary was in her mid-teens, still living away from

home (although spending more and more time with Jane at Blundell Hall) when she made her first voyage. The seas around the
Caribbean were somewhat safer after British victory over Napoleon
at Waterloo in 1815, and if her father had died the same year, as
might be supposed from the Army List, he could have provided his
children and their mother with an unofficial legacy. It often happened: a disapproving Lady Nugent mentioned just such a case in
her journal.

> One of the Lieutenants of the Apostles' battery came as we were
> going to breakfast to announce the death of poor wretched
> Captain Dobbin. He died without seeing his children, and it is
> said has left all he is worth to his black mistress and her child.
> This is, I am afraid, but too common a case in Jamaica.[26]

Mary travelled to London with Creole companions, most probably
aboard a merchantman.[27] Crossing the Atlantic took on average six
to eight weeks, and would hardly have been a comfortable experience, even for a female Ulysses. Apart from the near inevitability of
sea-sickness, and the volatile mood of the weather, there were
some awkward practicalities to cope with. These ranged from mild
inconveniences – fielding the crew's attentions, for example, or
dining in an impossibly enclosed space from a shifting, sloping board
– to the more taxing problem of keeping smart and healthy (both
important to Mary) when things were so easily spilt or soiled and linen
couldn't be dried. A considerable and understandable preoccupation
of most lady passengers during the age of sail involved the indignity of
answering nature's call. This had to be done as discreetly as possible
on, or over, the deck. The quandary was described in 1829 as being
responsible in extreme cases for loss of life: modest Englishwomen
were too apt, through abstention, to poison their systems beyond
repair.[28] The robust and pragmatic Miss Grant was unlikely to be
troubled, however. She overcame all, relished the voyage, and disembarked in the finest of health and spirits.

If Mary's patroness ever urged her to keep a journal, as any lady of quality might be encouraged to do, it has failed to survive. If she wrote letters home to the family at Blundell Hall, so have they. Mary's first impressions of London would make captivating reading. Merchant shipping was allowed to sail right into the commercial heart of London. The magnificent West India Dock had become one of the sights of the city since its completion in 1802. It occupied 54 acres of the Isle of Dogs on the northern shore of the Thames between Blackwall and Limehouse Reach, hemmed in by a 6m (20ft) wall, and with breadth and depth enough for twenty ships at a time.[29] Imposing five-storey warehouses surrounded its import basin and the wharf was teeming with people: it took four days to discharge a cargo, requiring the combined ministrations of merchants, agents, captains and crew, clerks, stevedores, dockhands, messenger-boys and customs officials. Watching would be groups of sightseers and the occasional passenger, and watching *them*, the ubiquitous pick-pockets and assorted opportunists of London's industrious under-world.

Mary stayed in London for a year. Where she lived during this time, we don't know. A recommended lodging-house would be a possibility, although expensive: perhaps she was a guest of the relations with whom she had sailed. Certainly, her enthusiasm for the capital suggests that she must have felt both physically and temperamentally comfortable there. Yet it would be hard to envisage a city more different than the one she had left a few weeks before. Here, everything was new. There was a new king: George IV was crowned in July 1821, pasty and jaded after the profligacy of the Regency years, but offering his people the tenuous hope of a more prudent and peaceful future. His estranged queen, the deeply unengaging Caroline of Brunswick, had the final grace to die within weeks of the coronation, as did Napoleon Bonaparte, for so long national bogeyman. Britain's colonies were making it rich, and at home the Industrial Revolution was spewing rewards out of its mills, mines and factories. Engineers were the alchemists of the new era, promising to transmute steam and iron into locomotives and ships, and to celebrate (and advertise) all this, London, the embodiment of British aspiration, was being remodelled on a fantastic scale. Regent Street was just finished, along with stuccoed chunks of Mayfair; the more modest elegance of Bloomsbury was busy building in black brick and glass, and further out, uniform terraces governed by the strictest of regulations regarding height, width and aspect, were spreading with a dignified air along the streets of Marylebone, Kennington, and beyond.

On her frequent sorties from her lodgings, Mary would have found much to enthuse her. Apart from the usual pursuits – visits to the pleasure gardens and theatres, the British Museum or St Paul's Cathedral (already charcoal-black with grime), or to Rotten Row on a summer Sunday afternoon to watch the swells and dandies flaunt their finery – she would have enjoyed watching the Household Cavalry exercising in Hyde Park, or wandering through the markets which reminded her of home. Not just Covent Garden (fruit, vegetables and flowers), Billingsgate (fish), and Smithfield (meat), but Leadenhall market, where herbs were sold, or the New Cut at Lambeth, where anyone could sell anything of an evening with the help of a loud voice and a candle to see by, stuck in a turnip. There were barrowmen everywhere, and women stationed at street corners offering violets, ribbons, sweetmeats, song-sheets, or – if Mary had turned one corner too many – themselves.

For propriety's sake these sorties should only have been conducted in the company of a chaperone. But it's part of Mary's attraction that all through her life one is never quite sure how proper she really was. It's easy to picture her slipping out on her own, intoxicated by the vigour of the city. The only occasion on which Mary ever felt threatened during this first visit to London was during a jaunt with a young girlfriend from Kingston. Mary insisted it was only a vicarious uneasiness, due to children in the streets taunting her friend about her complexion: 'I am only a little brown – a few shades duskier than the brunettes whom you all admire so much; but my companion was very dark, and a fair (if I can apply the term to her) subject for their rude wit. She was hot-tempered, poor thing!'. Prejudice was an unwelcome novelty.

But then so, to some, were apparently respectable young coloured women out on the streets of London. African attendants had been a feature of British high society since the sixteenth century, when merchants brought them back to England as servants, novelties, or – as time went on – fashion accessories. By 1764 an alarmist article in the *Gentleman's Magazine* reckoned the number of blacks in London to be nearly 20,000; in reality it was more like 15,000 in the whole of Britain.[30] But the majority of these were in domestic or other service, and the number of 'free' black and coloured individuals was low. One or two had been famous, like Ignatius Sancho (1729–80), a London grocer with a musical and literary bent whose letters were published posthumously in 1782; Francis Barber (c1735–1801), Samuel Johnson's erstwhile valet who was educated in his thirties at grammar school and later became a schoolmaster himself, or Olaudah Equiano (c1745–97), ex-slave and ardent campaigner for the abolition of slavery. Most were anonymous, though, hidden in the houses or institutions they served, and by the time Mary and her friend were to be seen confidently swinging down the street, arm-in-arm, in the early 1820s, their numbers were dwindling anyway.[31] The most familiar black figure to most Londoners then would have been the unfortunate Sara Baartman, the so-called 'Hottentot Venus' stolen from the African Cape in 1810 and toured around the circuses, theatres and pubs of England for the next four years as a freak. Her owner kept her naked in a cage, and charged people to come and gawp at her highly developed buttocks and genitalia, and guess whether or not she might be human.[32] So no wonder the urchins were shocked into jeers. This isolated incident didn't take the shine off London for Mary, however. Miss Grant was nobody's victim.

It was London that made Mary into an entrepreneur. Along with the other female members of her family, she would be well used to selling home-grown produce on the Sunday stalls in Kingston (if there was any left over after the hotel took what it needed). Part of her domestic education would be learning to pickle fruit and vegetables to keep them beyond their season, and boil jams and jellies for the table. It always excited Mary to make money, and there was nowhere like London for commerce. Her merchant friends could tell her that: it was the hub of an empire-wide market with an apparently insatiable appetite for the exotic. The cargoes stored in its majestic warehouses were worth some £20,000,000, of which everyone who handled them, directly or indirectly, would claim their share.[33] It was a place for adventurers, where Mary came to the realization that that's exactly what *she* was. 'All my life long,' she wrote later, 'I have followed the impulse which led me to be up and doing; and so far from resting idle anywhere, I have never wanted inclination to rove, nor will powerful enough to carry out my wishes.'

In about 1823, a year after returning home to Kingston, Mary was back in London. This time she went on her own, and as a business-woman. She was eighteen. She took with her 'a large stock of West Indian pickles and preserves for sale', which she must have spent a good deal of the previous year at Blundell Hall preparing, and surely an even larger consignment of self-confidence. Women travelling 'unprotected', as Mary chose to do (although it is possible she may have had, as on subsequent expeditions, a maid or servant) were not unknown then, but hardly common. One might travel alone, as an emigrant aunt going out to join the family, a missionary heading for her heathen sisters abroad, a member of the so-called 'fishing fleet' sailing to India to find a husband, or an apprehensive governess on the way to a new appointment in St Petersburg or somewhere, but never without the protection of a sponsor, a missionary society, a government organization or an employer. Yet if Mary had the capital and really was as sure of herself and her ability to cope as she appears, there was nothing to stop her, least of all a lack of precedent.

This time she spent two years in the capital, during which time she obviously made enough to keep herself and to buy the passage home in 1825. There would have been various ways of doing this. She would use her contacts first, and sell to friends and those to whom she had been recommended by friends. But she may have approached hotels and restaurants too, or officers' messes and other army and navy establishments across the capital. She might even have hired herself a barrow for a few coppers a day, or a wooden stall, and sat with the others in the crowded market aisles of Leather Lane or Tottenham Court Road. It's inconceivable that Mary would not have travelled within the country (humming 'The Roast-Beef of Old England' the while), both to satisfy her much-vaunted curiosity and wanderlust, and to find new markets for the goods she must have continued to produce in London from imported ingredients or commissioned ready-made from home. This was a country renowned for its appetite, after all, where a hearty squire at a single sitting

> absorbed a plateful of haddock, another of veal, two of tongue, three of mutton, two of roast pig, a wing of duck, and half the tail of a lobster. It was not surprising that bulging veins, mottled noses and what was politely termed a full habit were common among the English upper and middle classes. Statesmen, judges, merchants, poets, all engaged in the national vice of stuffing.[34]

Even Jane Austen, who can never have stuffed in her life, admitted that 'good apple pies are a considerable part of our domestic happiness'.[35] These were people after Mary Seacole's own heart.

In an unwonted excursion into detail, Mary recorded in her autobiography the name of the vessel on which she eventually left England for Kingston on 22 November 1825. It was the *Volusia*, remarkable for the fact that it almost failed to make the voyage at all.

> Christmas-day had been kept very merrily on board our ship . . . and on the following day a fire broke out in the hold. I dare say it would have resisted all the crew's efforts to put it out, had not another ship appeared in sight; upon which the fire quietly allowed itself to be extinguished. Although considerably alarmed, I did not lose my senses; but during the time when the contest between fire and water was doubtful, I entered into

an amicable arrangement with the ship's cook, whereby, in consideration of two pounds – which I was not, however, to pay until the crisis arrived – he agreed to lash me on to a large hencoop.[36]

Nobody's victim, indeed.

2

Daughter and Doctress

I saw so much of [my mother], and of her patients, that the
ambition to become a doctress early took firm root in my mind.

The unfortunate *Volusia* finally made it to Kingston at the beginning
of February 1826, the hen-coop empty but still reassuringly strapped
in place on the deck. The crossing had lasted some ten weeks, and
desperate as Mary had been back in 1823 to 'see the blue hills of
Jamaica fade into the distance', the sight of them smudged above the
horizon as the crippled ship neared harbour must have been
annoyingly welcome. News travelled fast. By the time the *Volusia*
was alongside the wharves there was an excited crowd clamouring
for the wanderer returned: one can imagine Louisa, now ten, with
her half-brother Edward in his teens, and perhaps Mary's favourite
young cousins Amelia, Matilda and another Louisa;[1] the old lady's
grandchildren with whom she had grown up, and enough noisy
friends and relations to turn the occasion into a regular Kingston
party.

Jane would have been there, if her clients could spare her. But her feelings about this prodigal daughter must have been mixed. Perhaps Mary took after her father. She might look at first glance like her mother, share her mother's skills, enjoy what Mary herself recognized as the impetuosity and unreserved warmth of her mother's family, and be blessed with the sense of pride and enterprise that had served Jane so well. But Mary had salt blood in her veins, like the Grants. She felt compelled to explore the world and her place in it on her own terms: a true colonial. Jane must have been aware of Mary's egotism, occasionally swollen into arrogance, and a domineering and intractable air which would prove Mary a staunch friend to those she loved through life, but a difficult companion. Jane would be aware, too, that none of these characteristics came with a guarantee of happiness.

In 1826 Mary turned twenty-one. Sometime during the next few years her patroness died, and Mary went to live at Blundell Hall permanently. There was more than enough work for her to do. The wives of officers stationed at Up-Park Camp on the northern edge of the town tended to stay either at Jane's, at the Fairbrothers' neighbouring establishment Date Tree Hall (16 East Street) or at Charlotte Beckford's slightly more upmarket hotel a few miles away in Spanish Town. For straightforward guests like these, Mary would be busy in the kitchen with her sauces and stews, and supervising the staff, which included black servants. Here she learned the arts of hotel management, administration and catering on which she based her later career. More involving than any of these, however, and much more charismatic, was the art of healing.

Jamaica already had a medical infrastructure by this time, with Western conventional methods built rather flimsily on a solid folk foundation. A few generations ago African slaves had brought with them the uncompromising traditions of Obeah and Myal. Obeah was 'bad' medicine, a powerful cult of malevolence and harm involving chiefs, charms, elaborate rituals and fear. Myalism was its benevolent counterpart: more direct and tactile a method of influencing health and well-being. It developed into the healing culture of using simples and sympathy Mary inherited from her mother. The white authorities, shocked, disgusted and more than a little alarmed by the violence of the Obeah men, tried to stamp their practices out. They had the sense to encourage Myalism, though, albeit in a moderated and sanitized form. Its practitioners – mostly women, as African healers had always tended to be – slotted their skills profitably into the shaky superstructure of orthodox Western medicine the British felt they ought to impose on the Empire. There were plenty of hospitals (of dubious hygiene), including a spanking new naval one built on the remains of Port Royal in 1819, and even one for slaves a few miles north of Kingston at Half-Way Tree. The public hospital in Kingston itself was founded in 1776, three years before the military and slave hospitals opened in the town, and by 1830 there were some 300 Western doctors resident on the island, including army and naval surgeons, civil surgeons employed in the hospitals, and private or plantation doctors.[2] But there were also nurses. Coloured nurses. In Jamaica, as in Britain, they worked in parish hospitals or on call amongst the private homes of those who could afford their services, and in lodging-houses. Mary mentioned being in charge, like a hospital matron, of a number of nurses on occasions at Blundell Hall, and she was called upon herself to do duty on the ward at Up-Park.

All this, of course, was long before nursing was recognized as a genteel or even respectable profession for anyone but nuns. This breakthrough is generally put at 1833 in the West, when an institute for training lay 'deaconesses' in the care of the sick was founded in Kaiserwerth by a German pastor (one of its students was Florence Nightingale).[3] Organized nurses existed, demonstrably, before then, but none was supposed to be remotely like a lady, either in name or disposition. They were Sarah Gamp's unlovely forebears, and Jamaica had its fair share. Comments in the Kingston Council Minutes complain of their recidivist brutality, and one in particular, concerning the town's hospital, smacks of the reports Florence Nightingale herself was to write of similarly undesirable characters at work in the Crimea:

> . . . the abusive language made use of by the nurses to the patients is too bad to be made mention of and should you complain to the [white] matron she gives you no kind of satisfaction . . . [she] gets drunk mostly every evening. She associates with [the black – or more probably coloured – nurses] in consequence of which all is neglect . . . for it cannot be expected that Negroes will care anything about a white person who makes a companion of them.[4]

Perhaps there was too pungent a whiff of Obeah about some of these women to inspire the complete confidence of all their patients. Governor Nugent's wife Maria employed a local character, Flora, to assist at the birth of her son in 1802, but when push came to shove, rather lost confidence in her less than orthodox approach:

> [T]he old black nurse brought a cargo of herbs, and wished to try various charms, to expedite the birth of the child, and told me so many stories of pinching and tying women to the bed-post, to hasten matters, that sometimes, in spite of my agony, I could not help laughing, and, at others, I was really in a fright, for fear she would try some of her experiments upon me. But the maids took all her herbs from her, and made her remove all the smoking apparatus she had prepared for my benefit.[5]

Mary's bedside manner was rather more charming. She and her mother possessed an instinct not only to nurse – i.e. care for their patients – but to heal them. We would call them nursing practitioners now, but the local contemporary term of 'doctress' suits them well. Not only did Creole doctresses administer their own medicines, but they inoculated their patients, and were confident osteopaths, even minor surgeons, given the circumstances (i.e. when no Western gentleman was available).[6] Mary certainly never flinched at dressing wounds. And most of all, they had permission – being female – to talk to patients, listen to them, soothe them, hold them and hug them, to *mother* them. Mary was a wonderful mother.

Her favourite 'sons' were the poorly officers and men of the army. During the decade between her return from London and her marriage, she nursed soldiers of varying ranks from ten different regiments stationed in Jamaica, some of whom she would come across much, much later and very far away.[7] The majority were suffering from yellow fever – 'yellow jack' – which hit quickly and hard as soon as new recruits arrived. A discomfiting guidebook to the island warned them what to expect:

> It is most fatal to new-comers; persons long resident in the island, and consequently inured to the climate, generally escape it, while hundreds of the former are perishing around them. It is attended by a highly inflammatory febrile affection of the whole system, with a particular determination to the head, violent headache, nausea and irritation of the stomach, restlessness, pain and weakness of the spine, delirium, and an utter prostration of strength.

The usual remedy in Jamaica comprised 'powerful doses of calomel, in the outset, and, afterwards, milder laxatives as occasion requires' together with 'Peruvian bark mixed up in brandy and water'.[8]

If the patient survived the onslaught of the disease in hospital, he might well be moved to a place of convalescence like Blundell Hall, where Miss Jane and Mary, with the aid of hired help and little Louisa Grant, would coax them back to health with herbs and good humour. At this stage in her career Mary was more involved in aftercare than in treating the attack itself, although she never lost an opportunity to learn from the surgeons and physicians with whom she came into contact, whether at Up-Park or at home. She made her eagerness to work at the medical front line obvious, even then, and remembered that most professionals indulged her with practical and theoretical advice 'with a readiness and kindness I am never likely to forget'.

She was not allowed, though, to act as doctor herself. Not as long as she was amongst real 'college', or qualified, men. She could only do what other women of her kind did. Defined achievement never appealed to Mary much. Freakishly for a young woman, she liked to set her own limits, to decide her own accomplishments without reference to others' permission or expectation. It soon became obvious that for her own peace of mind she needed more satisfying a challenge than that not insubstantial one posed by running her mother's house in her mother's company. She was only allowed to deal with those Creole patients Jane, as the family's chief doctress, chose to pass on to her, or those European ones the army doctors had done with. She was restless, craving the exhilarating independence of the heady years in London. It was time for a change again. Which always meant, in Mary Ulysses' case, time for travel.

Whoever Mary's 'kind patroness' was, she does not appear to have left her enough money to finance another business trip to Britain, and there was obviously not enough capital left over from the last one to warrant a repeat, so Mary had to scale down the scope of her market a little. This time, she decided to equip herself more modestly and embark for New Providence, an island some 800km (500 miles) north of Jamaica and 320km (200 miles) west of Miami in the Bahamas. New Providence had been a British colony since 1718: it was the home of the capital of the Bahamas chain, Nassau, and there Mary felt amongst friends. Having sold her usual stock of foodstuffs, she spent the rest of her stay negotiating with the profits for necklaces and other items made from small shells, and collecting the larger shells herself (principally conches, helmet shells, tusks and red cones: all gleaming pinks, papery whites, weird spiralling spikes and pepper-speckled ridges). Even to a Jamaican these seemed exotic, and Mary carried them home to take to market in Kingston where, she was gratified to note, they made 'quite a sensation . . . and had a rapid sale'.

Tempting as it might have been, Mary did not confine her travels to British Caribbean islands. She went to Cuba 'with a view to gain' sometime during this period. It was still Spanish, and by now the world's biggest sugar producer and Jamaica's direct competitor. It is difficult to imagine what the prosperous Cubans could have wanted of Mary, a visitor from one of their closest and least favoured neighbours. Nor can Mary have found much there, except for tobacco and a different flavour of rum, to sell back home. She does not enlighten us, but judging from her comments on the Spanish during a subsequent stay in Panama, it is safe to assume this was not a place she would hurry to visit again.

Mary's next expedition to Haiti, formerly Saint-Domingue, was probably more satisfying from a cultural than a financial point of view. Following a long civil war after the declaration of independence in 1804, which culminated in an unpopular leader's assassination in 1820, the administration of the island was now in the hands of a mulatto elite. It would be interesting to know where Mary's sympathies lay.

We have no dates for these speculative voyages. Mary implied in her autobiography (typically vaguely) that they followed hot on the heels of her return from London, but it would make more sense for them to have been spread over a number of years, to give her time to build up stock and become an influential part of the establishment at Blundell Hall. Whether she was at home or abroad when one of the most significant events in Jamaica's history occurred in 1834 is unclear: she never mentioned it in print at all. Momentously, on 1 August that year, slavery was abolished throughout the British Empire. The Afro-Caribbean people – Mary's people – were free.

Jamaica had played its part in hastening the declaration: although none was as cataclysmic as Saint-Domingue's revolution, several slave uprisings had seriously disturbed the planters' prosperity during the last century and a half, culminating in the Christmas Rebellion of 1831. This, led by an educated and inspiring black preacher by the name of 'Daddy' Sam Sharpe, was designed by him to be a peaceful mass protest against the physical and moral injustices of slavery, but passions ran high, and it blazed into a full-blown mutiny. Twenty thousand men and women ran amok through plantations and mills all over the island, destroying their former masters' homes and estates, and in many cases killing those who stood in their way. Martial law was declared; troops, including the militia, were deployed to quash the revolt, and a full pardon was mendaciously promised to all who surrendered. As soon as the slaves submitted, however, over 400 of them were hanged, and many more were horribly punished. When reports of the whole ghastly episode reached the House of Commons in London – already minded to accede to the fashionably humanistic policies of the abolitionists – the case for emancipation was sharply boosted. This was a barbaric way to behave, it was thought: barbaric that the slaves should have been driven to such extremity, and even more so that the authorities, in loco parentis, should have reacted as dishonourably as they did, and besmirched the mother-country's reputation.

All slaves over the age of twenty-one were liberated in 1834; those younger were required to stay in bondage until they came of age, and then they too were released. Economically, the effect of eman- cipation on Jamaica was disastrous. Those estates still in business after the exigencies of foreign competition and the Christmas Rebellion suddenly lost their workforce. Planters could not afford to pay their former slaves wages, which in hundreds of cases meant mutual ruin. Meanwhile ex-slaves may have had their freedom, but they no longer had employment. Most chose to work their own plots of land, and survive as best they could. It was a proud time for the island's African people, but a grim one too.

Again, one wonders whose side Mary took. Mulatto women like her mother may have been well-respected and established members of Creole society; a comparatively pale skin may have opened certain doors; but privilege depended on one thing: colour. Merit, potential, achievement, all these came into consideration, but only after one's colour had defined the boundaries. So, idealistically, just as a white woman would be prevented because of her colour from sailing off to Cuba or Haiti with a cargo of jam pots and self-confidence to make her fortune, a coloured woman would be prevented from being taken seriously, as a true equal, in anything she did amongst her white peers. Exceptions always prove rules, but Mary Seacole was not an exception. For all the admiration and affection she engendered in her later life, I fail to think of anyone who ever spoke about her in public – in London, at least – without some degree of patronization. Whether she was aware of this, and bothered about it, is a question to face later.

Meanwhile, Mary made it clear that she was a Creole, and Creoles, like whites, did not approve of recalcitrant negroes. Did not even, according to one contemporary observer, 'deign to mingle' with them at all.[9] Far from identifying with the plight of slaves, those removed from bondage by a mere generation or two, like Mary, were apt to be frightened and therefore angered by them. As a compassionate woman, Mary would have been appalled and saddened by the bloodshed of the Christmas Rebellion, but – certainly at this stage of her career – more ashamed of the slaves' behaviour than the authorities'. Jamaica, like the whole of the British Empire, was a strictly hierarchical place. All her life Mary looked upwards and ahead, but never down.

No doubt there were a few souls ungenerous enough to mutter that Miss Mary Jane was looking a little too far above herself when, on Thursday 10 November 1836, she married Edwin Horatio Hamilton Seacole in Kingston.[10] First, it was exceedingly unusual at that time for a white man to marry a coloured woman at all. Liaisons, life-long sometimes, were still common and locally respectable. The owner of a smart hotel in Spanish Town, Charlotte Beckford, ran her business with her two sons, George and Edward French, whose father was the Crown Solicitor. Someone said, with fascinated horror, that the Mayor of Kingston lived with a 'brown' woman, and even the consort of the Receiver General, an Englishman, was somewhat less than white.[11] Cynric Williams, a visitor to Kingston in the 1820s, noticed that mulatto women (using the term, as usual, for coloured women in general) tended not to marry officially because white women disdained to welcome them into their society, and they were never treated as 'real' wives. Instead they married 'after their own fashion'.[12] But Mary was proud, Edwin was keen, and both intended to do things properly.

The first time Mary mentioned coming across Edwin was at Blundell Hall in the mid-1830s. With her customary coyness, she declared that she spent her days there quite contentedly

making myself useful in a variety of ways, and learning a great
deal of Creole medical art, until I couldn't find courage to say
'no' to a certain arrangement by Mr Seacole, but married
him . . .[13]

Who this Mr Seacole was, and where she originally met him, she
declined to say. It is possible they encountered each other in
London: he was certainly English, and described (on Mary's death
certificate) as a merchant. But it's just as likely that he found himself
a patient at Blundell Hall, like Mary's father, having recently arrived
in Kingston and succumbed to the enthusiastic welcome of yellow
jack. He had relations in Black River, then an important port in the
south-west of the island: a C.W. Seacole was acting as harbourmaster
there in 1824 (he was later a captain in the local militia), and a
company called Seacole and Miller held slaves and stock nearby in
1833.[14] Whatever brought them together, it was a fascinating match.

Edwin Horatio Hamilton Seacole was baptized, and probably
born, in Prittlewell, Essex, in 1803. He was the sixth child of Thomas
Seacole and his first wife Ann. Thomas was officially described as a
'surgeon, apothecary, and man midwife' – the only one in the area –
and Seacole family legend has it that it was he who first forged an
unlikely connection with one of the two great British heroes of the
age, Admiral Lord Nelson.[15]

It's an intriguing story. Prittlewell, where Thomas and his family
lived, is part of Southend, which in the early nineteenth century was
a fashionable resort. Nelson sent his mistress Emma, Lady Hamilton,
there in September 1803 while he was away on naval duty in the
Mediterranean and she was secretly 'indisposed', i.e. pregnant, with
their second child. The first, Horatia, was born in 1801 and had been
baptized under a false name, a false date of birth, and with the
parents' names absent from the certificate. She was secretly handed
to a nurse, and later 'adopted' by Emma and Nelson. The second was
well on the way by August 1803, when Nelson's reply to a letter of
Emma's giving him the news was radiant with heavily encoded joy:

You will readily conceive, my dear Emma, the sensations which the sight and reading even your few lines [occasioned]. They cannot be understood, but by those of such mutual and truly sincere attachment as your's [sic] and mine. Although you said little, I understood a great deal, and most heartily approve of your plan and society for next winter . . . I am sure, that I shall admire all your alterations, even to planting a gooseberry bush.[16]

But the poor child had no future. Nelson wrote in April 1804 that he was desolate to hear that 'little Emma' – the name agreed upon before its birth – was 'no more'. The subject was closed. From that letter (all we have first-hand, since Nelson burned all Emma's correspondence) history has assumed that another daughter was born in Surrey, where Emma lived in late 1803 and early 1804, and that the infant promptly died.

The proud descendants of Thomas Seacole, however, make different assumptions. They cherish a family legend that has Thomas, as the only midwife available, delivering Emma's baby in Southend in September 1803; the baby is a boy, called Edwin and then 'Horatio Hamilton' for his natural parents; he is speedily baptized (perhaps he is sickly) and, like his sister, immediately given away – to Thomas.

It is just possible. But the baby would surely have been desperately premature in September, if Emma had only just realized her pregnancy in the letter Nelson received in August. Why did she take so long to let him know? Why imply it was a girl? And why tell its father it had died? Perhaps it *was* premature, and that's why it was so quickly christened and given to a medical man to care for. Perhaps Emma was ashamed of the baby's weak state, and couldn't cope with the thought of admitting it to her strange and precious family. Perhaps she thought it unworthy of Nelson and their heroic love for one another, and that it was better to fictionalize it as a beautiful girl (allowed to be frail) and consider it dead. Believe what you will.

What is indisputable is that for some reason, Edwin was christened with Nelson's and Emma's names, and that in Mary Seacole's will she bequeathed to her friend Lord Rokeby a diamond ring, 'given to my late husband by his Godfather Viscount Nelson'.[17]

The adult Edwin was certainly far from strong, according to his fond new wife.

> [I] took him down to Black River, where we established a store. Poor man! He was very delicate; and before I undertook charge of him, several doctors had expressed most unfavourable opinions of his health. I kept him alive by kind nursing and attention as long as I could . . .[18]

It can hardly have been a particularly vigorous marriage.

The next few years were marred by stress and ill-health. Black River was a propitious place to set up business, being at the head of the only navigable river on the island, and benefiting from the growing logwood trade on Jamaica. It was busy and reasonably fashionable, with a racetrack and a mineral spa, and there should have been plenty of trade for the Seacoles' general store. To make a success of it, though, the couple would have needed more than the support of Edwin's relations. With her husband's increasing feebleness, Mary's attentions were distracted from the meaty business of making money, and turned instead to nursing him. They neither prospered nor thrived, and in the early 1840s both gave up, returned to Kingston, and waited for Edwin to die.[19]

The last year of Edwin's life was traumatic, and not just because of his failing health. On Saturday 29 August 1843 a fire broke out at a foundry in the east of Kingston; it spread to a sawmill next door and soon, thanks to a brisk wind blowing sparks and flaming cedar shakes to neighbouring roofs, a tenth of the town was ablaze. The flames consumed first one side of East Street and then the other. Mary insisted on staying until the last possible moment to empty the house of everything she could, including, presumably, her ailing husband. Nothing survived of the original building. Losses in Kingston overall ran to some £250,000; the Seacoles, together with Mary's family, can only have salvaged what Mary rescued herself.[20] Bit by bit another hotel, New Blundell Hall, was constructed at 7 East Street. It was 'better than before', said Mary, but not without considerable cost.

Edwin Horatio Hamilton Seacole finally died in October 1844, at the age of forty-one, and was buried in Kingston by the same clergyman who had married him eight years earlier.[21] His exhausted widow was distraught.

> For days I never stirred – lost to all that passed around me in a dull stupor of despair. If you had told me that the time would soon come when I should remember this sorrow calmly, I should not have believed it possible; and yet it was so. I do not think that we hot-blooded Creoles sorrow less for showing it so impetuously; but I do think that the sharp edge of our grief wears down sooner than theirs who preserve an outward demeanour of calmness, and nurse their woe secretly in their hearts.[22]

Mary rarely acknowledged her instincts to be different from her European readers', but here she made an exception. She grieved loud and keenly for the acquiescent, trusting English husband she had lost. However unjustly, she felt that having taken responsibility for his life, she had failed him. The blue hills of Jamaica were closing in again.

Mary described the death of Edwin as her 'first great trouble'. Even the losses of her father and Blundell Hall couldn't compare. After eight years living on her own terms as a married woman, she was back in her mother's house at the age of thirty-nine, with Edward and Louisa, to start again at the beginning. It was humiliating, as well as dispiriting.

Her second great trouble followed hard on the first. Exactly when is unknown, but very soon after Seacole's death, Miss Jane died too. Her three children were left to take care of New Blundell Hall (hereafter referred to by Mary as 'my house') and Mary, being the eldest – and being Mary – took charge.

Responsibility suited her. 'I was left alone to battle with the world
as best I might,' she declared, '[b]ut I have always turned a bold
front to fortune.' There may have been debts to pay off in Black
River; finances certainly appear to have been in a pretty parlous state
at this stage, with the hotel not up to full strength yet, and Mary
complained – slightly ingenuously – about how hard it was for a
widow 'to make ends meet'. But she was naturally buoyant. 'I never
allowed myself to know what repining or depression was,' she
insisted, and staunchly carried on with her preserves and guava
jelly, and the hotel. She rather darkly refers to a number of 'speculations' in which she dabbled, emerging sometimes spectacularly
successful, but often with less than she had before. But as the next
few years ground by, and Mary entered her forties, things did not, by
and large, turn out too badly. By dint of constant hard work (a useful
anaesthetic for the restless and disappointed) and the goodwill of
others, Mrs Seacole became as successful as her mother. Maybe even
more so:

> I never thought too exclusively of money, believing that we
> were born to be happy, and that the surest way to be wretched is
> to prize it over much . . . [but still] succeeded in gaining not
> only my daily bread, but many comforts besides. Indeed, my
> experience of the world – it is not finished yet, but I do not
> think it will give me reason to change my opinion – leads me to
> the conclusion that it is by no means the hard bad world which
> some selfish people would have us believe it.[23]

After a suitable period of mourning for both her husband and her
mother, suitors began rapping at the jalousies of 7 East Street,
'candidates for the late Mr Seacole's shoes'. Mary would have none
of them: her independence was not to be mortgaged to anyone now.
If she could not be Mr Seacole's wife, she was proud to be his widow,
and his widow she would stay.

While the Seacoles had been over in Black River, the British
authorities had finally come to the conclusion that decisive action

against yellow fever had become an economic imperative. In the autumn of 1840, a quarter of the men in the 60th Rifles – James Grant's old regiment – had died in the space of a few weeks, and the hospital at Up-Park was beginning to look more like a morgue.[24] The army was having to budget for overwhelming loss of life, and though its doctors were working as hard as they could (when they themselves happened to be healthy), and Creole doctresses were playing their part in nursing the survivors back to health, it was not enough. Those regiments stationed outside Kingston, in Stony Hill, for example, up in the high ground to the north of the town, fared far better than the poor souls at sea-level. Perhaps the clear air helped? Attempts were made to hack down the vegetation encroaching on Up-Park's perimeters, but nothing changed. It seemed to be the altitude, and the cool breeze that went with it, that made the difference. So a mountain barracks was proposed, on the flanks of the Blue Mountains at Newcastle, and by 1841 it was built, occupied by the survivors of the 60th, and flourishing.

Newcastle consisted (and still does) of a parade square and a number of neat, white attendant buildings clinging to the steep slope of the mountain as though in danger of slipping off. Mary could have walked out of her front door, looked towards the hills, and seen it there, some 14 miles (22km) away and gleaming through the haze. The foundation of Newcastle relieved the medical authorities at Up-Park considerably, and saved scores of lives. It had its own small hospital, too, and whether or not Mary was ever called upon to visit patients there, she certainly came to know the medical personnel. They patronized New Blundell Hall, and would stay to dinner at Mary's table to discuss difficult patients and eccentric colleagues, treating her to the military shop-talk she found so tasty all her life. Newcastle was not large, and occasionally visiting top brass, with or without wives, would be billeted at the hotel for lack of room at the barracks. Those of the 97th regiment, whose reserve battalion arrived in Jamaica in 1848, were particular favourites. To them – officers and men alike – Mary became known affectionately as 'Aunty Seacole', and their well-being in terms of comfort and health became her first and proudest priority. It's during this period that the first likeness we have of her was taken: a watercolour portrait to the waist, showing a fine, broad-shouldered woman in a pin-tucked dress with white lace at the sleeves and neck. She hardly looks demure, though: the sleeves are gathered up above the elbow, her plump arms ready for work, and the neckline dips deeply to a brooch at the breast. Strings of beads are wound around her neck and disappear beneath her bodice, and beautiful, hefty pearl earrings hang from her ears. Threaded through her neatly dressed hair are elaborate pearl ornaments: she looks thoroughly feminine, but prepared to be useful. Her face is striking. With raised eyebrows, almond eyes, and an amused rather than obliging smile, Mary looks almost challenging, and utterly self-possessed.

Who commissioned the painting? Was it Mary herself, rather grandly, or an admirer? Perhaps it hung in the lodging-house, in Mary's private room. I suspect a young army officer did it as a favour to Mary. It's full of good humour and affection, and although she probably roared with laughter when she saw it, and pretended to cuff the artist's ear, it surely must have made her very happy.

Two years after the arrival of the 97th, another visitor landed at Kingston harbour. This one was a stowaway – Mary reckoned on a steamer from New Orleans – and smuggled itself on shore in some clothes sent to Dolly Johnson the washerwoman. It killed poor Dolly, and scores more at the harbour, before turning towards Black River and Montego Bay. By the time it had finished in Jamaica, 32,000 were dead. It was cholera.

This was part of the great Asiatic pandemic which swept westwards from China at the end of the 1840s and with terrifying speed dispatched millions of victims. Mary had never witnessed the disease before (although it was to become all too familiar in the future), and could only watch with horror as it cut down African, Creole and European alike. She tried to treat it, with the help of a military doctor living at New Blundell Hall at the time, and watched its terrible progress for clues to its remedy, but not until she got to Panama in 1851 did she claim to have cured anyone. There, and later in the Crimea, she was to become dangerously intimate with the disease.

As suddenly as cholera had struck Jamaica, it left, leaving the population depleted, weakened and shocked. The ailing island was suffering on several fronts by now. Planters were abandoning the properties they had been struggling to maintain, and leaving for home. Their former slaves had neither the money nor the strength to take over, and so estates were rapidly reclaimed by a brushwood wilderness and left to decay. With the planters gone, the island's tax revenue fell dramatically. A railway had been opened in 1845, rather uselessly running the dozen or so miles (19km) between Kingston and Spanish Town, but it didn't prosper. Hurricanes and earthquakes of varying intensity came and went, leaving more or less destruction in their wake, and even though the establishment of Newcastle had improved their prospects somewhat, soldiers and sailors still dreaded a posting to this reputedly dismal island. A Captain in the 33rd, writing home from Barbados, assured his family that ugly and dirty as he considered his Eastern Caribbean quarters to be, he would far rather be there than Jamaica, where 'the 68th are dying very fast, four or five a day'. Mind you, he doesn't appear to be the sort of guest Mary would have welcomed at New Blundell Hall, even had he wished to come:

In the character of the Creoles, or 'Bims' as they are called, there seems to be nothing whatever to admire, they are proud, ignorant, bigoted, quarrelsome . . . I never saw such an ugly race of people before, and sincerely hope I never may again. I speak of the Creoles and brown people, really the true niggers are better looking . . . much preferable to the mongrel yellow faces of the 'Bims'.[25]

It must have been profoundly galling to proud and hard-working people like Mary when visitors such as this turned up at the hotel. Not even the phoenix-like splendour of New Blundell Hall was enough to satisfy a certain Mr Bigelow on his visit to Kingston in 1850:

There are no first-class hotels in Kingston, and the best accommodations for travellers are to be found at boarding houses, of which there are two or three claiming precedence, which compare with the others, as warts compare with corns. They are all kept and served by coloured people, who enjoy the princely prerogative which attaches only to indolent people and kings; entire immunity from all the penalties of lapsed time.[26]

Notwithstanding the delights of military company, Mary thought there must be more to life than cooking beef stew and dumplings for men like Mr Bigelow. Until she found it, she would keep her sleeves rolled up, her medicine chest at the ready, and her eyes and ears wide open.

3

Up and Doing

All my life long I have followed the impulse which led me to be up and doing.

It is hardly surprising that local routine was beginning to pall for Mary by 1851. She was in her mid-forties, ambitious, solvent, comfortably 'unprotected', and bored. Her grasp was exceeding her reach, and she felt restless and underemployed. One wonders what would have happened had her husband not died. The Seacoles might have prospered excellently had he been strong and she unhindered by caring for him – with an import/export business, perhaps. Mary could have indulged her twin passions for travel and commerce by expanding the scale of her previous and comparatively parochial ventures to take in the whole of the Empire – via the Seacole Line, of course, smartly liveried in her favourite parroty shades of scarlet, blue and yellow. There (in the realms of fantasy) would be Mary, splendidly upholstered in gleaming silk and directing imaginatively named ships loaded with exotic and desirable cargoes around the very globe she used wistfully to trace her fingers over as a girl. She would attribute her success to instincts and acumen inherited from her mother; the fruits of it would be all the sweeter for being her birthright, courtesy of her father, as an Imperial Briton. She would be magnificent, and increasingly well-connected to the English establishment, but always careful to remember the names of her employees' families, and never harsh.

Here she was now, however, fifteen years a widow, preparing simples for the treatment of distinctly unlovely diseases, and managing the second-best hotel in slowly crumbling Kingston. She was learning more about Western medicine to complement the traditional knowledge her mother and her own experience gave her, but was astute enough to recognize that no matter how proficient a practitioner she became, it would lead her so far in colonial Jamaica, and no further. Mary flourished best all her life where there was no competition, which isn't a snide implication that she was never as accomplished as she liked to suggest: she derived confidence from her own idiosyncrasy and did not respond well to comparisons. That impulse she had talked about to be 'up and doing' was never stronger than now. So it was now that she had to leave, while still possessing the energy, need and funds to achieve remarkable things.

Never one to delay, having made a decision to do something Mary briskly decided precisely what that something should be. Kingston was temporarily revived at the time by the news that a railway was being built across the Isthmus of Panama, four days' voyage south across the Caribbean Sea, which meant work for Jamaican labourers (death, too, for many of them) and opportunities for victuallers and hoteliers prepared to invest a little money and risk the venture. At the end of 1848 the sensational discovery of gold in California was made public. During 1849 some poor souls were trekking thousands of miles across the unforgiving bulk of north America to reach it by wagon (a journey that could last over half a year, if one survived), and others were spending four to six months on one of the most dangerous passages on earth lurching around Cape Horn. But those with imagination were sailing from New York to Navy Bay (now Colon) on the north coast of the Republic of New Granada

(Panama). Admittedly, there followed a fairly foul mixture of swamp, mountain and jungle stretching to the city of Panama on the south coast, but once that was negotiated an easy run to San Francisco completed the trip. Each voyage sandwiching the overland crossing lasted about two weeks, and the crossing itself a week or so, depending on the season and the weather. So any treasure-hunters choosing the latter route could save themselves months, reaching the goldfields that much quicker, or returning home with their spoils that much sooner.

Meanwhile the mistress of New Blundell Hall, occasionally with the time to sit on the peeling veranda in her rocking chair, read of vessels of all kinds, from spanking new steamers to game little tubs, all making for the coast of New Granada. The settlements along the preferred route across the Isthmus were apparently burgeoning with grandly named hotels, optimistic salesmen and trade. The decision was easy: Mary was more than ready to go.

There can be no doubt that Mary's entrepreneurial instincts tempted her to join the venturesome forty-niners herself and sail for California and a fortune. Several hard facts mutinied against the romance, however, and realism, as usual, won. For one thing, American society was unlikely, even in its rawest state in California, to countenance a person like her with anything like the respect and accommodation she would require. It's not just that she was a female. In fact there was a surprising number of those on the California trail. Some, mere women, were of disquieting name and dubious intention like the infamous Madame Moustache or Kitty the Schemer.[1] But there exist photographs of *ladies* dressed smartly in plaid and bonnet panning for gold with aplomb in a wilderness feverish with promise. Mary would gladly have done the same.

What held her back was her colour, and a keen awareness of caricature. To Mary, all Americans were Yankees: rude, recidivist and racist. And to all Yankees, she reckoned, a coloured face, even a face as delicately tinted as hers, was a slave's face. The old stereotypes were not supposed to obtain in New Granada, however. There, society had started again. It was a republic, founded in 1831, where blacks were not only encouraged to settle, but, along with the native population of what used to be Spanish Central America, to govern.[2] Mary's African blood was stirred by the ethos of freedom and potential power. 'Against the negroes,' she noted when she got there, 'who almost invariably filled the municipal offices, and took the lead in every way, the Yankees had a strong prejudice; but it was wonderful to see how freedom and equality elevate men, and the same Negro who perhaps in Tennessee would have cowered like a beaten child or dog beneath an American's uplifted hand, would face him boldly here.' It was an exhilarating place to be, theoretically. What's more, as an instinctive businesswoman Mary never underestimated the value of experience, nor of the self-confidence experience can breed. And to make money from those, mostly American, who might or might not be making money themselves on speculations in the goldfields appealed not only to her business sense, but to her own prejudices too.

Most compellingly of all, Mary's half-brother Edward Ambleton had already left Kingston for New Granada in 1850. He had established what Mary called a 'considerable' stores and hotel in Cruces, some 70km (45 miles) up the Chagres River from the Caribbean coast. He sent news home to East Street of the hordes of travellers passing through the settlement, all of whom needed servicing in one way or another. For Mary to join him (and I don't suppose for a minute that he invited her) she would need courage to face the journey and the climate, determination to compete with those entrepreneurs like Edward already there, and the self-possession to cope with inevitable harassment from clients and competitors alike. It could be good for her career, or it could quash it altogether, since she'd need to risk a good chunk of her new-found capital to succeed. Perfect.

Like so many other women travel writers of the nineteenth century, who for reputation's sake felt they needed to justify their 'disposition to roam' by calling it a prescription for ill-health or an unorthodox means to a charitable or otherwise altruistic end, Mary made up an excuse for her New Granadian adventure. One gets the impression, though, that this was not so much for other people's benefit, as for her own peace of mind. It was a deeply unfeminine thing to be contemplating, and that worried her vanity. And she needed to be *useful*, whatever she did in life. Usefulness validated everything. The trick, and this is where she scored over her meeker Victorian sisters, was to make sure her own urges and desires could effectively be disguised by, or subsumed in, the service ethic. Mary was somewhat better at that than many of her contemporaries – Florence Nightingale springs to mind – and on this occasion successfully persuaded herself that as her brother had always been 'far from strong', like most of the men in her life, he would surely welcome her help and support. It was no less than her sisterly duty to arrange for one of her cousins to help Louisa with the management of New Blundell Hall, and during the weeks before her embarkation for Navy Bay, to engage a crowd of tailors and seamstresses to make coats and shirts to sell, to fill the lodging-house kitchen with cooks making jams, jellies, pickles and preserves to the celebrated family recipes, and to lay in supplies of carefully packed and salted meats, and those bloated-looking eggs in isinglass. It was a frantically busy, expensive and exciting time.

Things quietened down considerably for the now middle-aged Louisa and her cousin once Mary's preparations had been made, and all the goods from the temporary clothing factory and cookhouse at New Blundell Hall were packed, labelled for Edward's Independent Hotel in Cruces, trundled along to the wharves a few minutes down East Street, and safely stowed aboard the steamer for Navy Bay. In fact the whole of Kingston must have seemed that little bit calmer with the departure of Aunty Seacole. She took with her a black servant, Mac, a young and probably terrified mulatto maid called Mary, and together with heaps of assorted foodstuffs and merchandise, and a precious, well-stocked travelling medicine chest, they left – probably in the early summer of 1851 – to rescue Edward.

The voyage south was unremarkable (Jamaican navvies, merchants and supply ships were making it routinely); by the time New Granada hove into view that thrill of anticipation which

accompanies the outset of any venture was still intact. It was only as
the steamer coasted past the dilapidated settlement of Chagres on
the north shore of the Isthmus of Panama that Mary's robust spirits
began to feel a little dampened. Navy Bay was even more disheart-
ening:

> I thought I had never seen a more luckless, dreary spot.
> Three sides of the place were a mere swamp, and the town
> itself stood on a sand-reef, the houses being built upon piles,
> which someone told me rotted regularly every three years . . .
> As we arrived, a steady downpour of rain was falling from an
> inky sky; the white men who met us on the wharf appeared
> ghostly and wraith-like, and the very Negroes seemed pale
> and wan.[3]

In fact, Navy Bay was being asphyxiated. Other writers visiting at
the same time found it vile, and vastly overcrowded.[4] The building of
the railway to Panama had begun just a few months before Mary's
arrival, and this being the rainy season, which there stretches from
June to December, the makeshift streets of the town were clammy
with mud, filth and disease. It was not only the depot for new arrivals
from New York and elsewhere, arriving in shiploads of perhaps 1,200
at a time, but for those returning home again from California, along
with hundreds of railway workers commissioned by the Panama
Railroad Company. Tossed into the mixture were all those, like
Mary, who were there to take advantage of the rest. It was chaotic
and utterly uninviting. Pretty pestilential, too: even though Mary and
her little retinue only stayed for one night, she spent much of her
time raiding her medicine chest for the benefit of the more
unfortunate of Navy Bay's inhabitants suffering mostly, she noted,
from dropsy (morbid fluid retention in various parts of the body) or
ague, a malarial fever passed generously around by mosquitoes. She
comforted where she could, but was depressed to admit, with
prescience, that what these sufferers really needed was 'warmth,
nourishment, and fresh air', and these she couldn't provide. People

were putrefying, or dying of exhaustion and exposure, and she was impotent. This was not why she had come.

Mary left Navy Bay as soon as possible. It was a melancholy onward journey. The railway, flanked by the unmarked graves of the men who built it, took her and the hundreds of prospectors travelling with her as far as Gatun, 19km (12 miles) along the line. Then it was a question of hiring one of the large, flat-bottomed canoes available to take the party and its luggage upriver to Gorgona. This was not an easy task at the best of times: there were quite simply too few canoes for all those who needed them. Alternative boats might be hired in the daintier form of one-man cayucas, but Mary was more than one man. She was also multiply handicapped, of course. She was a woman, unaccompanied by an influential male, and to all American intents and purposes, black.

> [M]y experience of travel had not failed to teach me that Americans (even from the Northern states) are always uncom-fortable in the company of coloured people, and very often show this feeling in stronger ways than sour looks and rude words.[5]

Because of her easy identification with those Africans England once enslaved (and America still did), a bond she was proud to acknowl-edge, she couldn't expect whites to share a boat with her. She wouldn't want them to. So, ever practical, she sat down by the high bank of the Chagres river, surrounded herself protectively with a mysteriously diminishing edifice of packages, and sent Mac, ac-cepted as one black servant amongst many, to conduct her business.

Mac managed to find a dirty but serviceable vessel for £10 (not cheap), complete with an awning and a hammock. Mary was satis-fied, and once she had supervised the acquisitive porters in the loading of what was left of her cargo, she made to climb the slimy river bank towards the boats.

At this point in her story Mary reminds me of her namesake Mary Kingsley, who used a smaller but similar canoe to explore the rivers of West Africa some forty years later.[6] It was Miss Kingsley who said that one should never go about Africa in clothes one would be ashamed to be seen in at home: she was always impeccably dressed – booted, bonneted, corseted – no matter where she was. She nearly expired of embarrassment once when forced by local circumstances to substitute a black bootlace for a broken white stay-lace, and insisted on that particular day's expedition through the malodorous and leechy swamps of Cameroon that she should walk behind her African porters, so that none of them should witness through her damp white blouse this mortifying badge of moral turpitude.

So it was, to a slightly less earnest degree, with Mrs Seacole:

Now, although the surveyors of the Darien highways[7] had considerably cut steps up the steep incline [to the river], they had become worse than useless, so I floundered about terribly, more than once losing my footing altogether. And as with that due regard to personal appearance, which I have always deemed a duty as well as a pleasure to study, I had, before leaving Navy Bay, attired myself in a delicate light blue dress, a white bonnet prettily trimmed, and an equally chaste shawl, the reader can sympathise with my distress. However, I gained the summit, and after an arduous descent, of a few minutes' duration, reached the river-side; in a most piteous plight, however, for my pretty dress, from its contact with the Gatun clay, looked as red as if, in the pursuit of science, I had passed it through a strong solution of muriatic [chloride] acid.[8]

No matter: once she had installed herself in her hammock there were no witnesses, and the clay would brush off when, if ever, it dried. The passage up the Chagres should have taken a matter of hours. So heavy was the rain, however, and so wild the wind when the river banks were low enough for it to whip across Mary's hammock, that the boatmen were forced to moor by the bank for the night. Mary was tired, stiff and hungry, and spent the night ruminatively munching the few guavas Mac had managed to find growing wild by the river, and listening uneasily to the stir of alligators and the boat crew's snores.

The morning brought calmer weather, and it didn't take long for the Seacole party to reach Gorgona. This was a hastily erected settlement, almost deserted at this time of year since the river was full enough to allow navigation further up the trail towards Panama. Here Mary was able to locate a butcher selling alarmingly unidentifiable strips of meat, and a grubby bakery. Mac obliged with a meal before the last leg of the journey landed them that evening at Cruces.

Edward was there on the wharf to meet his sister, who must have looked amazing. She staggered stiffly off the canoe, beaming at him, her bonnet no doubt slightly awry, her dress still smeared and crispy with the clay, and her arms outstretched to clasp him to her stout and rather soiled bosom. He gave her 'the kindest welcome', though, and after arranging for the luggage to be transferred, led Mary up the sole street of Cruces to the Independent Hotel.

The Las Cruces trail, between Panama on the Pacific coast and the navigable head of the Chagres river on the way to Navy Bay, had been used by generations of speculators already. Gold and silver from Peru had been carried over its heights, along its rivers and through its reed-beds, since the fabled Camino Real fell out of favour amongst the Spanish in the early seventeenth century. Travelling via Cruces, instead of further east through San Lorenzo, was both easier and quicker, and – between Panama and Cruces at least – not an unattractive trek. One nineteenth-century traveller declared the approach to Cruces from the south to be 'extremely pretty', with a well-maintained road winding delightfully round the side of a hill, a lovely view at each turn, before leading down into the 'town'.[9] If Edward was determined to follow his mother's profession, then Cruces was an enterprising place to choose, or so it appeared in 1851.

Recognizing the potential, it took only minutes for Mary's fingers to start itching. As she and Edward walked arm-in-arm up the narrow street, they became engulfed in a crowd of gold-diggers who had just arrived from Panama by mule on their journey home. During the rainy season Cruces was the pivotal point for those coming and going across the Isthmus, and was heaving with people needing somewhere to eat and stay for the night. In fact Edward had already apologized that he couldn't accommodate Mary and her party at the expense of paying guests.

There were other hotels besides Edward's, of course. Most were owned by Americans, with gaudy signs outside advertising a range of over-optimistic services and nothing but vaguely organized squalor within. And their owners could charge extortionately for the dubious comforts they provided, supply and demand being so unequally met. What was not immediately obvious to Mary, however, was the cyclical and transient nature of the hotel trade. Only for the night or so a week when the latest budget of travellers was passing through Cruces from opposite shores did it flourish, gorged on temporary richness, before shrinking into fitful calm again. It was a parasitic place, for the most part dull, lonely and unprofitable. But it made the most of its few hours of fatness: lucrative gambling dens emerged in back rooms, tinselly Spanish dancers lingered seductively along the street in the fizzily illuminated dark, and no one slept till the place was empty and quiet once more.

Edward professed not to allow gambling at the Independent Hotel, but otherwise, Mary was appalled to realize, his establishment was typical of Cruces.

Picture to yourself, sympathising reader, a long, low hut, built of rough, unhewn, unplaned logs, filled up with mud and split bamboo; a long, sloping roof and a large verandah, already full of visitors. And the interior: a long room, gaily hung with dirty calico, in stripes of red and white; above it another room, in which the guests slept, having the benefit of sharing any orgies which might be going on below them, through the broad chinks between the rough, irregular planks which formed its floor. At the further end, a small corner, partitioned roughly off, formed a bar, and around it were shelves laden with stores for the travellers, while behind it was a little room used by my brother as his private apartment; but three female travellers had hired it for their own especial use for the night, paying the enormous sum of £10 for so exclusive a luxury. At the entrance sat a black man, taking toll of the comers-in, giving them in exchange for a coin or gold-dust (he had a rusty pair of scales to weigh the latter) a dirty ticket, which guaranteed them supper, a night's lodging, and breakfast.[10]

Obviously, what Cruces lacked in its hotels, as well as its general society, was the feminine touch. Not for the first time in her life, and far from the last, Mary Seacole found herself the right woman in the right place for the job.

Unusually, being the right woman in the right place did not evoke any evangelical zeal in Mary. I say unusually, because so many independent Victorian women travel writers, both during their journeys and in the books that followed, found credence in the public affirmation of their Christianity. Mary Kingsley didn't, it's true, but the arch 'globe-trotteress' Ida Pfeiffer, who was to pass through Panama soon after Mary's departure, undertook her first expedition by way of the Holy Land to disguise it as a slightly extended pilgrimage, and Isabella Bird – a vicar's daughter – was a staunch supporter of the Church Missionary Society on her travels. Closer to home, Nancy Prince, a black American woman who sailed to Jamaica in 1840, did so for the sake of spreading the Baptist word (and denouncing the slave trade into which she'd been born). After all, Christianity was supposed – with certain qualifications – to be the great leveller, and so a useful tool in the hands of women wishing to impress the Western world in some way. A tool Mary Seacole could apparently do without, however: she was not interested at this stage in her power to convert souls. Her mission was simply to heal the body.

Within a week of her arrival at Cruces, Mary started hunting for premises of her own. She was spurred by the extreme discomfort of her quarters at the Independent, where she was forced to sleep in an ad hoc tent under the dining table with her maid, while Edward, Mac and assorted staff slept on its top. It was neither dignified nor practical. The food was either far too expensive, eggs especially; inedibly heavy ('hard dumplings, hams, great dishes of rice, jugs of molasses and treacle for sauce'); or a dismal routine of flour-and-water pancakes. One guest at a hotel in Chagres at the time recalled being so desperate for a good square meal that he was forced to go out and hunt down emaciated chickens with a shotgun,[11] and it was not uncommon to find hungry diners poking around their neighbours' middens in a wretched search for something tasty.[12] Then there was the company to consider: the ill-mannered Yankees and a shocking number of women dressed in men's clothing (to make travelling easier) soon made Mary wish herself at home in New Blundell Hall.

But she was not yet done with her brother. Shortly after the weekly crowds had dispersed in opposite directions, something happened at the Independent that was to occupy Mary for several months to come. A friend of Edward, a Spaniard, fell ill after dining at the hotel one night, and promptly died. It was assumed that Edward's food had poisoned him, either by accident or design, and for want of any other distractions, Cruces's blood was up. Mary was intrigued by the suddenness of the victim's demise, and by reports of his bizarre appearance, and much to Edward's disgust, she asked to view the corpse.

> A single glance at the poor fellow showed me the terrible truth. The distressed face, sunken eyes, cramped limbs, and discoloured shrivelled skin were all symptoms which I had been familiar with very recently; and at once I pronounced the cause of death to be cholera.[13]

At the time of writing about cholera at Cruces in her autobiography, seven years after its outbreak, Mary was careful to point out that it was still imperfectly understood. The argument amongst the medical profession during this mid-nineteenth-century pandemic was that it was spread either by person-to-person contact, or by the 'miasma', or vapours, prevalent in the environment at the time. Mary had long supported the former view, following traditional Afro-Caribbean belief, and blamed the crowd of travellers with whom she had come for leaving this unwelcome guest in their wake.

Edward, with everyone else whose living depended on welcoming guests, was outraged at the suggestion that cholera had arrived, and refused to believe it. But by lunchtime a close friend of the Spaniard had also succumbed. Mary was by his side within minutes, having selected preparations of mustard and calomel (mercuric chloride) for blistering her patient which, she tells us, succeeded in saving the man's life. She was still regarded somewhat warily by the locals, but as the sickness spread and it became apparent that the only medical alternative to her ministrations was 'a timid little dentist' who had lost his nerve, she was overwhelmed with patients, visitors and locals alike.

Visitors fared better than locals. Foreigners often tended to have stronger constitutions and were more resolute in trying to withstand illness. Even the Americans refused to let cholera beat them without a fight, and their attitude served them well. Those Mary called 'the natives' were just too feeble, both of mind and spirit:

Beyond filling the poor church, and making the priests bring out into the streets figures of tawdry dirty saints, supposed to possess some miraculous influence which they never exerted

[I think it's safe to assume, by the way, that Mary was not yet a Catholic herself]

. . . they did nothing. Very likely the saints would have got the credit of helping them if they had helped themselves; but the poor cowards never stirred a finger to clean out their close, reeking huts, or rid the damp streets of the rotting accumulation of months. I think their chief reliance was on 'the yellow woman from Jamaica with the cholera medicine'.[14]

This was hardly surprising, since the Spanish doctor summoned from Panama to deal with the outbreak proved about as much use as the dentist.

For a while, Mary made a living out of cholera. Her 'best' patients were the American hoteliers and storekeepers who paid her as handsomely as they could, and would gladly advertise her expertise. This, of course, was useful, since there was no hope of expanding the hotel business – no point in doing so – until the epidemic was over. But welcome as it was, the money did not satisfy her as much as the work itself. She was busiest amongst her 'worst' patients, those too poor to pay and, usually, to survive. Their squalid circumstances taught her much about the epidemiology of cholera, and their sheer numbers presented her with a control group, as it were, from which she learned to recognize variations in the presentation and progress of the disease, the comparative effectiveness of treating individual patients according to their particular symptoms, and even the pathology of their illness. This last she managed when an infant, about a year old, who had already lost its parents, died in her arms one ghastly night at the height of the 1851 epidemic. The impotence Mary felt at having failed to save this little life made her angry, and she determined to cheat the disease by uncovering how it worked. The only way to do this, she realized, was to perform a post-mortem examination. But she didn't balk: 'I was not afraid to use my baby patient thus. I knew its fled spirit would not reproach me, for I had done all I could for it in life – had shed tears over it, and prayed for it.'

For delicacy's sake (and, more urgently, for her own credibility) Mary had to do the operation in private. But she needed to be quick. As soon as the baby's body was taken from the room in which it died she followed and bribed the man sent to bury it. Before putting it in its grave, he carried it down an overgrown path for her to a river bank, and then across the river itself. (Mary already had on a pair of high boots, lent to her that night to save her legs from the flooded fields on her calls.) Once there, and hidden in dense bushes, a little more money persuaded the man, horribly fascinated by now, to stay and assist Mary as she tried to surprise the secrets of cholera from its stiffening body. Mary dismissed the episode somewhat hurriedly in her autobiography: 'I need not linger on the scene, nor give the readers the results of my operation; although novel to me, and decidedly useful, they were what every medical man well knows.' Which was, presumably, that cholera sucks the body's fluids into the bowel like a sponge, preying on warmth, flesh, strength and nourishment, and exchanging them for useless, bitter water. Why it did this no one could yet be sure. But Mary had seen the evidence from the inside now, and it made stark sense to her to replace in the living patient that which was so obviously being stolen by the disease. This secret autopsy was the work of an instinctive pioneer, and an astonishingly brave thing to do.

Mary said afterwards that thanks to the baby, she gained confidence in her treatment of the disease, and became more successful at calling its bluff (she always referred to cholera in personal terms). As in Jamaica, her methods were, in retrospect, more likely to be effective as prevention than cure. She recommended fresh air, cleanliness, good food and a positive outlook. She conformed to conventional contemporary practice by prescribing poultices to warm and stimulate, mercury rubs to disinfect, emetics to purge, and acetate, or 'sugars of lead', to irritate the stomach into life. Only very rarely did she advocate the common remedy of opium, however, arguing that 'its effect is to incapacitate the system from making any exertion, and it lulls the patient into a sleep which is often the sleep of death.' Crucially, Mary also believed in giving thirsty patients plenty of cinnamon water, or otherwise fortified liquids, equating with the most modern treatment for diarrhoea: plenty of fluid, as soon and as often as possible, mixed with electrolytes of sugars and salts. She made much of her success in curing cholera, of course, but the fact remains that if someone survived, there was a good chance that he never had true cholera at all.

The disease was nothing if not fickle, however. Mary knew by now that what she gave one patient by way of medicine might well help finish off another with the same symptoms, and while some poor souls floated for days between life and death, plenty were sinking like stones. It was not to be trusted. This became chillingly evident when, after ignoring her through months of exposure both at home and in Cruces, it suddenly decided that the yellow woman's turn had come. Mary felt the onset of symptoms with horror. She counted them as they settled into her shivering body, limbering up for their battle with (as she put it) their greatest foe.

During the first night of Mary's illness, and the following morning, the morbid question of her survival diverted the ailing settlement of Cruces very nicely. She had a room of her own at the Independent by then, it being a quiet time of the week, but its door was rarely closed. Past patients were constantly and rather loudly tiptoeing in, ostensibly to leave little scraps of flannel or blanket to keep her warm, but really to see if 'Aunty' Seacole was dead yet. No chance: if it was cholera, it had met its match in Mary, and fled after one day, empty-handed.

Not for the first time, it is difficult to anchor Mary down to precise dates after her recovery. When the future President of the United States, Ulysses Simpson Grant, passed through New Granada on military duty in July 1852, he said that Cruces was still tightly in the grip of cholera, so much so that about 120 men, or a third of his party, perished either there or on the way to Panama shortly afterwards. Mary, however, reckons that the disease lasted only 'for some months', and since she implies that the epidemic began only a week or two after her arrival in 1851, and was well over before she left the town in the early weeks of 1852, this puts her account of the major outbreak a year too early. I suppose one is inclined to believe the President, but that doesn't mean we have to discount Mary's story. In fact, cholera first reached the Isthmus from New Orleans in 1849, and was a more or less permanent guest there, waxing and waning, until the pandemic was done some five or six years later.

Naturally Mary made the most of the outbreak. By the time it had slunk temporarily away from Cruces at the end of 1851 it had gifted her as thorough an understanding of its progress as was possible, given the time and place. She had been able to observe and try treating scores of different cases; she had discovered for herself the pathological proof of its effects on the body; most precious of all, she now knew what it felt like to suffer cholera – or what she recognized as cholera – herself. All this knowledge she stored away for future use, sadly sure that the opportunity to act on it would come again, as it did with a vengeance in the Crimea.

Meanwhile, there was work to be done. Aunty Seacole was now the unofficial medical authority in Cruces across the social board. It didn't take long for the pace of life to pick up again, and soon the town was as crowded and brutal as ever. Mary used to wince at the coarseness, remembering that 'if you happened to be near the river when a crowd were arriving or departing, your ears would be regaled with a choice chorus of threats, of which ear-splitting, eye-gouging, cow-hiding, and the application of revolvers was the mildest.' Literally ear-splitting: Mary was called upon one night by a boatman whose ears were in tatters, thanks to 'some hasty citizen of the United States' and a knife. She calmly sewed up the shreds for him and sent him on his way. 'Few tales of horror in Panama could be questioned on the grounds of improbability,' she surmised, and it was increasingly she who was summoned to deal with the consequences of stabbings and shootings in Cruces.

All this excitement kept Mary busy enough, and in reasonable funds, but she still hankered after the business she knew best. She began to send out scouts to find a likely site to open up an hotel of her own. What Edward thought when, with a gleam in her eye, she took possession of a building right opposite his own, is not recorded. But it's not hard to guess. It wasn't the most attractive place: a two-roomed hut of ramshackle wood and wattle, with a mouldering thatch to which the mules of Cruces seemed particularly partial and a monthly rent of £20. But Mary was delighted. She cleaned it out, hung cheerful calico on the walls – brighter and fresher than Edward's – and decorated them 'with an exuberance of fringes, frills, and bows' for the benefit of the fussy. She found and dressed tables for fifty diners; filled up the shelves and the cook-hut;

smartened up Mac, the maid and a local cook; copied her brother's tariff list (exactly, or with slightly lower prices?), and proudly announced at last the opening, not of another Blundell Hall this time, but of Mrs Seacole's magnificent British Hotel.

4

An Inclination to Rove

*I have never wanted inclination to rove, nor will powerful enough
to find a way to carry out my wishes.*

It is unlikely to have been either whimsy or irony that moved Mrs
Seacole to call her tropical confection of third-hand wood and
rotting reeds the British Hotel. In fact it's difficult to think of anyone
less whimsical than Mary. There were already several American
Hotels dotted about the Isthmus; she wouldn't be adding another
of those. There was an Empire City Hotel at the threadbare village of
Chagres, and doubtless she could have chosen some similarly stately
name without too much ridicule. But false grandeur was not Mary's
style, and even had hers been the only such establishment in the
whole of New Granada, it would still have remained the British
Hotel. Mary considered herself unassailably British, like the rest of
Jamaica's countrymen and women. She would have expected any
British guests to respect her kinship, just as they did at New Blundell
Hall.

One wonders just how naïve Mary was in this. When she

remembered incidents of racial discrimination and abuse in her autobiography, *Wonderful Adventures of Mrs Seacole*, they were always (save on a couple of occasions connected with the Crimea) at the hands – and, she thought, the ignorant mouths – of either Americans or children. That may have been a selective and intensely anglophilic memory at work. There is certainly a patronizing strain running through several travelogues by white British authors during the mid-nineteenth century which occasionally smacks of that bullying sense of superiority Mary so abhorred in others. Lady Emmeline Stuart Wortley, travelling through New Granada with her twelve-year-old daughter in 1850, provides a rather extreme example:

> The principal washerwoman [at the hotel] claims me as a countrywoman, and with a patronising inclination of her woolly head – she is black as the blackest raven – informs me graciously she is an Englishwoman. 'I Ingles tambien; I 'long to England; si.'
>   England! Did she come out of the Durham coal-mines, and had she never used soap and water since? She quickly solved the mystery by saying she was born in Jamaica.[1]

But another visitor, a Mr Hussey travelling two or three years later, noticed that at his hotel even the landlord – 'a gentleman of colour' – boasted to his guests of how effectively he could 'move' his 'nigger' staff with threats of violence. Mary herself, we know, was not above prejudice either.[2]

So the British Hotel it was, and if some of its white patrons sniggered behind their hands at the trenchantly patriotic yellow proprietress, it was not worth Mary's notice. Somehow, though, one doubts if they did. For she was a true patriot, and an intelligent, businesslike and feminine woman who cared about herself as well as for others. Unthreatening too, and nicely acquiescent (when necessary – Mary was nobody's fool): what more could the Victorian gentleman require? Apart, of course, from a pale, pure skin, the lack of which it would have been in the utmost bad taste, in the circumstances, to mention at all.

Mary decided before opening the British Hotel for business that she would not accept residents. She had neither the room to do so, nor the protection she felt she might need as a widow with no one but Mac, little Mary and a New Granadian cook to help keep place and person safe at night. She did once make an exception when she agreed to put up a couple of American women, but rued the lapse. They kept her awake all night with a shouting match climaxing in a bout of fisticuffs, and then absconded with as many of Mary's valuables as they could tuck up their skirts and elsewhere. Never again – or not in Cruces, anyway. Instead, she concentrated her energies on a fifty-cover table d'hôte. The clientele was not as select as she would have wished, but as long as her sense of humour – and honour – remained intact, she could cope with the roughest of customers.

To attract the diners Mary hit on the inspired idea of hiring Jose, a barber, who kept court in a specially built outhouse, 'well-provided with towels, and armed with plenty of razors, a brush of extraordinary size, and a foaming sea of lather'. A traveller through Cruces in 1852 mentioned 'the Razor-Strop Man' in a letter, crediting him with the sort of native wisdom we now expect from taxi-drivers.[3] Jose must have been a significant asset to the British Hotel. Itchy-chinned men would queue to visit and gossip with him, and then move on to the dining room, often accompanied by 'their coarser female companions', to eat and drink.

A careful watch was kept on the consumption and payment of food. When eggs were scarce, Mary felt she could charge as much as 8d each for them (the equivalent of about £2). They were usually served hardboiled, on a dish placed in the middle of the table for diners to help themselves, and a tally was kept of the number of shells on each plate. The honest, if they were really egg-desperate, would pay readily enough. But occasionally the less scrupulous would cheat. Not much got past Mary, though. One glutton was seen to be taking far more eggs than the frugal heap of shells in front of him suggested, and when Mary sent her maid exploring under the table, it was revealed that he was dropping and then deftly toeing the extra shells as far from his seat as possible. No problem: the maid was given a piece of chalk and told to collect the fragments, reassemble them as best she could, and record the resulting total on his tailcoat. Even though the rest of the clientele found his exposure a capital joke, his own reaction frightened Mary in its ferocity. Sometimes she rather lost faith in the privileges of her unprotected state.

Most of the guests at the British Hotel were more imprudent than menacing, and of dubious morality rather than evil intent. Mary blamed the females who preyed on them as much as the foolish men. The promise of gold-dust was overwhelmingly alluring to a certain type of woman, and some familiar figures crossed and re-crossed the Isthmus selling themselves to the highest bidder. Not offering accommodation, Mary did not have to worry about any implicit connivance in this business. Nor, like Edward, did she allow gambling under her roof. Which is not to say that there were no problems involved in running a comparatively respectable restaurant in Cruces. Her guests' bad manners pained her considerably: they kept spitting all the time. It was no good providing them with knives and forks: 'very often they laid their own down to insert a dirty hairy hand into a full dish,' she lamented, and although they rarely got drunk, their common fondness for copious amounts of tea and coffee soon threatened to erode Mary's profits. When she asked her brother for his advice (after one profligate chap had just downed his tenth cup of coffee), he let her into a trade secret. 'There was a merry twinkle in his eyes as he whispered, "I always put in a good spoonful of salt after the sixth cup. It chokes them off admirably." '

In fact Mary's greatest difficulties did not stem from her patrons at all, but from the inhabitants of the dangerous town around her. Thievery was endemic there, as elsewhere on the Isthmus, and she suffered no less than anyone. More, probably, because of the assumption that as a lone coloured woman she would offer little resistance. This was a dangerous inference, though, as more than one opportunist found to his (or her) cost. Mrs Seacole was not a woman to be trifled with. She remembered one night in particular, when she was woken from a heavy sleep by her maid. There was a vague noise in the thatch of their bedroom, and then unmistakable footsteps.

> [B]y the light of the dying fire, I saw a fellow stealing away with my dress, in the pocket of which was my purse. I was about to rush forward, when the fire gleamed on a villainous-looking knife in his hand; so I stood still, and screamed loudly, hoping to arouse my brother over the way. For a moment the thief seemed inclined to silence me, and had taken a few steps forward, when I took up an old rusty horse-pistol which my brother had given me that I might look determined, and snatching down the can of ground coffee, proceeded to prime it, still screaming as loudly as my strong lungs would permit, until the rascal turned tail and stole away through the roof. The thieves usually buried their spoil like dogs, as they were; but this fellow had only time to hide it behind a bush, where it was found on the following morning, and claimed by me.[4]

The climate was another factor making hotel life in Cruces less than easy. Once the rainy season was over, come January or February, the Chagres began to dwindle back to Gorgona, a few miles downriver. This meant that passenger traffic to and from Panama had no need to visit Cruces any more: from Gorgona there was a southerly short-cut to the Las Cruces trail which bypassed the town altogether. Consequently it was habitual, before the railway came, for everyone involved with servicing that traffic to shift to Gorgona when the time came. Mary, somewhat weary by now, prepared to do the same in the early spring of 1852.

There was lots to be done before she shut up the British Hotel and left. It was the tradition at this time of year for all the hoteliers and shopkeepers in the town to exchange formal farewell visits (or as formal as Cruces got), and Mary implied that she was an honoured guest, in recognition of her work during the cholera outbreak, at several of these get-togethers. Throughout her life Mary whole-heartedly relished her personal triumphs – politically indelicate in someone of her sex and assumed station – and one of these parties proved particularly gratifying to her. The occasion was a grand celebration held at Edward's Independent Hotel at which 'a score of zealous Americans dined most heartily' and lustily drank champagne at 12 shillings a bottle. There were toasts and there were speeches, one of which exclusively honoured Aunty Seacole for all she had done for the health of the town during the past months. It was delivered by a remarkably weedy gentleman, Mary recalled. 'God bless the best yaller woman he ever made,' he piped, before commiserating with her that He had not seen fit to make her either an American, or the right colour:

I calculate, gentlemen, you're all as vexed as I am that she's not wholly white — [the pauses allowed him to slurp a quid of tobacco around his mouth], but I du [sic] reckon on your rejoicing with me that she's so many shades removed from being entirely black —; and I guess, if we could bleach her by any means we would —, and thus make her acceptable in any company as she deserves to be —. Gentlemen, I give you Aunty Seacole!

Mary was incandescent. After a few minutes' hissing with Edward, who would have preferred her to keep quiet, she responded.

Gentlemen, – I return you my best thanks for your kindness in drinking my health. As for what I have done in Cruces, Providence evidently made me to be useful, and I can't help it. But I must say that I don't altogether appreciate your friend's kind wishes with respect to my complexion. If it had been as dark as any nigger's, I should have been just as happy and useful, and as much respected by those whose respect I value; and as to his offer of bleaching me, I should, even if it were practicable, decline it without any thanks. As to the society which the process might gain me admission to, all I can say is, that, judging from the specimens I have met with here and elsewhere, I don't think that I shall lose much by being excluded from it. So, gentlemen, I drink to you and the general reformation of American manners.[5]

The company laughed uneasily. Mary was honest enough to confess that she would have preferred them not to have laughed at all.

It might be asking a bit much to expect us to believe that some seven years after they were spoken, Mary remembered these speeches verbatim. But knowing her wit, her proud integrity, her facility with words, and her impulsiveness, they can't be far off. Of course this might just as well have been a boorish British dinner-table in India or Africa or somewhere, and even though she admitted once or twice that she had met some delightful Americans in her time, Mary was prone herself to that bigotry that deems a whole nation guilty of the sins of a few of its most unattractive individuals.

Once the parties in Cruces were over, the seasonal flit began. Mary was late leaving because she spent too long trying to persuade her brother to accompany her home instead. She claimed she was still worried about his health and, besides, the novelty of the New Granada adventure was wearing thin now. It was an uncongenial place in which to try to make a fortune and a future, and with no kindred spirits around, the going was hard for Mary. Edward, however, starkly refused to go. Maybe he had dependants in New Granada: his son was born in 1850, but whether in Kingston, before he left, or out here on the Isthmus is unclear. Certainly something tied him there, and his sister was loath to abandon her mission and him. So she scuttled down to Gorgona in the wake of everyone else to look for a new property. Nothing was left but a 'miserable little hut' by the river. Feeling desperate, she took it, and faithful to her (usually lucrative) philosophy of making the best of things, managed to acquire some land beside it. A friend she'd cured of cholera lent her his boat so that she could get at the wood and bamboo growing on the opposite bank; with the help of a few labourers she soon had at her disposal a comparatively splendid new hotel with an oil-lit

9m (30 foot) dining room, a storeroom, bar and modest sleeping quarters.

Actually the hotels across the Isthmus at this time were notoriously basic. Their floors were of packed earth (unless it had been raining again, in which case they were viscous with mud); flimsy screens of palm leaves were used for walls, and guests slept on lice-ridden mats or in hammocks. Neither privacy nor comfort featured much, but Mary did her best. She aimed rather higher in Gorgona than she had in Cruces: what she envisaged in these new premises was an establishment especially for the accommodation and entertainment of travelling ladies, with facilities and nursing care for those whose constitutions had failed them on the journey. Much more, in fact, like Blundell Hall, but without the officers and gentlemen.

It was an astute idea, and in another location – Harrogate or Chamonix, for example – business might well have flourished. The concept of 'women only' hotels chimed well with the promotion during the second half of the nineteenth century of 'safe' tourism for ladies (pioneered, incidentally, by Thomas Cook himself).[6] But yet again, Mary had reckoned without her colour. The sort of clientele she hoped to attract, necessarily American, would rather stay in an American hotel, and there were not enough others (i.e. enlightened British ladies) to make the thing worth while. In New Granada, you took what you could get, or you failed.

Even though Mary recalled remaining in Gorgona for the rest of 1852, that's rather unlikely. It was a temporary place, and when the rains returned in summer, it would have been natural to travel upriver again to Cruces and reopen the British Hotel. This would explain a few of the discrepancies that arise in her record of this New Granadian episode. How, if Mary was in Gorgona, could she remember (as she does) the visit of the Irish soprano Catherine Hayes to Cruces, for example? The celebrated singer passed through while on tour in early November 1852, and disappointed the town by refusing to sing for her supper.[7] How too did Mary manage to avoid the floods she recalls afflicting Gorgona – but not her own hotel – if she really was, as she described, living by the river bank? Far more likely that the floods were in Cruces during the rainy season and that, being at the top of the street, she could watch their inexorable progress without worrying too much that the British Hotel would join the general flotsam. There is one inconsistency that cannot easily be reconciled, however, much as one would love it to be true. It's Mary's description, apparently first-hand, of Lola Montez.

Even in the early 1850s, Lola Montez was world-famous. It's as difficult now as it would have been then to pinpoint exactly why: like Mary, she enjoyed various talents, and several careers. Lola was a mistress of reinvention and an adventuress of the most glamorous kind. She was born Elizabeth Rosanna Gilbert in Ireland in 1821 without any particular privileges save an obviously lovely face, then brought up in India and Scotland (a somewhat confounding combination); at nineteen she eloped with an army captain called Thomas James. The young Mrs James was readily acknowledged the most decorative memsahib in the Indian station to which she and Thomas were posted in 1838, but the enforced passivity of conventional colonial life didn't suit her. Neither did Thomas, so she left him, embarking for London, and a subsequent life of scandal, in 1842. She acquired an aristocratic paramour to while away the voyage, but once home, with her lover's ardour cooled, it became urgently apparent to Mrs James that she must support herself and choose a career. She emerged from a hastily discarded history as 'Lola Montez, the Spanish Dancer': a stage performer of iridescent beauty and irresistible allure. She toured Europe as Lola for the next few years, settling for a while with King Ludwig of Bavaria, who became her besotted patron, confidant and pawn. Lola had pretensions to a new life of political power, but while His Majesty allowed her almost free rein of his country's government, rivals were quick to take advantage of his weakness and Lola's hubris. To cut a long and melodramatic story short: they rioted, he abdicated, and Lola left.

Next came a lucrative and increasingly high-profile period as an actress and lecturer, her circuit widened now to include North America. This is when Mary claims to have come across her, at a time when Lola was combining her stage career with a spot of prospective gold-digging in California.

Ostensibly she was unlike Aunty Seacole in every way, from the tip of her pert and pretty little (white) nose to the turn of her elegant and over-evident ankles, and Mary spat scornfully that 'the wretched woman' had no modesty at all. The hussy was known to wear men's clothes, for a start, and used publicly to whip those who dared displease her. She was 'at the full zenith of her evil fame', scoffed Mary, and looked it.

Lola, however, was never in Cruces. She did cross the Isthmus in April 1853, but by that time Mary was long gone. So when *Wonderful Adventures of Mrs Seacole* was published in 1857, with its libellous account of an episode which never occurred, Lola was incensed. In her own book, which appeared the following year, she made a very particular point of putting Mary right.[8] First she quoted the relevant passage from *Wonderful Adventures,* a book she noted (incorrectly) as being 'edited by no less of a literary man than the gifted correspondent of the London Times, W.H. Russell Esq.'. Then she went on to aver that she had *never* worn men's 'unmentionables', as Mary had prissily put it, except occasionally on stage and twice while undercover in Bavaria. She was not in the habit of walking around whipping people, and anyway, the time and the place were all wrong. 'The whole story is a base fabrication from beginning to end,' jeered Lola, before adding darkly that it was 'as false as Mrs Seacole's own name'.[9]

Why should it have mattered so much to Lola that she justify herself like this? Not only in print, but over and over again, live, in the autobiographical lecture on which this part of her book was based? It was an occupational hazard that as one of the world's most glamorous and voluntarily shocking women she should often be misrepresented and denounced. Yet it is Mary's short and relatively insignificant piece that is singled out for public rebuttal, and not just rebuttal: Lola ridiculed Mrs Seacole, lobbing insult for insult, and tried to damage her reputation by suggesting that not only was this so-called heroine of the Crimea unlikely to have been married to the man she called her husband, but that she had had to rely on a ghost-writer to make her book a success.

It could be the book that gives us the answer. *Wonderful Adventures* was indeed hugely successful, and its first edition predated the publication of Lola's lectures by only a few months. Ironically, Lola's book carried an advertisement for Mary's at the back. What's more, Mary and Lola shared the same publisher. I believe Lola was jealous of Mary. It stung that an elderly coloured hotelier from Jamaica, without the imagination to admire Miss Montez in her heyday, should be enjoying such celebrity, and selling so many books. In 1858 Mary Seacole was a national treasure, and utterly respectable. Perhaps Lola – far less wayward by then – feared the influence of Mary's disapproval, although quite why Mary should have disapproved so loudly in the first place is unclear.

They may not have been so different after all, these two celebrated women. Both had an acute business sense and were instinctive opportunists; both needed fairly heavy editing as writers (although in Mary's case it was more to do with adapting her native grammar and orthography than improving them); both were proud, and both made mistakes. Lola's were in implying Mary's marital shortcomings – though Lola, once arrested for bigamy, was a fine one to talk – and in suggesting, however obliquely, that Mary needed a prominent literary figure like *The Times* correspondent W.H. Russell to ensure her book's success. Mary's blunder, somewhat more substantial, was in publishing an extremely prejudiced view of Lola based on an acquaintanceship which didn't exist. In Mary's mitigation, there were apparently women going about impersonating the larger-than-life Miss Montez during the early 1850s,[10] to deflect a little of the adulation and notoriety their way for a while – the opprobrium, too. One of these, yet another opportunist, must have landed in Cruces in 1851 or 1852, foreshadowing Lola's visit and enjoying the in-decent liberty of caricaturing someone truly outrageous. Either that, or Mary made it all up, and I can't think why she should.

None of the reviewers picked up on this spat when Mary's and Lola's books were issued by James Blackwood in his cheap and cheerful 'London Library' series in 1857 and 1858: if the mutual insults were seriously supposed to defame, they failed, and now just add a little extra piquancy to the stories of two very striking women. If they really had met, each might have recognized in the other some of the drive and charisma they so prized in themselves, and admired it.

By the autumn of 1852 New Granada was beginning to dispirit Mary. Not, she says, that she ever made a habit of being depressed, but it was difficult to stay jolly in such a ramshackle, fly-by-night mess of a place. The hotel looked as good as she could get it, but suitable ladies and gentlemen rarely stayed there. Most visitors seemed to prefer the American establishments and, anyway, when the railway opened in a year or two there would be no need for any hotels at all. No dithering this time: she must return to Kingston and look for a challenge elsewhere. Edward still couldn't be persuaded to join her, and so Mary left him unrescued and departed for Jamaica. She never wasted much time on regret. Not only was she too sensible, but too proud. On this occasion though, she must have wondered whether she had made the right decision in coming to Cruces. She had achieved little as a businesswoman and had failed either to boost her brother's fortunes or bring him home again. The venture had cost time, energy, health, and possibly confidence.

But think what she had gained from it. She had established her own hotel(s) rather than managing her late mother's; she had looked after herself and held her own with considerable aplomb; she had travelled because she wanted to travel and gone where she wanted to go; and most of all she had been *useful.* Her core ambition of being the right woman in the right place at the right time had been realized during the cholera outbreak, and that vindicated most things.

Towards the end of 1852, when the rains had begun again and Gorgona, downriver, was in steamy hibernation, Mary, Mac and the maid packed up the medicine chest (probably augmented by supplies of local quinine and cedron)[11] and set off for Navy Bay. The first steamer due to leave for Kingston was an American one, which

Mary would rather have avoided, but, with her hallmark impulsiveness, she was too impatient to get home to wait for the next English ship, and booked herself aboard.

She soon wished she hadn't.

I passed through the crowd of female passengers on deck, and sought the privacy of the saloon. Before I had been long there, two ladies came to me, and in their cool, straightforward manner, questioned me.

'Where air you going?'

'To Kingston.'

'And how air you going?'

'By sea.'

'Don't be impertinent, yaller woman. By what conveyance are you going?'

'By this steamer, of course. I've paid for my passage.' . . .

'Guess a nigger woman don't go along with us in this saloon,' said one. 'I never travelled with a nigger yet, and I expect I shan't begin now,' said another . . . At last an old American lady came to where I sat, and gave me some staid advice. 'Well, now, I tell you for your good, you'd better quit this, and not drive my people to extremities. If you do, you'll be sorry for it, I expect.' Thus harassed, I appealed to the stewardess . . . But the stewardess was not to be moved.

'There's nowhere but the saloon, and you can't expect to stay with the white people, that's clear. Flesh and blood can stand a good deal of aggravation; but not that. If the Britishers is so took up with coloured people, that's their business; but it won't do here.'[12]

Mary lost her temper, and stormed off to the captain, who sympathized, but could only give her a promise of her passage money back. He would not risk taking Mary on the voyage. Furious and humiliated, she, Mac and the young maid Mary (who had been spat at in the face) were dumped back on the wharf at midnight, and left to their own devices. They stayed with friends in Navy Bay, possibly connections of her late husband, who assuaged Mary's anger with their own, and two days later the English *Eagle* arrived. This time she was welcomed on board by the captain – another friend – and all was well.

Less well at home, however: during 1853 Jamaica was blighted by one of the fiercest outbreaks of yellow fever the island has ever borne. It is a fact, recognized gladly by Mary, that Afro-Caribbeans are almost immune to the disease, but so brutal was this bout that even they were dying. Like malaria, yellow fever is spread by mosquitoes, although this was unknown in the 1850s. Its symptoms, though less dramatic than those of cholera, still led during this outbreak to an average mortality in the West Indies of about one in ten. Its aches, fevers and vomiting result in necrosis of the liver and jaundice (hence its name) and it responds badly to any treatment but time. Mary set up New Blundell Hall as a hospital, mostly for officers, their wives and children, and engaged local women as nurses and extra staff to help her care for her patients. She treated them with plantain juice to ease internal bleeding, with soothing lemon grass and ginger tea for the fever, and waited.

Mary attributed her sanguinity about death to this epidemic. One of its victims was a young surgeon to whom she felt especially close. It was probably foolish, she admitted, to have loved him so, but he came as close to a real son as anyone. He was one of her New Blundell Hall patients, and as it became obvious the disease was going to claim him, she insisted on staying by his side until the end. She was there when he dictated his will ('his dog to one friend, his ring to another, his books to a third, his love and kind wishes to all'); there when he asked her to hold him to her bosom; there when he called uncertainly for his mother; still there, still holding him and weeping, when he died.

How could she be afraid of death herself, she asked, when she'd seen it embraced with such calm resolve by so many others? This son of hers had rallied at the very end and smiled. He told her he was almost home, and she believed him.

Intriguingly, Mary mentions at this point in her life a hugely significant event as though it were something entirely mundane. Perhaps, to her, it was. At the height of the yellow fever outbreak she was sent for by the medical authorities at Up-Park Camp. They commissioned her to provide a nursing service for the hospital there, probably of traditional and supposedly immune Afro-Caribbean 'doctresses' and their unofficial trainees. This she was glad to do, leaving another budget of nurses at New Blundell Hall with the loyal Louisa in charge once again.

It is not true that Florence Nightingale, as is popularly believed, was the first person to administer and organize a military nursing service. There was already a history of women (often soldiers' wives) being put 'on the strength', i.e. paid to accompany army campaigns, long before the Crimean War. General George Washington requested the engagement of salaried nurses to attend wounded soldiers of the Continental Army in 1775: it's frustratingly unclear where he found them, together with the matrons who supervised them, or what sort of training they had.[13] Similarly, there are no personal details of the American nurses contracted (according to ships' logs) during the naval war of 1812–15. We know a little more of the professionals across the Atlantic who, like Mary, applied to join Miss Nightingale's outfit in the Crimea, however, thanks to their own testimonials. Of the thirty-eight women who accompanied Florence to Turkey in 1854, fourteen already had hospital experience. Elizabeth Smith, for example, had nursed at St Thomas's in London for six or seven years, and Mrs Grundy had been seven years at the Middlesex Hospital.[14] Florence drew the rest of her recruits from the various genuinely or quasi-religious sisterhoods and orders around at the time, like the Catholic Sisters of Mercy founded by Catherine McAuley in Ireland in 1827, or the Institute run by a Miss Sellon in Devonport for Protestant nurses: these tended to be seminaries both for healers of the body and, just as importantly, saviours of the soul.

Mary appears to stand alone in the early 1850s as a practitioner totally uncluttered by overt religious persuasion or sentiment, managing a professional nursing service for the British Army. It is an important precedent, even though her experience at Up-Park was small-scale and severely limited by the exigencies of the disease, which was so fast-moving and severe that most attempts to alleviate the symptoms were bound to fail.

Once the yellow fever epidemic in Kingston was on the wane, Mary was (predictably) seized by another fit of restlessness. Just as well, this time: there was business to be done. Edward did not want the responsibility of his sister's hotels in Cruces and Gorgona (river passenger numbers were steadily diminishing thanks to the progress of the railway) and Mary was obliged to return to New Granada from Jamaica in the spring of 1854 to wind up her affairs. The place had not improved, but Mary was tempted to stay by the promise of a new venture. If there was still money to be made in New Granada, it was not in the interior any more, but at the bustling railway termini: either at Navy Bay, renamed Aspinwall in 1852 in honour of the president of the Pacific Mail Steamship Company, or at the other end of the line in Panama. She had visited Panama with Edward and it wasn't worth the journey. Even the *journey* wasn't worth the journey: a day on mule-back was hardly a thrill for Mary. So it was Navy Bay (as she continued steadfastly to call it) or nothing.

Mary had had enough of hotels for a while: this time she harked back to Black River days and opened a store, but it didn't thrive. After three months she was only too glad to accept an invitation to work at Escribanos, a coastal village (then) some 113 km (70 miles) east of Navy Bay at which the New Granada Gold-Mining Company was stationed. She was lured to Escribanos by Thomas Day, an entrepreneurial relative of Edwin Seacole, who at that time was engaged as superintendent of the Fort Bowen Mine at Escribanos. I assume Mary was asked along to act as a sort of Nellie Cashman[15] to provide, care and possibly cook for the Company's staff. After a brief recce, during which she was a guest of the local alcade, or magistrate, she nipped back to Navy Bay, stocked up on stores, and returned to Escribanos excited and happy for the first time since leaving Kingston for Cruces back in 1851.

Fort Bowen was not a particularly productive mine. The labour and costs involved in coaxing the ore from the quartz in which it was embedded made it barely profitable. To Mary, though, the area was a potential treasure-chest. She used to take long, rambling walks which involved lots of kicking of stones, just in case she stumbled on the nugget that would make her fortune. Once, she thought she had, and guiltily keeping the secret of her stash, she waited until her next visit to Navy Bay and then smuggled it in high anticipation to the broker. It was worthless: fool's gold.

Never mind: Escribanos needed her. She nursed its inhabitants when they were ill (including Mr Day on one occasion) and fed them when they were well. There wasn't much to choose from when preparing her menus: the roasted monkeys' heads she was offered looked like black babies (a rather crass observation on Mary's part) and tasted miserable stewed in soup. Parrots were all right, and squirrel went down well, but iguana, the most popular local titbit, was foul.

Mary never refused the opportunity to rove while she was stationed at Escribanos. When a Company surveyor announced that he was about to canoe up the uncharted Palmilla river, Mary jumped at the chance to accompany him. The maid came too, and it was a delicious journey in every way. The vegetation by the river's quartzy banks was impossibly lush and contorted; through its impenetrable depths Mary caught the odd glimmer of a hummingbird or rustle of a wild boar, and when the guides stopped the canoe at a chosen tree to slice its bark and collect the sap on a biscuit, she was transported with delight. 'I was so charmed by its flavour that I should soon have taken more than was good for me had not Mr Little interfered with some judicious advice.'

It was a pleasant interlude, this, but not to last. For, much as Mary enjoyed Escribanos, there was something niggling away at her peace of mind all the time she was there. Indeed, she may have gone expressly to think over the implications of taking on what she termed this 'novel speculation'. If she decided to commit herself, it would mean exchanging her home, family and half her heritage for uncertainty, danger and the finest life (or death) she could imagine.

Late in August 1854, the decision made, widow Mary Jane Seacole (forty-nine), quadroon, of Kingston, Jamaica, put her affairs in order, left Escribanos for Navy Bay, and then Navy Bay for London. She was going to war.

5

Pomp, Pride and Circumstance

My father was a soldier, of an old Scotch family; and to him I often trace my affection for a camp-life, and my sympathy with what I have heard my friends call 'the pomp, pride, and circumstance of glorious war.'

The Crimean War was a godsend to Mary Seacole. Without it she would probably have spent the rest of her life still looking, with increasing frustration, for fulfilment. Always concerned with marketing herself as well her businesses, she had so far met with limited success. And that success enjoyed a limited audience. She may have been respected in Kingston around the guest-rooms and sick-beds she frequented, but Kingston was a peripheral place. There were too few British in Panama to render her work there remarkable. She was a public person, to whom recognition and approval by those she considered to be in authority were just as important as self-satisfaction. In fact the two were indistinguishable to a great extent: the greatest achievement would signify little without influential witnesses.

Fame and fortune were Mary's chief ambitions, but unlike many would-be celebrities of the early Victorian age (or any other), she intended to use industry, honesty and integrity to achieve them, and to be as generous to others as to herself. She was the ultimate positive thinker, rarely wasting time on cynicism and always ready to get out a cloth and buff up promising silver linings rather than complain about the clouds.

Mary must have read the news in the early spring of 1854, before leaving for Escribanos. Limp and well-travelled copies of *The Times* usually arrived in Kingston several weeks after publication. This one reported a crucial episode in the recently declared war between Russia and Turkey in the region of the Black Sea:

London, Friday, December 23, 1853.
Among the bulletins of the Russian forces, – which must be read with due allowance for the source they proceed from, – the account of the battle of Sinope [in Turkey] is by far the most interesting, and, from the wide-spread destruction which overtook the Turks on that occasion, we must probably accept the testimony of the victors as our chief evidence . . . Admiral Nachimoff was cruising on the coast of Anatolia, when he perceived a squadron of Turkish ships in the roads of Sinope. He must have seen that the Turkish flotilla was already inferior in strength to his own squadron for he had then with him three two-deckers and six frigates; but, not content with this advantage, he sent the steamer *Bessarabia* back to Sevastopol to fetch three line-of-battle ships of 120 guns each . . . On the 30th [November], between 9 and 10 a.m., with a favourable north-east breeze, the Russians entered the roads . . . The heavy three-deckers did terrific execution, and several of the Turkish ships were blown up by shells from the Russian guns. At 2 o'clock the firing ceased; . . . nothing remained of the twelve vessels composing the Turkish squadron except a sloop and a corvette run on shore, and . . . the [Turkish] Admiral, wounded in the leg, a few officers, and about 80 men. These

appear to be the sole survivors of an armament which must
have numbered the day before several thousands . . .

Such are the facts upon which the Governments of England
and France, are now called upon to take a prompt decision . . .
The manner in which these attacks have been conducted, and
the tone in which these victories have been celebrated, is
sufficient proof that [Russia] will not easily desist from this
war, and, though we regret none of the protracted efforts which
have been made to avert so great an evil, we are not the less
prepared to meet it in the last resort by a vigorous resistance.

Rumours that Britain was preparing to join Turkey at war against
Russia had been scuttling between the harbour and Up-Park Camp
along Kingston's juicy grapevine for a few weeks already, but this was
in black and white. To most local readers it would be interesting,
even exciting, news. Britain had been at peace since Waterloo nearly
forty years ago: this war, if it did come off, would be the first great
conflict of the modern age and was bound to involve officers and
men of the 97th Regiment, currently stationed in Jamaica. Turkey
and Russia, being halfway round the world, were too far away to
worry about personally (even Mary had to resort to her childhood
globe to find them), but the colonial connection promised a self-
righteous and entertaining few months ahead. It would be a remote
sort of war to most West Indian Britons, but a satisfying one as long as
the mother-country and her sons were victorious over those avar-
icious Russians. As they were bound to be, of course, given the
pedigree of God Himself.

That newspaper report must have galvanized Mary. Its awful (and
highly subjective) story outraged her sense of justice, given that
Britain was supporting the feeble Turkish underdogs, and recalled
the tales of derring-do she relished as a child. Her father was a
military man, and she had spent much of her working life amongst
soldiers. She loved Britain, was a whole-hearted patriot, and could
not resist an urge to answer individually this general call to arms. She
had long been listening for it, after all: the bouts of restlessness she'd

suffered since before her marriage were never completely quelled by activity, however adventurous. To be content she needed full physical occupation, and a mission combining practical altruism with personal heroism. Reading that piece in *The Times* would have been an epiphany for Mary: a moment of almost Messianic certainty that now, at last, her time had come. War was imminent. It would take courage to respond, but after due consideration (not something she had been much given to in the past) she decided – in Escribanos – that she must do her duty. She would enlist.

The background to what was known at first as 'the War in the East', and later exclusively as the Crimean War, was ostensibly rather complicated.[1] It arose from an argument in 1850 between the clergymen of Russia and France over which denomination should be responsible for protecting the twelve million Greek Orthodox Christians resident in the Islamic Ottoman (Turkish) Empire. Tsar Nicholas I, in true expansionist spirit, claimed the Russian Orthodox Church to be their natural champion, hoping to consolidate Russian influence over his strategically significant Turkish neighbour. Equally rapacious, however, was Prince Louis Napoleon of France, nephew of Bonaparte and soon to become Emperor Napoleon III. In opposing the Russian claim he saw an opportunity of aggrandizement both for himself and for his country; he loudly threw his weight behind the claims of Roman Catholic Fathers based in the Holy Land to oversee the Turkish Christians. The conflict was concentrated in a single episode in 1852 when the sacred custody of the keys to the Church of the Nativity in Bethlehem (at that time still part of the Ottoman Empire) came into dispute. The Turkish Sultan Abd al-Majid, after much diplomatic deliberation, decided to bestow the keys on the Catholics. Tsar Nicholas was incensed. It was an insult to himself, his country and his religion, he stormed, which must either be revoked or avenged.

An envoy was sent to Constantinople (Istanbul), in the overbearing person of Prince Alexander Menshikov, to persuade the Sultan to reverse his decision. Menshikov kept ominous company on this mission: he took with him the Russian Admiral currently in charge of

Mary Seacole's neighbourhood in downtown Kingston, Jamaica.

Up-Park Camp, Kingston, where Mary and her mother nursed British servicemen.

The earliest known likeness of Mary, in her mid-forties.

The infamous Lola Montez. She and Mary disapproved strongly of each other.

The Dutch screw-steamer *Hollander*, which took Mary to Istanbul on its maiden voyage in 1855.

Balaklava Harbour at the time of Mary's arrival in the Crimea,
photographed by James Robertson.

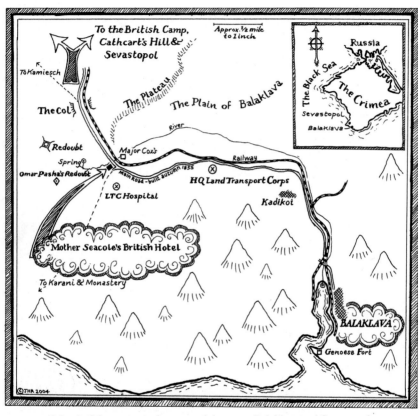

Mary's Crimean stamping ground, between Balaklava and Sevastopol.

A powerfully eloquent portrait of Mary painted in 1869 by A.C. Challen.

The original cover of Mary's autobiography, 1857.

the Black Sea naval fleet and the chief-of-staff of the Russian forces stationed in the Danubian provinces of Moldavia and Wallachia, now in Romania. These provinces were proving troublesome to the Sultan: they were autonomous, but still nominally Ottoman, and although Russian soldiers were entitled by treaty to be there as long as they were only engaged in helping to maintain order, Abd al-Majid suspected the Tsar of planning to appropriate them to launch a full-scale invasion on the rest of the vulnerable Turkish Empire. Distant Montenegro was at risk too: Christian uprisings there were endangering the fragile integrity of the whole area west of the Black Sea. Menshikov threatened the Sultan by vowing Russian support to the Danubian and Montenegran rebels unless al-Majid changed his mind about the keys.

War was not inevitable, even when the Sultan ignored the Russian ultimatum and the Tsar's troops did indeed occupy the Danubian provinces in July 1853. Turkey alone was not strong enough to withstand Russia. But by now the British and French had dispatched naval fleets to the Dardanelles to display moral support for the Turks. Canny Abd al-Majid recognized the vested interests of both European nations in stymieing Russian Imperialism, and confident they would leap to his defence if really necessary, he forced the issue by formally declaring war against Russia on 5 October 1853.

Still Britain and France hung back, not committing themselves to hostilities. But at the beginning of November their ships passed through the Dardanelles to the Sea of Marmara, a little closer to the action (in which the Turks seemed currently to have the upper hand). This was too close to the Russians' Crimean headquarters at Sevastopol for comfort, and soon afterwards a number of ships from the fearsome Black Sea fleet launched an attack on part of the Turkish navy moored on the northern coast of Anatolia at Sinope. This is what Mary read about in Kingston. Sixteen Turkish ships were destroyed. Three thousand Turks perished, and Britain and France, presenting this as a massacre of the most barbaric nature, a moral outrage, pledged that unless Russia withdrew its troops from the Danube and its navy from the Black Sea, they too would declare war.

The importance of the Bethlehem church keys was largely symbolic, of course. Behind the elaborate scenes of diplomatic outrage and religious sensitivity lurked the real reasons for this war. Turkey was to some extent a buffer zone between Russia and India. It controlled the overland route from Britain to its treasure-house on the subcontinent; it guarded the Dardanelles and the strategic city of Constantinople (Istanbul) which, should they fall into the hands of the Tsar, would release the Russian navy into the Mediterranean and who knows how far beyond. The Ottoman Empire – famously labelled 'the sick man of Europe'[2] – had been growing gradually more feeble for decades, and the Crimean War was essentially a bone-picking exercise.

What Mary responded to was the probability that Britain was to send its soldiers and sailors thousands of miles away from home to defend the Right. She knew many of those soldiers and sailors personally from the Blundell Hall days: they were the bravest and best of men, but needed looking after, whether at peace in Kingston or at war in the East. It was her duty to them – her own people – to offer her support. Her duty to her country, too, and to herself. But what about her family? Whether she was working in Kingston or Cruces, there were people depending on her. Her unmarried sister Louisa, no doubt members of the extended family: should she not return to Jamaica for their sakes, and in homage to Miss Jane? And what about her patients at Up-Park and Newcastle? Cholera might return and yellow jack was never far away; her medical skills, well-known by now, would always be needed at home.

Mary failed to negotiate the emotionally charged waters of the Rubicon in Kingston, preferring to think things over while profitably engaged in Escribanos. But once she was back in the comparative civilization of Navy Bay, her feet still itchy, she caught up with the news that Britain had declared war on Russia on 28 March 1854. This finally gave her the confidence (or excuse) to trust her instincts, indulge that 'inclination to rove' again, and leave for London. Her first consideration was how to get to the battlefield. What she would do there came later.

. . . no sooner had I heard of war somewhere, than I longed to witness it; and when I was told that many of the regiments I had known so well in Jamaica had left England for the scene of action, the desire to join them became stronger than ever. I used to stand for hours in silent thought before an old map of the world, in a little corner of which some one had chalked a red cross, to enable me to distinguish where the Crimea was, and as I traced the route thither, all difficulties would vanish . . .[3]

She was not the first woman to succumb to the fickle allure of warfare. Several women disguised themselves as spies or soldiers during the English Civil War, and others during the eighteenth century ran away to sea, as the Royal Marine Hannah Snell did, or joined the army, like infantryman Phoebe Hessel.[4] What most of these women had in common was the need to disguise their sex in order to realize an unsuitable ambition to operate on the battlefield. That was never an option for Mary. She was too proud of her womanliness to wish to hide it. Nor was she much good at dissembling. Her whole philosophy of life was founded on the right to be accepted for who she was, not what she was, or appeared to be to others.

Besides, tempting as it might have seemed, Mary never seriously considered becoming a soldier herself. It wasn't necessary: while dabbling for gold in the rivers of New Granada, it had come to her how she could enlist as herself. She would offer her services to the British Government as a doctress, skilled and experienced in the management and treatment of fever, disease and trauma. She would be a familiar face to many of the men in her care; as a woman she could give them emotional comfort as well as bodily ease; her natural gentleness and cheerfulness would boost morale amongst the sick and wounded, and she'd become a heroine. It was the perfect plan. At this stage, of course, she'd never heard of Florence Nightingale.

Mary's passage from Navy Bay was probably taken aboard the mail ship *La Plata*, which arrived in Southampton on 18 October 1854.[5]

Nothing very honourable had happened to the British Army during the months since war was declared. Back in March an expeditionary force of 20,000 men had been sent first to Scutari, via Malta and Gallipoli, then on to Varna, on the Black Sea coast of Bulgaria. Here it was to make camp (in tents that had last been used during the Peninsular War in 1808) and to sit out Russia and Turkey's Danubian squabbles until the time was judged right to attack the Russian naval base of Sevastopol in the Crimea. Once Sevastopol was taken – originally estimated as a mere six weeks' work – the war would be over. Over, indeed, by Christmas.

The word to sail to the Crimean peninsula did not come from the British and French Governments until August 1854. By then the refreshing novelty of Varna in the springtime had curdled into a hot and cholera-ridden reality of boredom, apathy and general malaise. Hundreds died of fever – especially if they went anywhere near the makeshift hospital – and the rest whiled away the weeks picking lice out of their hair, watching the rats and heavily drinking the local schnapps. Morale lifted a little when orders were eventually received to embark for the Crimea. Action was infinitely preferable to this squalid sort of stasis, even if it did mean death. At least it would be death in action.

By the time Mary arrived in London in the middle of October, the papers were sizzling with news fresh from the Front. *The Times* had sent its own special correspondent out to 'the seat of war', William Howard (or Billy) Russell, and his sensational dispatches were appearing daily. The biggest news so far was the Battle of the Alma, fought on 20 September – six days after the troops landed on the Crimean coast at Kalamita Bay – and reported on 9 October. It was described as a great British victory (the French being relegated almost to spectator status) during which 'the Englishman' was able to rout some 33,000 Russians from the high ground above the river Alma in the space of three hours, and so continue his southerly progress towards the enemy stronghold of Sevastopol. Russian casualties ran to 1,755 dead and over 4,000 wounded; the allies only lost 362 men, with 1,600 sent back to the hospital in Scutari, hastily fashioned out of a rambling and rather putrid Turkish barracks just across the Bosphorus from Constantinople. All this was splendid news, but what really impressed the reading public was the aftermath of Alma, as witnessed by another *Times* correspondent, Thomas Chenery.

> For the last week the commandant, Major Sillery, and the medical staff have been fully occupied. The number of men sent down from the Crimea as invalids was much beyond the expectations of anyone; and, though the majority of cases was by no means serious, yet the trouble of transportation and attendance was the same. The horrible episode of the *Kangaroo* may have created some alarm in the minds of the English public. It appears that nearly 1,500 sick and invalids were placed on board this vessel in Kalamita Bay. The captain made signals of distress, and remained at anchor for sheer inability to go to sea with his decks encumbered with dying and dead. At last the *Dunbar* sailing transport was sent to his assistance, and took off nearly half of what was left of his miserable freight. The *Kangaroo* brought 600, the *Dunbar* 500 sick, who were at once placed in the hospital, although many of them were already convalescent. About 300 more arrived in another vessel the next day. The numbers in hospital were originally about 1,000, which were raised to 2,200 by this new influx – a number, of course, having expired during the voyage, or soon after their landing . . . The affair of the *Kangaroo* may have cost many their lives; how many died it is impossible for me to learn; but from what is said there can be no doubt that during the passage the loss on board both the *Kangaroo* and the *Dunbar* was very great . . .[6]

Chenery explained that not only the wounded and sick, but the merely exhausted were also being evacuated from the Front in overcrowded ships like these, and that those who might have been comparatively healthy at the beginning of the short voyage across the

Black Sea often ended up as ill as the rest by the time they got to Scutari. There had been relentless rainfall during the night of the landing at Kalamita, before the tents had been disembarked, which Russell reckoned had fetched up latent cholera amongst the weaker men. Once that started spreading again, it would jeopardize the health of the whole army. There were not enough ambulance wagons (or wagons of any sort) to carry sick or injured men from the camp, battlefield or grisly 'amputation fields' to the transport ships; palpably too few ships to ferry patients down to Scutari, and when they arrived there, only handfuls of men to treat and care for them. And this, according to *The Times*, was supposed to be 'the finest army that has ever left [British] shores'.

Chenery continued his dispatch:

> By the way there is one experiment which has been a perfect failure. At the commencement of this war a plan was invented, and carried out, by which a number of Chelsea pensioners were sent out as an ambulance corps to attend on the sick. Whether it was a scheme for saving money by utilizing the poor old men or shortening the duration of their lives and pensions, is difficult to say, but they have been found in practice rather to require nurses themselves than be able to nurse others . . . To attend the sick who lie by hundreds in the wards of a vast hospital, and require unceasing care by night and day, is no easy task, and certainly cannot be performed by such old men as may be seen at Scutari . . . The soldiers attend upon each other, and directly a man is able to walk he is made useful in nursing his less advanced comrades, but the few pensioners are not of the slightest use.[7]

There was an outraged response to *The Times* correspondents' reports in the days following their publication. One particular letter, signed 'A Sufferer by the Present War' and published on 14 October, could almost have been written by Mary herself:

Sir, – I venture to write to entreat that you will not drop your advocacy of the subject on which there is an article in today's Times – *viz*, the want of surgeons and nurses at Scutari . . . You cannot, perhaps, adequately conceive the deep solicitude felt in the matter by mothers, wives, and children at home, in the humbler as well as in the higher classes.

We sit at home trying to picture the last moments of those dear to us, and our agony is increased by the fear that all was not done that might have been done to relieve their sufferings, or, may be, to save their lives. The question will arise with regard to someone who has fallen – 'Was there no-one near to relieve his sufferings, to speak a word of kindness or hope, to receive some last message, perhaps, for some dear ones at home, or even to support his head or give him a drink of water?'

The strongest man becomes helpless and dependent like a child in his hour of need, and we all know how, in such a case, a humble nurse, with no other recommendations than a kind heart and skilful hands, appears to the sufferer as a saving angel . . .

The day after the above letter appeared in *The Times*, the British Government's Secretary-at-War, Sidney Herbert, wrote to a friend of his, formally asking her to organize and superintend a company of trained nurses to go to Scutari and save British lives. It was Florence Nightingale. She would need her parents' permission first (she was thirty-four) but if they agreed, she should get to work as quickly as possible recruiting suitable staff. Florence had already decided, the day before, that she would go out herself on a private mission, taking a few trusted ladies with her, to do what she could; this commission from the Government widened her scope considerably. But speed was of the essence: reports were coming in that there were no bandages left in Scutari, and doctors were having to resort to tearing up rags already stiff with dirt to dress wounds. All the medical supplies sent east at the outbreak of war seemed to have been stranded at Varna. The French, annoyingly, were faring much better, with a proper ambulance corps, many more surgeons, ten hospitals, and a band of Sisters of Charity to tend to their sick. That only added to British humiliation, and to the sense of urgency that for appearance's sake as well as medical expediency, something must be done without delay.

It was: Herbert's wife Elizabeth, together with two lady friends, advertised for suitable companions for Florence and frantically began interviewing applicants at the Herberts' London house, 14 Belgrave Square.[8] Enquiries were made at the Anglican 'sisterhoods' of Miss Sellon in Devon, St John's House in London, a Catholic convent in Bermondsey, and an orphanage run by nuns in Norwood; these four Houses, all of which trained nurses in a more or less rudimentary way, provided twenty-one women to form a 'Female Nursing Establishment in the East' with Florence. The rest were civilians. Everyone had to promise submission to Miss Nightingale, and a set of rather tart rules and regulations was drawn up to keep the group cohesive and (in theory) easily controlled.

Florence Nightingale was as well aware as anyone of the popular reputation of nurses. She had been only seventeen when she recognized her own vocation, but her parents forbade her to do anything so vulgar as medicine. They did not want their daughter sullied by the sort of company she would be forced to keep on a hospital ward (staff included). Eventually Florence engineered a visit to the nursing Institute in Kaiserwerth – once in 1850 and again the next year – and in 1853 her connections and (scant) experience led to an appointment as Superintendent of the Hospital for Invalid Gentlewomen at Harley Street in Mayfair. That all sounds quite proper, but the professional nurses she'd come across in her short career could not always afford to remain aloof from or untouched by the crudity with which they came into contact at work. Discipline was everything: no good would be done in Scutari if every nurse who went did only what she chose, or behaved as she liked. One of her Rules and Regulations summed up Florence's attitude: 'It having been found that some of the Nurses have believed they were to be on equality with the Ladies or Sisters, it is necessary that they should understand that they will remain in exactly the same relative position as that in which they were in England.'[9] They must be like soldiers – angel soldiers – under the general command and strict direction of Miss Nightingale.

Florence and her party left England on 21 October, less than a week after Herbert had first requested her help. Thirty-seven nurses went with her. Many more had applied and been interviewed; some were held in reserve for the future (a maximum of forty being thought the optimum number to accompany Florence), while others were promptly dismissed. The first deadline had now come and gone.

Mary Seacole missed it. Not that she had been idle: since arriving in Southampton three days previously on 18 October, she had travelled up to London, found somewhere reasonably central to stay, organized letters of introduction (including a glowing one from the Medical Officer of the West Granada Mining Company)[10], and set about her own personal Crimean campaign. First, she applied directly to the War Office to be sent out as a hospital nurse, 'knowing I was well fitted for the work, and would be the right woman in the right place'. Dressed most probably (and unfashionably) in her favourite yellow dress and bonnet with scarlet ribbons, she presented herself with a confident smile at Whitehall and stated her business.

I have reason to believe that I considerably interfered with the repose of sundry messengers, and disturbed, to an alarming degree, the official gravity of some nice gentlemanly young fellows, who were working out their salaries in an easy, off-hand way. But my ridiculous endeavours to gain an interview with the Secretary-at-War [Sidney Herbert] of course failed, and glad at last to oblige a distracted messenger, I transferred my attentions to the Quartermaster-general's department. Here I saw another gentleman, who listened to me with a great deal of polite enjoyment, and – his amusement ended – hinted, had I not better apply to the Medical Department; and accordingly I attached myself to their quarters with the same unwearying ardour. But, of course, I grew tired at last, and then I changed my plans.[11]

Mary couldn't bring herself to blame the authorities: London grandees had no reason, when one really thought about it, to listen seriously to 'a motherly yellow woman' improbably claiming practical expertise in tropical medicine. Things would have been different back home in Jamaica, but here, no one knew any better than to laugh, before dismissing her as an embarrassing eccentric. Predictably, Mary was not to be put off.

Miss Nightingale had left England for the Crimea, but other nurses were still to follow, and my new plan was simply to offer myself to Mrs H[erbert] as a recruit. Feeling that I was one of the very women they most wanted, experienced and fond of the work, I jumped at once to the conclusion that they would gladly enrol me in their number. To go to Cox's, the army agents, who were most obliging to me, and obtain the Secretary-at-War's private address, did not take long; and that done, I laid the same pertinacious siege to his great house in [Belgrave] Square as I had previously done to his place of business.

Many a long hour did I wait in his great hall, while scores passed in and out; many of them looking curiously at me. The flunkeys, noble creatures! marvelled exceedingly at the yellow woman whom no excuses could get rid of, nor impertinence dismay, and showed me very clearly that they resented my persisting in remaining there . . . At last I gave that up, after a message from Mrs H. that the full complement of nurses had been secured, and that my offer could not be entertained. Once again I tried, and had an interview this time with one of Miss Nightingale's companions [possibly Mary Stanley].[12] She gave me the same reply, and I read in her face the fact, that had there been a vacancy, I should not have been chosen to fill it.[13]

Mary was right to be sceptical. Recruiting was still going on at this time, but only following written application, and under very strict conditions. There is no letter from Mary to Mrs Herbert amongst the copious archive of these applications in the Public Record Office in London, nor any official mention of the interview at Belgrave Square. But we do still have the comments scribbled by Mrs Herbert and her colleagues on other candidates' letters to explain why they were refused. Miss Brickdale, for example, seemed to be 'rather wanting in tact'; Jane Bevan appeared very suitable but proved to be 'a Bad Character'. Nurse Cator's sobriety was called into question, along with Miss Eccle's morals; Miss Downing was obviously impossible, being unmarried with 'a baby at the breast'. Emily Bailey was deemed too young at twenty-three, and Mary Jarman too old and 'peculiar' at forty-eight (Mary Seacole was nearing fifty). Attached to the application of Elizabeth Purcell of Shepherd's Bush in London is a highly satisfactory reference: she was sober, honest, cleanly, active, intelligent and good-tempered, and came by recommendation of a surgeon apothecary and a chemist. But not only was her age – fifty-two – against her: she was noted, with revulsion, as being 'almost black'.[14]

Mary never had a chance. She must have mentioned her hospital work in her application, as must her letters of recommendation from medical officers in Jamaica. It would be obvious to those in charge of appointments in London, however, that anyone used to the authority Mary enjoyed at Up-Park, and with her breadth of experience, was highly unlikely to submit to orders without question (which is exactly what was required of the Nightingale nurses). Besides, Mary wasn't just anyone, she was a mature, confident, opinionated, impulsive and deeply compassionate woman. She would far rather follow her own instincts than some lady with a lamp and a letter from the Government. On those grounds, Florence's people were absolutely right to refuse her. But to Mary, at the time, the rejection appeared morally unjustifiable, and it stung.

I stood in the twilight, which was fast deepening into wintry night, and looked back upon the ruins of my last castle in the

air. The disappointment seemed a cruel one. I was so conscious
of the unselfishness of the motives which induced me to leave
England – so certain of the service I could render among the
sick soldiery, and yet I found it so difficult to convince others of
these facts. Doubts and suspicions arose in my heart for the first
and last time, thank Heaven. Was it possible that American
prejudices against colour had some root here? Did these ladies
shrink from accepting my aid because my blood flowed beneath a somewhat duskier skin than theirs? Tears streamed
down my foolish cheeks, as I stood in the fast thinning streets;
tears of grief . . .[15]

She had been told what all unsuccessful applicants were told: 'no
more nurses are needed at present, thank you', and that was that.

There was one more place to try: a Crimean Fund had recently
been set up to administer the donations of money and aid elicited by
reports of the wounded of Alma, the poor sick soldiers at Scutari,
and the noble fallen of the battles of Balaklava and Inkerman. By the
beginning of December everyone knew about the gloriously disastrous Charge of the Light Brigade, and of the great storm in
Balaklava harbour on 14 November which had robbed the British
of ships, stores and scores of lives. Thousands of pounds had been
collected already, and Mary decided to ask if the Fund might like to
sponsor her to work at the Front in their name.[16] Again, no written
application from her survives, but she was clearly unsuccessful.

Mary despaired – but only temporarily. The morning after that
lonely emotional breakdown in the gleaming streets of Belgravia, she
decided to commission herself to travel to the Crimea. She was a
businesswoman as well as a doctress, after all: if no one would make a
professional nurse of her, she would just have to resort to her other
profession, and nurse when she could on the side.

There were those there who had known me in Jamaica, who
had been under my care; doctors who would vouch for my skill
and willingness to aid them, and a general who had more than

once helped me, and would do so still.[17] Why not trust to their welcome and kindness, and start at once? If the authorities had allowed me, I would willingly have given them my services as a nurse; but as they declined them, should I not open an hotel for invalids in the Crimea in my own way?[18]

It was an outrageous proposition, but certainly succeeded in restoring Mary's spirits. She quickly had some cards printed announcing the imminent opening of another 'British Hotel', and sent them in advance to Balaklava so that by the time she got there herself, her public would be ready. They were addressed to the 'former kind friends of Mrs Mary Seacole (Late of Kingston, Jamaica)' and to 'the Officers of the Army and Navy generally', and promised 'a mess-table and comfortable quarters for sick and convalescent officers'.[19] Her patrons would thus subsidize Mary's nursing, for which she would not expect (but would nevertheless welcome) payment.

Shortly after the cards had been dispatched to arrive in the Crimea at the beginning of the following February, the entrepreneur Thomas Day turned up in London. He was the relative of Edwin Seacole's she had last seen in New Granada. Like her, he was an opportunist who had recently left Navy Bay and was bound for Balaklava on business. Grateful for the nursing care she had given him in the past, and with a mixture of family loyalty and acumen, he agreed to back Mary's scheme with the wherewithal to open a store as well as an hotel.

To Mary, success seemed certain. The firm of Seacole and Day was founded, and while one principal embarked immediately for the Crimea, the other, Mary, booked an expensive passage on the splendid new Dutch screw-steamer *Hollander* bound for Constantinople via Malta on her maiden voyage.[20] Goods were bought and laden into packing cases. The trusty medicine chest was overhauled and carefully restocked. No doubt Mary had a moment to boil up a few dozen jars of jams and jellies too, and write a hasty letter to various Grants and Seacoles back home to break the improbable news.

On 27 January the sleek and gleaming *Hollander* left England with a large Creole lady and an embryonic hotel aboard. Luckily, the chap in charge of the ship's cargo was the brother of that young surgeon Mary had so loved and lost to yellow fever a few months ago in Kingston. He welcomed Mary with delight, and soon declared himself convinced that her Crimean adventure, though perhaps a touch unconventional, was sure to end in triumph. Never burdened by false modesty, Mary was bound to agree.

6

Enjoying it Amazingly

I enjoyed the voyage amazingly. And as day by day we drew nearer to the scene of action, my doubts of success grew less and less, until I had a conviction of the rightness of the step I had taken, which would have carried me buoyantly through any difficulties.

There isn't any frost in Jamaica. You can't even see your winter breath in the mountains beyond Newcastle, and down at Kingston the temperature rarely dips below 60°F. Nor is Central America known for its chilliness. England was the coldest place Mary had ever known. There the rancid fog, while pretending to comfort you with a billowy embrace, was really only interested in working its clammy way through your woollen wraps, your close-tied bonnets, your very boots, until it had succeeded in sucking out your marrow. You could sit by a fire and be toasted on one side while the other still shivered. If you took coffee or chocolate your nose dripped and your stiff fingers throbbed against the warmth of the cup. The hem of your dress got caked in slush and clunked as you picked your way along the street, and your lips and cheeks cracked without the careful application of emollients and unguents. In fact, enduring an English winter in the 1850s was, for a tropical soul like Mary, an odorous, messy and uncomfortable business.

Once aboard ship, however, the astringency of the sea breeze and ebullience of Mary's spirits changed the mood. The *Hollander* left the freezing fog in London, and though still cold, the weather grew clear and invigorating. Mary never suffered from sea-sickness; swathed in an abundance of shawls, and fortunate enough to be provided by nature with stout insulation (both mental and physical), she savoured every minute of the voyage to the East.

It did not take long. Screw-steamers like the *Hollander* were modern and efficient vessels, favoured for their elegance, speed, cargo capacity and fuel economy. Mary was travelling upmarket – a thrill in itself – and was damned if she was going to waste her money by failing to make the most of the experience.

The first episode of any note en route to Constantinople was the passing of Trafalgar at the tip of Cape St Vincent, visible early one morning on the port side. Mary was woken up and shown the site of Nelson's victory, and duly 'expected to feel deeply impressed'. Just how impressed she did feel, she doesn't say, and 'expected' is a curious choice of word, given that Nelson himself was (at least) her own godfather-in-law. Mind you, the great man had done little for the sickly Seacole but leave him a diamond ring and a ridiculously noble name: one can imagine Mary feeling indignant, even vicariously snubbed, by that.[1]

A few hours later the *Hollander* reached Gibraltar, her first port of call. Any lady – especially an 'unprotected' lady – with the means to travel to a tourist spot like Gibraltar was bound to attract attention. Her fellow passengers would naturally offer their services as chaperone and guide, and once a champion had been chosen, he in turn would engage a local cicerone to show them the sights. They would gaze at the Rock, be pruriently fascinated by the monkeys, and happily absorb the general air of familiarity about the place. Henry Swinburne, an English tourist at the end of the eighteenth century, was delighted to be amongst the 'jolly roast-beef faces' of his countrymen there: it was the best of all possible worlds, being foreign without the foreigners.[2]

Mary Seacole, however, preferred to do things differently. Frankly, she didn't care for polite society's females. She felt no need to ape their assumed inadequacies and fashionable feebleness. 'I never found women so quick to understand me as the men,' she commented once, finding that if she behaved with integrity and benevolent common sense, with sympathy, good humour and (most of all) true womanliness, she could always command a gentleman's respect. Being 'womanly', to her, was the female equivalent of being a gentleman – much more important than being merely 'ladylike' – and implied a right to the same high regard gentlemen enjoyed. 'I had an idea that I should do better alone,' she declared on clambering off the *Hollander*, and firmly refused any offers of help, sharing the philosophy of a contemporary independent tourist, Emily Lowe:

Ladies *alone* get on in travelling much better than with gentlemen: they set about things in a quieter manner, and always have their own way; while men are sure to get into passions and make rows, if things are not right immediately. Should ladies have no [British] escort with them, then everyone is so civil, and trying of what use they can be; while, when there is a gentleman of the party, no one thinks of interfering, but all take it for granted they are well provided for.

The only use of a gentleman in travelling is to look after the luggage, and we take care to have no luggage.[3]

Once ashore, Mary chose the most intelligent-looking of the guides who immediately swarmed around her, and marched him off with instructions to show her the British garrison's fortifications. She dismissed him after a brisk hour's tour, and decided to rest in the market-place before re-embarking. It was there that she met two officers of the 48th, old habitués of New Blundell Hall, who lustily bawled her name ('good old Mother Seacole!') across the square and invited her, like any old mess-mate, to join them for a drink. Over some 'very nasty' Spanish wine, she told them of her great plan, and listened politely as they forbade her to go to the Crimean hell-hole they had just escaped as invalids. Her response was to enquire whether or not she might be useful there, never mind safe or comfortable, and when they were forced to admit that she would, she laughed, raised a glass to toast their future health, and hers, and left for her cabin in high spirits.

The next stop was Malta, which Mary, in typically trenchant mood, found disappointing. The Maltese were 'lazy', and their island too dull to merit any sort of description in her autobiography, which is a shame. Valletta had played a poignant part in the war already, being the place where surplus British women tended to be jettisoned en route to the Crimea. Some chose to stay there, close but not too close to their husbands at war, but most were casualties of the military administration's derisive attitude to soldiers' dependants. Non-commissioned officers in the British Army were not encouraged to marry, but a few wives per regiment were grudgingly accepted 'on the strength', entitled to a modicum of provision from their husband's pay. No married quarters were available: official wives and children had to be accommodated in curtained-off corners of the barracks, or in private rooms elsewhere. When the time came to march, in this case to war, each regiment would receive an allocation of small white cards. On most of the cards three stark words were printed: 'not to go'. Half a dozen or so read 'to go', however, and those NCOs lucky enough to draw the latter cards were allowed to bring their wives as camp followers, so long as no children were involved. The 'not-to-go's tried various ways of bypassing the ballot by presenting themselves to the authorities as laundresses, cooks or even nurses, because once their husbands had been drafted away, there was no further guarantee of subsistence money.[4] One of them, Matilda Norman, even applied to Florence Nightingale:

I am a Soldgers Wife and my Husband is just gone out to the East . . . the Colonel been [being] well satisfied with my

Carertor [character] thought I should be very useful in the Regt but having heard that was being Nurses sent out I would do any thing to go for I there might be able to help him in is dieing moments. I am Young and Strong and do not mind what I suffer . . .[5]

Another desperate 'not-to-go' disguised herself as a rifleman aboard her husband's ship and was allowed to continue, even when discovered, in tribute to her soldierly pluck and loyalty.[6] Yet more scraped the money together to get as far as they could along the route to the East, be that London, Gibraltar, Malta or Constantinople, and trusted to luck for the rest. But luck rarely obliged, and wherever women were found by the authorities to be without means or patronage, as in Malta, they were unceremoniously dumped and left to fend for themselves.

Commissioned officers' wives were a different matter. Even though official opinion on the wisdom of allowing them into the theatre of war was divided (on this matter as on almost every other in the Crimea), they were unhindered by army regulations. Some said high-caste ladies were bound to boost morale while the lower orders did valuable work in the canteens and wash-tents. Others spat fire at the thought of any female presence at all on the battlefield, including nurses. While wounded men clasped those nurses' hands and wept with gratitude on the wards of Scutari, General Lord Lucan (commander of the cavalry) used furiously to scan the ranks 'to find traces of a lady'.[7] And caught in-between were the ordinary women desperate to stay with their men and survive. Few – including Mary – discussed these women with any degree of humanity: without subsidy, and without a home of their own, the only alternative for far too many dependants was destitution, which would automatically confer on them the badge of the social and moral outcast.

Mary was no outcast herself, of course, although well aware of her ostensible apartness from almost everyone else bound for or already in the Crimea. She was utterly, anachronistically, convinced of her right to choose to be where she was, and to be respected for that decision. But she was astute enough by now to realize that any help to persuade others of that right was much to be welcomed, and when she chanced to meet a doctor she knew on the streets of Valletta – another admiring contact from Kingston days – she set to work. This doctor had just left Scutari, where he had been working with Miss Nightingale: a letter of introduction from him to the great lady would be invaluable to Mary. It would be a fillip to her self-esteem, and endorse her credibility as a medical practitioner most satisfactorily.

Letters of introduction, the remote equivalent of verbal introductions, played a significant part in the fabric of nineteenth-century social life. They operated, as did everything else, along strictly hierarchical lines and their purpose was to open doors which would otherwise remain intractably shut. Person A would approach person B for a letter of introduction to person C (or be offered one, like Mary). Generally C's social rank was equal to or higher than A's, and B was never of lower rank than C. Any solecism caused great offence. Failure to produce such a letter when seeking to meet someone of higher rank to whom one had not formally or formerly been introduced usually resulted in suspicion and disappointment. The letters were networking tools, which when properly used, like a passport (which is, after all, a glorified letter of introduction), smoothed the path of progress. When abused or neglected, they could destroy one's social credibility. Perhaps worse: I remember reading a journal entry written by a desperate Victorian wife at a small station in some godforsaken outpost of the British Empire. She felt unbearably lonely and so bored she ached. Yet all she could do, day after day, was sit at home and stare out of the window: her husband had not bothered to provide her either with a verbal introduction to her neighbours or a suitable letter, so she could neither visit them, nor be visited. In the end, she used to walk to the local cemetery of an evening to chat to the dead, which was 'relatively pleasant', she said, under the circumstances.[8]

This offer of the doctor's, then, was real boon to Mary. She had not intended to visit Miss Nightingale, nor expected to. Given the way she had been treated by the London branch of Florence's nursing outfit, she probably felt too affronted to wish to visit. But the doctor's letter was irresistible. 'There is that in [it] which prevents my request being refused,' she noted rather smugly, and the thought that Florence Nightingale would be unable to avoid an interview with 'old Mother Seacole' (at last) was quite delicious. She accepted, of course, and safely stowed the document away.

By now the wintry memory of London was far behind the *Hollander*. After leaving Malta and approaching the Greek archipelago the weather grew softer and the whole voyage assumed an air of romance for Mary. She started twittering indulgently, and rather unwontedly, about 'beautiful islands' and legends of star-crossed lovers until 'the good ship's anchor plunge[d] down fathoms deep into the blue waters of the Bosphorus' and the minarets and domes of Constantinople (Istanbul) shimmered exotically into view.

Keen to add to her tourist portfolio, which by now included memories of England, the Bahamas, Cuba, Saint-Domingue, New Granada, Gibraltar and Malta, the first thing Mary did on disembarking from the *Hollander* at Pera (the port of Constantinople) was to hold her customarily subjective interviews for the post of cicerone and engage the likeliest lad. She named him in the traditional spirit of British imperialism: he was a Greek Jew with a quite unnecessarily complicated name, 'whom I called by the one common name over there – "Johnny". Wishing, however, to distinguish my Johnny from the legion of other Johnnies, I prefixed the term Jew to his other name, and addressed him as Jew Johnny.' Unlike Mary, when caricatured by that inebriate American at the dinner in Cruces, Jew Johnny did not object, and eventually became her 'best and faithfulest servant' both here and in the Crimea. Jew Johnny was probably completely transfixed by his new employer. Few enough British women had visited Turkey by that time in their own right, and independent Creole ladies doing the same were unheard of. Mary was keenly aware of being a pioneer, and predictably proud of it. Proud too, perversely, of being underwhelmed by the fabled city she explored:

I do not think that Constantinople impressed me so much as I had expected; and I thought its streets would match those of Navy Bay not unfairly. The caiques [slim Turkish rowing boats], also, of which I had ample experience – for I spent six days here, wandering about Pera and Stamboul in the daytime, and returning to the 'Hollander' at nightfall – might be made more safe and commodious for stout ladies, even if the process interfered a little with their ornament. Time and trouble combined have left me with a well-filled-out, portly frame . . . and more than once, it was in danger of becoming too intimately acquainted with the temperature of the Bosphorus . . . Somewhat surprised . . . seemed the cunning-eyed Greeks, who throng the streets of Pera, at the unprotected Creole woman who took Constantinople so coolly (it would require something more to surprise her); while the grave English raised their eyebrows wonderingly, and the more vivacious French shrugged their pliant shoulders into the strangest contortions. I accepted it all as a compliment to a stout female tourist.[9]

There was work to be done here: letters to be collected from the post office (mostly from miserable Thomas Day, her business part-ner, who had gone ahead to Balaklava and hated it); stores for the hotel must be ordered, and arrangements made for her onward passage across the Black Sea. Shortly before leaving Pera aboard the *Albatross*, a transport ship currently laden with 'cattle and commis-sariat officers', Mary hired the most robust caique she could find and set off to pay her respects – as one doctress to another – to the newly famous Miss Nightingale.

Florence and her original band of nurses had been at work on the hospital wards of Scutari, just across the Bosphorus from Constan-tinople, since November 1854. They had since been joined by more nurses recruited by Mary Stanley, and by the spring of 1855 British or Irish women were employed not only in the huge Scutari barrack hospital, but at several other hospitals including another 'general' one in Scutari, at Koulali (slightly north of Scutari, on the coast of Asia minor), at Renkioi and Smyrna (further south), and even up at Balaklava.[10] At first, only one doctor at the Scutari barracks had deigned to allow them to treat patients; the others were hampered by prejudice, lack of imagination or the absence of specific orders indicating exactly what authority this Miss Nightingale and her 'nurses' had been allowed. But gradually the women's duties crept from the kitchens and laundries to the wards and even the temporary operating theatres of the hospitals, as Florence battled to wrest some sort of constructive order from the administrative and practical chaos swaddling the army's and Government's officials.

Mary somehow managed to hoist herself out of her caique on landing at Scutari, and once she had adjusted her blue bonnet with the scarlet streamers and carefully plumped her canary-coloured dress, she looked up the slope ahead of her to the huge and dreary hospital. It stood – still stands – bleak and four-square, rearing up to form a vast quadrangle, pocked with little black windows and chillingly quiet and still. One side of it had been damaged by fire and was unusable, but that still left some 4 miles of wards with an average of 2,349 patients in them, and a network of cellars underneath housing some 200 women camp-followers, who 'drank, starved, gave birth to infants, carried on their trade as prostitutes and died of cholera'.[11] Men wounded in the skirmishes were arriving from the Front in transport ships all the time (even though the last major engagement with the Russian enemy had been five months ago at Inkerman); the sick were unloaded in even greater numbers than the injured, and if a patient had managed to avoid fever before, he soon succumbed at Scutari. Two thousand three hundred and fifteen men are recorded as having died in the hospital during the two months preceding Mary's arrival;[12] there must have been many more who ebbed away in transit before reaching hospital. *This* is why Mary had come: not, like Florence, to challenge statistics and change the system, but simply to make life – or death – a little more comfortable for its individual victims. To be to as many of her 'sons' as possible a 'mother', and if not to heal them, at least to love them, one by one.

With her doctor friend's letter ready for inspection, Mary walked briskly up the path towards the forbidding-looking building.

> [D]irectly I entered the hospital, and came upon the long wards of sufferers lying there so quiet and still, a rush of tears came to my eyes, and blotted out the sight for a few minutes. But I soon felt at home, and looked about me with great interest. The men there were, many of them, very quiet. Some of the convalescent formed themselves into little groups around one who read a newspaper; others had books in their hands, or by their side, where they had fallen when slumber overtook the readers, while hospital orderlies moved to and fro, and now and then the female nurses, in their quiet uniform, passed noiselessly on some mission of kindness.[13]

Mary soon (naturally) found a sergeant she had known in the 97th at Up-Park, and appointing himself her guide, he took her to see all the patients she was likely to have met in Kingston. They greeted her, like the men in Gibraltar, with cries of 'Mother Seacole!' and tears in their eyes. Sensitive to the danger of offending hospital staff, Mary could still not resist adjusting the odd bandage or replacing a dressing or two on her rounds, and was gratified to be congratulated by a harassed doctor on her skills. The whole day was thus spent on the wards, with a growing conviction on Mary's part that the path she had chosen must be the right one. If she could be useful to the sick and wounded here on the wards of Scutari, think how much more so she could be at Balaklava, that much nearer to the source of their injury and disease.

The day, meanwhile, was done. It was almost dark outside, and much too late to summon another caique to ferry Mary back to the *Hollander*. What's more, the principal object of the mission to Scutari had been forgotten in all the bustle: the letter was still in Mary's pocket, unread by Florence Nightingale. Someone who knew Mary, another doctor, suggested she take the letter to Florence's companion Selina Bracebridge,[14] and ask whether it might be possible to spend the night at Scutari before returning to Pera in the morning. Mrs Bracebridge was found in the nurses' quarters, and the letter duly presented. Politely, Mary was questioned about her reason for being at Scutari. Was she perhaps looking for employment? Because Mrs Bracebridge didn't think any vacancy was available at present (familiar stuff). Mary assured her that she was on her way to the Front, and merely, for courtesy's sake, wished to present her compliments to Miss Nightingale whom, after half-an-hour's wait, she was conducted to meet. Mary saw a slight figure

> . . . in the nurses' dress; with a pale, gentle, and withal firm face, resting lightly in the palm of one white hand, while the other supports the elbow – a position which gives to her keen inquiring expression, which is rather marked. Standing thus in repose, and yet keenly observant . . . was Florence Nightingale – that English woman whose name shall never die, but sound like music on the lips of British men until the hour of doom.[15]

This initial impression was recorded in Mary's autobiography in 1857, when Florence was at the height of her hagiographic fame. It was written for an audience who adored Florence Nightingale, and very properly implies similar adoration. Mary knew which side her bread was buttered, and she always spoke of Florence in terms of great respect, obsequiousness, even – when she spoke of her at all.[16] What Florence thought of Mrs Seacole on first meeting her is, regrettably, unknown. She was uncompromisingly candid in her comments about Mary after the war, as we shall see, and had no time for 'dark' women like that unfortunate nursing applicant Mrs Purcell, nor for the naturally well-upholstered, insisting (when arranging interviews) that 'fat drunken old dames of fourteen stone and over, must be barred. The provision of bedsteads is not strong enough.'[17] Whatever her instinctive reaction to seeing this dark, fat, comparatively elderly widow done up like a fairground attraction in her own neat and orderly little office, Florence managed to suppress

it. The doctor's testimony lay open on the desk in front of her, and
with a perfectly civil, if slightly brusque enquiry, she asked what Mary
wanted, and offered any help in her power.

Mary launched into her story of missing the boat home, and
suggested she might be allowed to stay in the hospital, perhaps
nursing the sick for the night. Florence seems to have ignored the
offer of medical help, but did acquiesce to Mary occupying a bed in
the washerwoman's quarters somewhere down in the bowels of the
old barracks. This might sound like a slight, but space at Scutari
really was tight. Florence shared a 'closet' with Selina Bracebridge; in
one room were fourteen nurses, ten nuns in another,[18] and when
Mary found her way to the washerwoman, it was to find several
invalid nurses already billeted there. No matter: Mary and the
laundress got on famously ('my experience of washerwomen, all
the world over, is the same – that they are kind soft-hearted folks').
They spent the night swapping life-stories and fighting off the fattest
fleas Mary had ever met.

The day before the *Albatross* steamed across the Black Sea for
Balaklava was ominously stormy. Mary had to transfer her cargo from
the *Hollander* in the winter wind and rain, and make sure that those
stores left over could safely be stowed aboard the *Nonpareil*, another
vessel bound for the Crimea. The voyage took three or four days,
during which time Mary barely dried out, and when she reached
Balaklava, she was cold, tired and unusually tense.

It was an impressive harbour, guarded by dolphins and milky
jellyfish, hidden on the approach by a funnel of sheer cliffs and only
opening out a couple of hundred metres or so in breadth. Like a
little fjord it curved towards a valley at its foot, the land rising steeply
on either side. Looking over her shoulder, once the harbour had
been entered, Mary saw the cliffs slide closed behind her and hide
the open sea. On the right, as the *Albatross* inched through towards
her mooring, the pale, ruined towers of a Genoese fort crouched on
the skyline. At the water's edge, again on the right, and obscured by
all the shipping jammed in-between, she glimpsed the crowded
wharf, narrowly stretching along the water's edge and lined with

peeling, pantiled buildings and wooden shacks. It felt claustrophobic: deep, dark and enclosed on three sides – including, apparently, the seaward – by scrubby, grey-green walls of rock.

Thomas Day was horrified by the place: arriving a few weeks earlier than Mary, he had probably seen it near its worst. British morale plummeted after the twin disasters of the Charge of the Light Brigade and the tragically destructive storm of 14 November, and the management of Balaklava's traffic, both shipping and human, was at its most haphazard then. Fanny Duberly, a pert and tenacious officer's wife present throughout most of the Crimean campaign, described the port in her journal on 12 December.

If anybody should ever wish to erect a 'Model Balaklava' in England I will tell him the ingredients necessary. Take a village of ruined hovels and houses in the extremest state of all imaginable dirt; allow the rain to pour into and outside them, until the whole place is a swamp of filth and ankle deep; catch about, on average, 1000 sick Turks with the plague, and cram them into the houses indiscriminately; kill about 100 a day, and bury them so as to be scarcely covered with earth, leaving them to rot at leisure. On to one part of the beach drive all the exhausted bat [pack] ponies, dying bullocks and worn-out camels, and leave them to die of starvation. They will generally do so in about three days. Collect together from the water of the harbour all the offal from the animals slaughtered for the use of about 100 ships, to say nothing of the inhabitants of the town – which together with an occasional floating human body whole or in parts, and the driftwood of wrecks, pretty well covers the water – and stew them all together in a narrow harbour, and you will have imitation of the real essence of Balaklava. If this is not *piquante* enough, let some men be instructed to sit and smoke on the powder-barrels landing on the quay, which I myself saw two men doing today.[19]

No wonder the hospitals were filling fast with cases of dysentery or worse. Balaklava was such a confined place, hemmed in by high cliffs, with a near constant swell to the sea and loathsomely messy conditions inland; so crowded and so disorganized. Contemporary photographs show the leaden water heaving with masts and rigging, the wharf near-impassable with clutter of every sort (animate and otherwise), and the landward approaches ill-defined and dilapidated. The stench is almost palpable. Yet at the beginning of March the relentlessly positive Mary professed to find the place better than Mr Day's letters had led her to believe. 'Whatever might have been the case at one time,' she wrote, 'there is order in Balaklava Harbour now.'

It was all comparative: it still took all of Mary's mental and physical power to get her stores unloaded from the departing *Albatross* to the shore, where there was no better protection against the weather and endemic culture of thievery than an old tarpaulin. Those goods stowed aboard the *Nonpareil*, now berthed not far from the *Albatross*, were safe for the time being, but Mary herself had nowhere to stay until Day suggested the *Medora*, an ammunition ship. It was hardly a tranquil solution, but for lack of anywhere else in the whole of Balaklava, it would have to do. Mary was damned, however, if she was going to abide by the mealy-mouthed rule of extinguishing lanterns at night if one's cabin, like hers, happened to be next to the gunpowder and cartridges.

Her first week in the Crimea was spent supervising the storage of her putative hotel's contents, discussing business with her partner, and sending letters to friends and acquaintances from Kingston – the more influential the better. When word came within days of her arrival that the *Nonpareil* had been ordered out of harbour before the firm of Seacole and Day's supplies had been fully unloaded, she was distraught. The only way to avoid watching much of her stock disappear through the defile to the open sea was to appeal directly to the officer in charge of harbour transport, the terrifying Port-Admiral Boxer. Day wouldn't do it: he was too scared. So Mary went and met him instead, waxed warm and reminiscent about the

Admiral's son (who, someone had told her, had been out in the West Indies), and emerged victorious. The *Nonpareil* could stay until Mary's business was done.

Boxer resented Mary's wheedling and his own susceptibility, until (according to her) he saw her at work during the next five weeks, while waiting to move out and build the hotel. Her efforts to help the sick and wounded were also witnessed by Dr Douglas Reid in the earliest independent picture of Mary Seacole we have:

> Here [on the landing stages of Balaklava] I first made the acquaintance of a celebrated person, Mrs Seacole, a coloured woman, who, out of the goodness of her heart and at her own expense, supplied hot tea to the poor sufferers while they were waiting to be lifted into the boats. I need not say how grateful they were for the warm and comforting beverage when they were benumbed with cold and exhausted . . . She did not spare herself if she could do any good to the suffering soldiers. In rain and snow, in storm and tempest, day after day she was at her self-chosen post, with her stove and kettle, in any shelter she could find, brewing tea for all who wanted it, and they were many. Sometimes more than 200 sick would be embarked on one day, but Mrs Seacole was always equal to the occasion.[20]

Mary scarcely mentioned the cold, but she was proud to record that the curmudgeonly Admiral shed tears when he saw her cheerful and practical compassion, and that the surgeons supervising the loading of their charges onto the hospital ships not only tolerated but welcomed her attention to the wounded and traumatized men. She eased tight bandages and renewed loose dressings, she gave them tea or water, held their hands, listened with love to their last words or joshed the more robust into something like good humour. Some remembered her (surely instantly recognizable, even so far from Kingston) and called her by the old familiar names of Aunty or Mother. Others just thanked the kind old lady unaccountably there on the stinking, ice-filmed quay of Balaklava expressly, it seemed, to make them feel better.

The next five weeks assumed a pattern. The nights were spent aboard the *Medora*; every morning Mary would find her way through the confusion of shipping in the harbour to the depot of stores she had stacked on the shore and check how much had been stolen in the night; Jew Johnny would be deputized to guard the depot if Mary had business elsewhere, otherwise he would be sent on errands while she received guests, dispensed tea and sold easily accessible portions of her stock to visiting customers. Amongst the first of her invited guests was the famously holy young Captain Hedley Vicars of the 97th, of whom she had been fond in Jamaica, and who sadly died of fever on 22 March 1855, soon after Mary's arrival. Another was her old friend Major-General Sir John Campbell, whose wife had stayed at New Blundell Hall in the past.

Whenever a caravan of wounded or ill soldiers and sailors arrived for transfer to Scutari, Mary dropped everything to help with their loading, and any chinks of spare time throughout the day were devoted to collecting, from the harbour and its surroundings, the flotsam and jetsam which would eventually become the fabric of the British Hotel. Evenings were passed with friends on other ships, or at home on the *Medora* baking sponge cakes and brewing lemonade for her 'sons'.

As the spring began to shift towards summer, Seacole and Day mounted expeditions along the crowded track next to the newly built railway line from Balaklava to the Camp south of Sevastopol some four miles away, to prospect for a suitable site. They settled on a place beyond the village of Kadikoi, up on the heights towards what was known as 'the Col', and about three-and-a-half miles away from the harbour. It was on the left going up, beside the railway at the foot of a small hill (on which were a couple of redoubts or small fortifications), and nestled between a stream leading down to Balaklava and the path to the picturesque Monastery of St George on the coast. Opposite stood the comparatively splendid quarters of Major Samuel Cox of the 56th, and a bizarre-looking striped hut belonging to a Mr Hort known as Zebra Vicarage, where Florence Nightingale's friend Alicia Blackwood was living.[21] Roses and wild herbs grow there now – descendants of Mary's pharmacopoeia? – and there are butterflies and constant birdsong in the surrounding vineyards. It looks a propitious place. Mary named the spot Spring Hill because of the stream, or (more fancifully) after a tiny settlement of the same name near home in Jamaica, and immediately engaged all the labour she could find to begin construction work.

All the labour she could find wasn't much. A couple of English sailors were hired as carpenters, along with two Turkish soldiers of dubious commitment and a keen and multi-talented Turkish officer, who became the site's unofficial and genial foreman. Because Spring Hill was situated close to a Turkish encampment, Mary decided it would be politic as well as useful to ride over to the local Pacha, or commanding officer, and present her compliments. It was a happy idea: the Pacha and Mary took to each other immediately, and struck an unlikely bargain, given the time and place. The noble Muslim Turk offered his elderly, female, infidel neighbour all the help at his disposal in terms of manpower and materials, and his protection from thieves and bandits; in return 'Madame Seacole' must teach him English, and tell him jokes. Mary hooted with laughter: that anyone should covet her rich, Creole accent tickled her pink, and even though, by the time the Pacha's Division moved on in a few weeks' time, all he had learned was her name, 'gentlemen, good morning', and 'more champagne', she and her pupil reckoned their lessons a huge success. He behaved 'like a Scotch Presbyterian on the Continent for a holiday' with her, said Mary, when she revealed to him the forbidden delights of bottled beer. Observers noticed their fondness for one another, and rumours began to fly.

Indeed, the wits of Spring Hill used to laugh, and say that the crafty Pacha was throwing his pocket-handkerchief at Madame Seacole, widow; but as the honest fellow candidly confessed he had three wives already at home, I acquit him of any desire to add to their number.[22]

That, of course, was not the point: it wasn't marriage the rumours hinted at, but something less honourable and possibly a lot more fun. Mary always had a vigorous sense of fun.

Slowly, the British Hotel began to emerge from the driftwood, packing-cases, iron sheeting and rafters its proprietors had managed to salvage from the meagre, war-torn landscape around them. Mary was sleeping there more and more, and began to spend the days on the trackside by the building site canvassing for future business. One illustrious visitor to the Crimea, the French chef Alexis Soyer, first came across her there in the early summer on his way from Balaklava to the British Headquarters. It was an unforgettable rendezvous.

As I was not well acquainted with the road across the country, I made up my mind to follow the high one which passes close to headquarters. When about halfway, I perceived a group of officers standing by the road-side round a kind of tent much like a gypsy tent. I was riding towards it when, much to my astonishment, several voices called out – 'Soyer! Soyer! come here – come this way!' I readily complied with the invitation, and found two or three gentlemen whom I had the pleasure of knowing. During our conversation, an old dame of a jovial appearance, but a few shades darker than the white lily, issued from the tent, bawling out, in order to make her voice heard above the noise, 'Who is my new son?' to which one of the officers replied, 'Monsieur Soyer, to be sure; don't you know him?'

'God bless me, my son, are you Monsieur Soyer of whom I heard so much in Jamaica? Well, to be sure! I have sold many and many a score of your Relish and other sauces – God knows how many.'[23]

Mary pressed Soyer to take a glass of champagne with Sir John Campbell who was sitting contentedly by her side, and bustled off to fetch more supplies, during which time Campbell divulged to Soyer who she was. It is highly significant that Soyer, when told, was flabbergasted. He could barely believe that at last he had met 'the celebrated Mrs Seacole'. Soyer's reminiscences of the Crimea, like Douglas Reid's, were published after the event, when Mary was indeed a celebrity. Nothing appeared in print about her (apart from her own business cards) until newspaper and then veterans' accounts started appearing in London from 1856 onwards. Yet Soyer implies here that she was already well known, even before the British Hotel proper had opened its gap-toothed doors. So, ever since those cannily written business cards had arrived back in February, the British establishment in the Crimea must have been buzzing with the news that Mother Seacole was on her way – which is, of course, what Mary herself implied, but it's always satisfying to have corroborative evidence. Satisfying, too, to realize just how powerful her character must have been, to carry such a fulsome reputation so far.

It wasn't long before Mary reappeared at the flap of her tent with a couple of bottles in her hands, declaring that she would treat the General and Monsieur Soyer to a drink herself.

We all declared it would never do for a lady to stand treat in the Crimea.

'Lord bless you, Monsieur Soyer,' said the lady, 'don't you know me?'

'Yes, I do now, my dear Madam.'

'Well, all those fine fellows you see here are my Jamaica sons – are you not?' said she, opening the champagne, and addressing the general.

'We are, Mrs Seacole, and a very good mother you have been to us.'[24]

They all drank each other's health and, just for a while, relaxed.

By about July, the hotel building was as complete as it would ever be. Mary claimed it had cost £800, somewhat incredibly equating to about £33,000 today. It neatly occupied an acre of ground.

The hotel and storehouse consisted of a long iron room, with counters, closets, and shelves; above it was another low room,

used by us for storing our goods, and above this floated a large
union-jack. Attached to this building was a little kitchen . . . In
addition to the iron house were two wooden houses, with
sleeping apartments for myself and Mr Day, outhouses for
our servants, a canteen for the soldiery, and a large enclosed
yard for our stock, full of stables, low huts, and sties. Everything,
although rough and unpolished, was comfortable and warm;
and there was a completeness about the whole which won
general admiration . . . The reader may judge of the manner in
which we stocked the interior of our store from the remark,
often repeated by the officers, that you might get everything at
Mother Seacole's, from an anchor down to a needle.[25]

Mary had realized her ambition. Her achievement in getting herself
from Navy Bay to Spring Hill, and establishing herself so quickly and
convincingly, is staggering. If anyone deserved to prosper, surely it
was she.

7

Comfort and Order

Mismanagement and privation there might have been, but my business was to make things right in my sphere, and whatever confusion and disorder existed elsewhere, comfort and order were always to be found at Spring Hill.

The British campaign in the Crimea might roughly be divided into five stages. The first dated from the earliest preparations for war in 1853 until August 1854 when the order came through for troops to sail from their pestilential camp at Varna, on the western coast of the Black Sea, to Kalamita Bay (you can guess its contemporary nickname) on the Crimean peninsula. The second, much more aggressive, involved marching towards and besieging the Russian headquarters at Sevastopol, and encompassed the Battle of the Alma on 20 September, the first bombardment of Sevastopol on 17 October, the Battle of Balaklava (including the Charge of the Light Brigade) on 25 October, and the Battle of Inkerman on 5 November. During the next stage things quietened down a little as winter bit in and exposed the appalling extent of the administrative and military mismanagement the whole British campaign had suffered from the start. After much bickering amongst – and between – generals, allies, government spokesmen, medical supervisors, and commissariat and transport officers, the spring accompanied a slow but steady growth of comparative order, sensitivity and confidence.

Mary arrived in March 1854 just as things were beginning to improve, and the fourth stage began. This period, stretching until the fall of Sevastopol on 8 September 1855, involved several more bombardments of the city and another major engagement (at the river Tchernaya on 16 August), which Mary witnessed herself. Almost every night throughout the summer British troops were stationed in stagnant trenches mined in front of Sevastopol's bastions, and were regularly picked off by enemy artillery and disease. Russian shells sometimes reached the British military camps, some three or four miles south of the city, and Mary remembered having to dive to the ground for cover on her rounds delivering food or medicine to various grateful clients. On one occasion she dislocated her thumb when her weight fell on it awkwardly, and in a dubious advertisement for her osteopathic skill, it never properly healed. (It was her right thumb: you can see it poking out of line on a photograph taken some fifteen years later.)

Part of the improvement in the general condition and efficiency of the British contingent during the spring of 1855 was due to political pressure (stirred up by W.H. Russell's melodramatic dispatches in *The Times*), and a bout of belated housekeeping in the corridors of power back in London. A suffocating tangle of rules and regulations that clung to everything like cobwebs began to be swept away. The odd gleam of common sense was allowed, occasionally, to peep through the mess, and resulted in the decision to send a Sanitary Commission to clear the wharf and streets of Balaklava of dead dogs (specifically) and any other putrescence liable to infect the troops with fever. Supplies started finding their way through to the men, after months of misadventure and confusion, and characters like Mary's new friend Monsieur Soyer arrived to do something constructive for the army. It shouldn't be forgotten that

Florence Nightingale nearly killed herself with frustration and fatigue in her efforts to inject yet more common sense and compassion into the system at Scutari; nor that the supplies that arrived, as the weather heated up nicely towards summer, were mostly thick woolly coats and 'balaclava' helmets knitted by fond fingers at home. Still, some sort of progress was being made. Particularly so in the case of Alexis Soyer.

Mary Seacole considered Soyer 'the great high priest of the mysteries of cookery'. He was a grocer's son, born in France in 1810, who launched his own catering career at the age of nine by working in a Paris kitchen with his elder brother Philippe.[1] Philippe was training to be a chef, and by 1831 had been appointed to the Duke of Cambridge's household in England. Alexis followed him to London and excelled, being asked in 1837 to become *chef de cuisine* – and help design the kitchens – of the new Reform Club in London, whose members included the most influential Liberal politicians of the day. Ten years later he requested a sabbatical, in order to travel to Ireland for the relief of famine victims there. The British Government commissioned him to set up the 'soup kitchen' he'd invented: a novel arrangement of boilers and utensils whereby up to 5,000 people daily could enjoy a bowl of special recipe 'famine soup', and stay alive.[2] To help finance soup kitchens in Dublin and, later, amongst the slums of London, he opened an art gallery (he had been married to the painter Elizabeth Emma Jones, who died in 1842) and donated the admission fees to charity.

Restless after the Irish episode, Soyer spent a lot of energy and too much money during the next few years on opening a vast restaurant complex opposite the gates of the Great Exhibition site in 1851, grandly named the 'Gastronomic Symposium of All Nations', and far too elaborate to thrive. He also wrote books; designed ever-more efficient stoves and kitchenware; and toured the country giving lectures on the art of cookery. Like Mary (in more ways than one), immediately he read newspaper reports in 1854 about the plight of the British troops in the Crimea, his enthusiasm and innate philanthropy drove him to insist on getting out there to help. Unlike

Mary, however, he was a gentleman, and well known enough, having run 'the finest kitchen in London',[3] to command instant respect; he was commissioned with alacrity to travel to Scutari to advise Miss Nightingale on optimizing the design, equipment and output of hospital kitchens.

Soyer revolutionized army catering, both within hospitals and further afield. Basic rations at this time consisted of 1lb of meat for each soldier (not necessarily fresh), 1lb bread, coffee (sometimes uselessly supplied in the form of unroasted, unground beans), tea (which was brewed by twisting first- or second-hand leaves in a rag and dunking them in a can of water), a little salt and sugar, and perhaps what was alarmingly known as 'boiled missionary', or extra salt-meat, if any were left over from the voyage out. Soyer augmented these by using offal, which the British butchers were apt to toss away in disgust, to make nourishing soups and jellies for the sick. He ordered dried vegetables to be sent from home; he wrote down simple but tempting recipes for his trainees to follow in their own mess kitchens; he sourced local supplies to add variety to menus, and developed cheap but practical utensils like 'Soyer's Scutari teapot' – a wonderfully elegant vessel with a little model minaret for its lid and a perforated tube inside to hold the leaves – and the famous field stove, designed to work beautifully on precious little fuel and in any weather. The book he wrote to describe his work in the Crimea, *A Culinary Campaign,* includes popular field recipes – for example 'Salt Pork with Mashed Peas, for One Hundred Men':

Put in two stoves 50lbs of pork each, divide [another] 24lbs in 4 pudding-cloths, rather loosely tied [if any were left over after the men had torn them up for much needed handkerchiefs]; putting [dried peas] to boil at the same time as your pork, let all boil till gently done, say about two hours; take out the pudding and peas, put all meat in one cauldron, remove the liquor [gravy] from the other pan, turning back the peas in it, add two teaspoonfuls of pepper, a pound of the fat, and with the wooden spatula smash the peas, and serve both. The addition of about half a pound of flour and two quarts of liquor, boiled ten minutes, makes a great improvement. Six sliced onions, fried and added to it, makes it very delicate.[4]

It's sobering to realize that dishes like this were hailed with such gastronomic delight: whatever must meals have been like before Soyer arrived?

Although Mary was no doubt familiar with the stringy, salt stews and pallid soups of traditional army fare (one wit dubbed her Balaklava's 'Creole with the tea mug', a more prosaic equivalent of Scutari's 'Lady with the Lamp'),[5] she was quite as capable of providing *nouvelle cuisine* for the troops as Soyer. But her kitchens at the British Hotel were often confidently aimed at the higher end of the market. Contrast the above soldiers' menu with one for the sort of officers' dinner party Mary liked to cater for:

Main Course:

Welsh rarebit
Fish
Irish Stew
Curry (chicken, beef, vegetable, mutton, goat)
Chicken with gravy
Saddle of mutton
Ham
Tongue

Dessert:

Rice Pudding (no milk)
Tarts with senna
Rhubarb pudding
Sponge cake
Pastry
Custard

Jelly
Blancmange
Plum pudding
Mince Pies

Beverages:

Claret Cup
Cider Cup
Sangria
Raspberry vinegar
Champagne

Coffee (with a lump of butter to substitute for milk)
Tea.[6]

Only an instinctive nutritionist would include two of nature's more palatable laxatives (and staples of Mary's pharmacopoeia) disguised amongst the puddings.

Despite her skills and forty-odd years' experience in hotel kitchens, Mary still sought Soyer's advice while the British Hotel was being built. She warmed to him. He dressed flamboyantly, like her, and spoke English as idiosyncratically as she must have done. He was non-judgemental, jolly, and quick to think the best of people, and Mary was proud to consider herself his equal. As one restaurateur to another she asked him not only what she should stock to most advantage (giving little away, he advised 'hams, wines, spirits, ale and port, sauces, pickles, and a few preserves and dried vegetables') but also, typically, how to make the most money from her venture. Soyer, perhaps better aware than Mary that he was not, given his business record, the best man to ask, vaguely assured her that with her reputation amongst 'all the army', she was bound to triumph as long as she was prudent. And Mary, benevolent snob that she undoubtedly was, heartily concurred. She assured him that the commander-in-chief himself, Lord Raglan, had only the other day called in and spoken to her for a full ten minutes, promising support for her venture. 'I know Miss Nightingale too,' she boasted, explaining about her stay at Scutari and making it sound more like a private house-party than a squat in the laundry-woman's quarters. Florence was on a tour of inspection in the Crimea at the time of this particular conversation between Mary and Soyer, and had fallen ill. If she had known before being struck down at Balaklava that Mrs Seacole was so near, Miss Nightingale would definitely have come to call, insisted Mary – and now that the angel was in need of medical help herself, Mary promised to return the intended call as soon as possible and sort 'the dear lady' out with some treatment.[7]

Armed with the support (real or imaginary) of the great and the good, Mary filled her newly constructed cupboards and shelves with hundreds of pounds worth of goods, brought from England or ordered since her arrival, reared in the pens behind the hotel, or haggled from the shops and bazaars at nearby Kamiesch (the French HQ) and Kadikoi. She proudly listed what was available at the height of the hotel's success, claiming that

> . . . the firm of Seacole and Day would have been happy to serve you with (I omit ordinary things) linen and hosiery, saddlery, caps, boots and shoes, for the outer man; and for the inner man, meat and soups of every variety in tins (you can scarcely conceive how disgusted we all became at last with preserved provisions); salmon, lobsters, and oysters, also in tins, which last beaten up into fritters, with onions, butter, eggs, pepper, and salt, were very good; game, wild fowl, vegetables, also preserved, eggs, sardines, curry powder, cigars, tobacco, snuff, cigarette papers, tea, coffee, tooth powder, and currant jelly. When cargoes came from Constantinople, we bought great supplies of potatoes, carrots, turnips, and greens. Ah! What a rush there used to be for the greens . . .[8]

Her succulent and miraculously milkless rice-puddings were famous, especially since most Crimean rice-puddings were 'dry as tinder';[9] equally famous were her sausage and mash and curiously addictive 'Welch rabbits'. On occasions her black cooks, including the faint-hearted Francis, helped her prepare West Indian dishes for her clientele: she longed to challenge Soyer to a culinary competition, French versus Jamaican, but sensibly he never dared accept.

Where Francis came from, and when he arrived at Spring Hill, are mysteries. He and his colleagues must have been mainstays of the whole operation at Spring Hill, but Mary only acknowledged him – 'my black man' – in *Wonderful Adventures* on a couple of occasions: once when he managed to apprehend a French thief, and again when he'd been outrageously gnawed by some of those legendarily gargantuan Crimean rats.

> On the following morning he came to me, his eyes rolling angrily, and his white teeth gleaming, to show me a mangled finger, which they had bitten, and ask me to dress it. He made a great fuss; and a few mornings later he came in a violent passion this time, and gave me instant notice to quit my service, although we were paying him two pounds a week, with board and rations. This time the rats had, it appeared, been bolder, and attacked his head, in a spot where its natural armour, the wool, was thinnest . . . Driven to such extremity, I made up my mind to scour the camp in search of a cat.[10]

Pinkie the Coldstream Guards' cat was duly detailed to sentry duty in Spring Hill's kitchens, but soon deserted. Poor Francis was prevailed upon to stay at the British Hotel, and left to fend for himself.

There was obviously no feeling of Afro-Caribbean kinship between Mary and those she considered her servants. She placed herself closer to her clients than to her staff, and during the summer and early autumn of 1855 was content to bask in the complete satisfaction that she was exactly where she wanted to be, with no one but herself (and maybe the shadowy Mr Day) to thank for it, doing just what she wanted to do, and being treated by many of the officers of the British Army with the affection and admiration she had always felt was her due. Life was good.

Until this comparatively late stage in her career, we have never had the grounds to argue with Mary's representation of herself, because no one has spoken about Mary but Mary herself. She has been completely in charge of her own image. Despite a few family facts and figures in the registers and record books of Jamaica, evidence of the nature of her upbringing there has been entirely circumstantial. She elaborated more on the Central American episode of her life, but again, we only have her word for how things were at the first British Hotel, and how she was perceived by others. Once she arrived in the Crimea, however, in a very public arena where she strove to become the focus of attention and approval, she began to run the risk of her future memoirs being undermined by others. She quoted a chapterful of letters in *Wonderful Adventures*, all stressing the importance of her work and saying what a sterling soul she was, from the likes of the high-falutin' adjutant-general of the British Army Lord William Paulet and John Hall (the Inspector-General of Hospitals), down to mere members of the rank and file. But these, given the lack of corresponding copies in their authors' papers, are inadmissible as independent tokens of esteem, though it would have been rash in the extreme for her spuriously to quote easily recognizable and high-profile gentlemen like Paulet and Hall in print.

In the canon of literature of all kinds which followed the war, however, entirely arbitrary mentions of Mary began to emerge. Dr Douglas Reid, who commented about her work on the wharves of Balaklava, obviously approved. So did William Howard Russell, the war artist William Simpson and Monsieur Soyer. Journalists sang her praises in the *Illustrated London News*, *Punch* and the *Morning Chronicle*. Other more ordinary mortals appreciated her hospitality, her cooking, her work with the sick and wounded, and her good-humoured ubiquity with more or less amusement. Often she was caricatured as a rather ridiculous creature – a surreal hybrid of Mad Sally Mapp (a famously bombastic but successful London quack) and Miss Nightingale – who, beneath the gaudy costumes and substantial brown bosom, possessed a glowing heart of gold. But inevitably, then as now, there were those who, like Lola Montez, suspected that the widow Seacole was a little too good to be true. Florence Nightingale was chief amongst them.

Alexis Soyer mentioned in *A Culinary Campaign* that Mary had promised to visit Florence when the latter had been taken ill on her visit of inspection to Balaklava; he also noted rather wearily that the Creole with the tea mug never lost the opportunity of telling anyone who would listen how 'fond' she and the Lady with the Lamp were of each other. Florence was aware of this loudly broadcast familiarity, and thoroughly uncomfortable with it. Although politely agreeing with Soyer that she was sure Mary had 'done much good',[11] privately she was revolted by the idea of any association at all with this dark, fat, opinionated, impertinent and rather vulgar old dame. Florence abhorred people who didn't recognize their place in society, claiming once that she was misunderstood by those who imagined her working amongst the sick and/or lower orders with equanimity. In reality, mixing with them often made her squirm: 'I don't suppose [people] had any idea of one's station in life, & thought one enjoyed coming there among the officers and men as a pleasant thing.'[12] She was appalled by any suggestion of drunkenness either in women or at women's hands, dismissing nurses at the first sign of intoxication and deploring (as did Mary) the harm the local Turkish spirit, raki, did to so many of the troops. Yet Soyer told her that Mary regularly prescribed brandy and water to 'strengthen the courage' of the wounded she was treating, and cheerfully served copious amounts of alcohol to the patrons of the British Hotel. No matter that Mary always insisted that here, as in Kingston, Cruces and Gorgona, she never condoned drunkenness on her premises (and would immediately evict the over-boisterous): to Florence, she was a pernicious influence on the morale and, ironically, the health of the men. 'She kept – I will not call it a "bad house" [i.e. a brothel] – but something not very unlike it – in the Crimean War,' wrote Florence of Mary in 1870, continuing

[s]he was very kind to the men &, what is more, to the Officers – & did some good – & made many drunk . . . I had the greatest difficulty in repelling Mrs Seacole's advances, & in preventing association between her and my Nurses (absolutely out of the question) when we established 2 Hospitals nursed by us between Kadikoi & the 'Seacole Establishment' (in the Crimea). But I was successful.[13]

On another occasion, Florence was somewhat less circumspect, recording disgustedly that Mary was a 'woman of bad character' who did indeed keep a 'bad house', and who had to be dissuaded from coming to 'quack' Florence during her illness at Balaklava.[14] It's not difficult to get to the bottom of this. I cannot imagine any two people more different in background, upbringing and experience than Florence and Mary. Besides which, Florence's character tended towards intolerance and defensiveness, while Mary's was more relaxed and self-assured. While Florence may have been worshipped for her wan-faced, angelic ministrations on the wards of Scutari, Mary was clapped on the back for her generous and impulsive readiness to help anyone (in uniform) she could – even if that did mean giving them the odd swig of sherry or claret cup. Florence was stringently clinical in her fight against the diseases that corrupted the military medical system, and burned with a cold fury at the suffering her patients faced unnecessarily thanks to maladministration and mismanagement. Mary met the victims of that suffering with a homely instinct to make things better – *feel* better – and to cheer them up enough to meet life, or imminent death, with good spirits. Yet both were dubbed by the press (and, each claimed, by the men they treated) the 'mother' of the army. Both were praised for caring for individuals in a military culture that before the Crimea had tended to deal only in units of men. I don't think Florence could even begin to understand how a woman like Mrs Seacole, with a personal history so utterly alien to Florence, could claim to be operating, and operating successfully, in the same general field as she. When the war was over, and Mary's book came out to such acclaim, it must have riled Florence that such a slapdash, morally dubious (from Florence's point of view) and socially iconoclastic character should have become the other heroine of the Crimean War. While not quite courageous enough – or perhaps too canny – to denigrate Mary in public, Florence spat venom in private and, perhaps, felt better for it.

What grounds Florence had for claiming the British Hotel to be a brothel, I don't know. Mary has always struck me as a person of integrity. If she had really believed that sex was therapeutic for British officers and men, then I'm sure she would have obliged to the best of her ability. The French, according to Billy Russell, quite readily availed themselves of the women attached to each regiment to cook and care for the men, the 'vivandieres'. He cracked a famous joke about them:

Two sailors walking up to the camp met a French *vivandiere* riding down. 'Hullo, Jack,' says one, 'is that what they call a She-Dragoon?' – 'Oh, no,' says the other, 'that's what they call their *Hors de Combat*!'.[15]

However, while that sort of thing might have been all right for foreigners, Mary worked hard at being British. Even though she was 'duskier' than many, and aware of the ungovernable libido black women like the 'Hottentot Venus' were supposed to possess, she was a true imperial Victorian, who preferred to espouse the traditional moral culture of her father's heritage rather than the more relaxed mores of her mother's. Officially, sex was not a business (literally) in which English ladies and gentlemen engaged. It happened in a sort of parallel existence, behind closed doors and unacknowledged. Besides which, Mary was – for all her banter and high spirits – a godfearing woman. As the future would show, she held highly developed religious convictions, and preached to dying men the sentimental promise of righteous reward. She also made a virtue of her own civilized nature, and liked to surprise prejudiced people into thinking her perhaps not quite as black as they'd thought. She would be extremely unlikely to have blotted her British copybook for posterity by risking exposure as a procuress. Florence was wrong. Or – given her own antipathy to Mary, and the general jollity and various comings and goings at the British Hotel – understandably mistaken.

As to Florence's charge of deliberate drunkenness: despite Mary's adamant statements in print that alcoholic over-indulgence was discouraged at Spring Hill 'in every way', and that 'my few unpleasant scenes arose chiefly from my refusing to sell liquor where I saw it was wanted to be abused,' I have no doubt that most people left the hotel in a merrier mood than when they had arrived, and that this must have been due – amongst other things – to Mary's copious cellar. Bodily comfort was just as important to her as spiritual salubrity, and she hadn't the heart to refuse her 'sons' a little of what they fancied now and then. But I can't see her abetting them in – as one officer put it – habitually getting so 'beastly drunk that they are carried home in sacks'.[16]

Part of Florence's discomfiture may have arisen from her inability to pigeonhole Mary's role in the campaign. Florence's work was hemmed in (or supported) by definitions, regulations and a tight structure. She was circumscribed, certainly at the beginning, by both the Government and the medical profession. In turn, she expected strict compliance from anyone under her authority. Discipline and obedience were everything. This might have been reasonable to those who had been trained in the religious or quasi-religious milieu of nursing sisterhoods. But lay people, more used to self-reliance, were not so easily subdued. Nurse Betsy Davis, for example, found Florence's methods repugnant to her own disorganized style of instinctive, highly sympathetic nursing. Betsy was an obstreperous Welsh woman, remarkably in her early sixties. She was appointed by Mrs Herbert to be sent out to Scutari soon after Florence's departure at the end of 1854 (at the same time as Mary applied) but Betsy knew, as soon as she clapped eyes on Florence, that working under Miss Nightingale was not feasible. 'I did not like the name of Nightingale. When I first hear a name, I am very apt to know by my feeling whether I shall like the person who bears it,' she declared, adding (harshly) that Florence was an arrogant and cold-hearted 'petticoat', out for power and glory at the expense of the sick.[17]

Mary, although not as reactionary as Betsy, was similarly idiosyncratic and therefore unsuitable for military service. Yet she undoubtedly possessed the experience and confidence to practise in the field, and it can't have escaped Florence how much affection and respect came Mary's way, especially during Florence's visit in 1855 to the Land Transport Hospital a few yards from the British Hotel and one of Mary's favourite haunts. How galling it must have been to Miss Nightingale that a woman she obviously despised should be so acclaimed. Indeed, there is a suggestion that so wary was Florence of Mary's influence at that particular hospital that she installed her staunchest ally, a Mrs Shaw Stewart, as superintendent there. A scribbled, abbreviated note, dictated by Florence after the war, states that she 'put Mrs S. at the LTH . . . in the front because near Mrs Seacole & the raki [alcohol]'.[18]

If she wasn't a credible nurse, according to Florence, then neither was Mary a typical sutler, which was the other profession claimed for her (though never by herself) in the Crimea. Sutlers – especially female sutlers – historically formed an established part of army culture all over the world. They were independent, usually small-time traders whose job it was to sell provisions to military personnel. They might keep a shop or barrow in a regimental garrison town (as Seacole and Day did in Aldershot after the war), or join camp followers on the march, like Brecht's Mother Courage. Essentially, they ran independent commissariats, and the Crimean theatre of war had more than one sutlers' 'village' right in camp. Outside camp, Kadikoi looked more like an English country fair by the beginning of 1856, so stuffed was every alleyway and open space with stalls. There was even a branch of Crockford's wine merchants from St James's Street in London to raise the tone. The French equivalent was in nearby Kamiesch, boasting some particularly fine restaurants and cafes.

Mary did more than the average sutler, however. She kept a restaurant *and* a hotel, the latter not just for the convenience of the odd convalescent officer, but to cater for the increasing number of sightseers who somewhat bizarrely sailed out from Britain during 1855 to see how the war was getting on. However, she had plenty of competition. A visitor to Kadikoi in May 1856 (when the British Hotel was still extant) mentioned several hotels there, all 'very curious' buildings

> . . . constructed of deal [timber planks], like every other building, but gaily decorated with little flags, fluttering all around, after the manner of the Crystal Palace, and bearing the high-sounding names of 'Hotel de l'Europe', [or] 'Hotel de la Paix', painted in large letters on their sides. A passing glance showed the single apartment of these hotels, neatly papered with the 'Illustrated London News', with here and there a few gayer scraps of art.[19]

It sounds reminiscent of the ad-hoc lodging-houses in Cruces and Gorgona, except that being mostly made of iron, the British Hotel was rather grander than the rest. It had a thriving take-away business, too, catering for everything from regimental banquets to chicken drumsticks twisted in a scrap of paper or a handkerchief (if either happened to be available). George Buchanan, a civilian surgeon, referred to Mary repeatedly in his memoirs of the campaign. He described a particularly enjoyable meal, heaping praise on its chef in the highest terms possible: 'he contrived wonderfully, and when it is considered that we did not have recourse to the *cuisine* of Mother Seacole, I am sure we had a capital bill of fare.'[20] Buchanan was entranced by Mother Seacole's HQ, which he came upon on his journey from Balaklava to the British Camp before Sevastopol.

> [A]t the top of the hill, before entering on the plateau, is situated the hut or house of 'Mother Seacole' called 'The British Hotel'. Here we called a halt, and refreshed ourselves with a draught of porter, and saw the active Creole at her occupations. This store was very conveniently situated, within

two miles of the Camp, and was always well supplied with all sorts of eatables. Things were a little more expensive than at Kadikoi, but you could always depend on their being good . . .[21]

Another patron was somewhat less charitable, but still grateful, when he recalled 'a capital [picnic] lunch on the ground, provided by an old black woman who kept a sort of eating-house on the heights'.[22]

At the hub of everything to do with the British Hotel – hardly anyone ever mentions Thomas Day – was this loud, loving woman, selling champagne to the (comparatively) rich to give tea to the poor. To Florence, she must have been a thoroughly distasteful conundrum. In fact, had Florence chosen to spread around the Crimea one of the more succulent rumours she came to hear involving Mary Seacole, I doubt whether Mary would have become quite the heroine she did. It involved a scandal of the juiciest kind, featuring a high-ranking officer serving in the 23rd, and a fourteen-year-old girl, with brown skin and blue eyes, called Sally. But Florence kept the 'secret' safe until much later on.

Someone else complained about Mary. He was present on one of the many occasions when Seacole and Day provided outside catering facilities in the Crimea, either in a bell-tent, or on a wagon: 'Mrs Seacole was there [at an army review on 24 February 1856] with a cart full of grub,' he noticed, but so great was the clamour to get at the heap of pastries and pies that 'none of us poor regimental officers could get near it.'[23] The implication, which I can well believe, is that Mary had favourites, and that those favourites were usually of lofty rank. Not always, because she was never slow to help those too weak or lowly to help themselves, but given the choice between middle-class or high-class money, she would much prefer the latter. Had she been a little less exclusive, and accepted the cash of slightly less illustrious patrons instead of the IOUs of the supposedly rich, she might just have survived in business. For now, however, she was happy with her lot.

Mary didn't have the weather to worry about at this time of year: after March, the spring and summer of 1855 were quite pleasant.

The track leading up from Balaklava to Kadikoi turned inexpressibly muddy in any rain, but a fine new road was being built to take its place, and the railway served to bring up stores if necessary. Those stores were arriving in plenty now that the harbour was better organized and communication with London had been speeded up by the installation of an electric telegraph line in April. Customers were never in short supply; indeed, Mary had to insist on closing the restaurant by 8 p.m. and on Sundays, to give her time to draw breath. And if money wasn't coming in now, it soon would: her friends were trustworthy and honourable men, and would surely pay their debts as promptly as possible. On the promise of their credit she ordered more and more goods for the British Hotel, to attract new clientele and increase its (putative) turnover.

Apart from the biblically sized population of rats, fleas and flies in the Crimea, it was the constant thievery that really made things difficult for Mary. Balaklava had been bad, but Spring Hill was far worse. Food and livestock were the main targets. In all, the firm of Seacole and Day lost over twenty horses (including Mary's own thirty-guinea mare Angelina), four mules, *eighty* goats, and numerous sheep, pigs and poultry. One fine, plump pig proved particularly alluring. Mary had bought him fresh from a newly arrived ship in the harbour, and was fattening him up to sell to her favourites, conferring promises of the best cuts to those she wanted most to impress, or to please.

> I could laugh heartily now, when I think of the amount of persuasion and courting I stood out for before I bound myself how its four legs were to be disposed of. I learnt more at that time of the trials and privileges of authority that I am ever likely to experience again . . . I baffled many a knavish trick to gain possession of the fine fellow; but, after all, I lost him in the middle of the day, when I thought the boldest rogues would not have run the risk . . . I rushed to the sty, found the nest warm, and with prompt decision prepared for speedy pursuit. Back I came to the horsemen [officers who had offered to help],

calling out – 'Off with you, my sons! – they can't have got very
far away yet. Do your best to save my bacon!' . . .

Not half a mile off we soon saw a horseman wave his cap; and
starting off into a run, came to a little hollow, where the poor
panting animal and two Greek thieves had been run down . . .
Piggy was brought home in triumph.[24]

Mary wasn't so lucky with Angelina. Although the horse was
spotted at various times after her disappearance from Spring Hill
– on one occasion nobly bearing an elderly naval officer and on
another a dandy member of the French cavalry – Mary never got her
back. Angelina had been bought by each of them in good faith at the
Kamiesch horse fair, and was nothing to do with Mary any more. So
she had to settle for a mangy old grey, whose coat she would dust up
with flour when riding out to meet important people (with predictably messy results in squally weather).

Embarrassingly, it wasn't only Mary's belongings that went missing
from the hotel: Soyer had his horse taken from outside the restaurant one day, and only after considerable efforts on the part of Mr
Day, turned detective, was it returned to him three days later. Mary's
partner featured somewhat shiftily in another stolen horse story
when a customer had his animal returned to him – again, a few days
after it went – by Day, who claimed vaguely that 'a sailor' had left it at
Spring Hill.[25]

Nor was it just food and livestock that vanished. All the laundry,
including the hotel's linen, was lost when Mary extravagantly sent it
to Constantinople to be cleaned one day, leaving her with the outfit
she stood up in and one more (besides a number of wholly
unsuitable fancy muslin gowns she'd naïvely packed for the adventure). The expense and sheer inconvenience of trying to cope with
the unremitting threat of burglary came closer to exhausting Mary
than anything else in the Crimea. She was running to stay still, and it
hurt.

With all the hard work of the hotel, it was easy to lose sight of the
main reason for Mary's presence in the Crimea. She had first come,

after all, to experience some of the 'pomp, pride and circumstance of glorious war', and even though this campaign had been running a bit short of pride and glory, she had no intention of spending all her time up to the elbows in flour and missing all the action. Mary had always considered she would be most useful on the battlefield, and whenever news came to Spring Hill of an impending engagement, it invigorated her wonderfully. She would immediately load up an enormous shoulder-bag with medicines, dressings, bandages, needles and thread, a bottle of sherry for rinsing hands and instruments, and some cheese sandwiches. Night or day, she would travel for 6km (3½ miles) across the wide plateau of the British Camp beyond the hotel to Cathcart's Hill. Unsurprisingly, 'conspicuous' is a word that often crops up in contemporary accounts to describe Mary; to one of the doctors working with the Turkish army, who witnessed these semi-commercial missions of mercy, no other word would do.

> Mounted on a horse, and conspicuous by her costume, which was bright blue in colour relieved by yellow, she made her way to the high ground overlooking the scene of action and, provided with a large basket of provisions and comforts, generously distributed refreshment to exhausted or wounded soldiers.[26]

Cathcart's Hill was a favourite viewing point for non-combatants, where spectators could gather out of the direct line of fire to watch the fighting (while enjoying sandwiches), and Mary often used it as a sort of satellite British Hotel. She supplied the sandwiches, helped with casualties dragged up to safety from the action in the valley of the Tchernaya or the trenches of Sevastopol down below, and savoured the vertiginous danger of the moment.

What Mary witnessed from Cathcart's Hill between Friday 7 and Sunday 9 September beat anything she'd ever seen before. It was the childhood stuff of her father's stories, and ever since, of her dreams: a real, live war at last. On the Friday evening, while selling snacks to other interested observers, she was able to look across to the north-east horizon and see 'fire after fire break out in Sevastopol, and . . . the beautiful yet terrible effect of a great ship blazing in the harbour, and lighting up the adjoining country for miles.' The allies were obviously working up towards some terrible climax after days of bombardment, and the next morning – suddenly bitterly cold – the constant cannonading continued until lunchtime. Then, in the distant silence, Mary noticed hundreds of French and British figures begin to spill out of the tiny-looking trenches in front of Sevastopol's two great bastions, the Malakoff and the Redan, and teem towards the deeply moated ramparts ahead of them. She watched as the French appeared to take the Malakoff from the beleaguered Russians, and turned with proud anticipation to see the British assault on the Redan. It was disastrous. Fanny Duberly, also perched on Cathcart's Hill, recalled the awful chaos in her journal.

The British, not troubling to silence the Redan guns, their advance trench still 200 yards distant, had leaped from their parapets and staggered across the open ground through a storm of fire. They had tumbled into the Redan ditch and struggled up the escarpment. The mass of British, ever increasing and clinging like a swarm of agitated bees to the outer parapet of the Redan, had suddenly grown petrified. Behind them lay corpses and screaming wounded. What awaited them beyond the parapet? Officer after officer [including Mary's friend Sir John Campbell] jumped into the Redan. None followed the waving swords. During an agonized pause the Russians, back on their parapet, beat at the crouching red mass below with stones, their muskets blazed at point-blank range, they stabbed and slashed, yelling with mad laughter . . . Too much had been entrusted to the young soldiers, who had come to think that defending trenches was the worst that war demanded of them.[27]

Some of the troops involved in this debacle belonged to Mary's favourite regiment, the 97th, and she was heartbroken to recognize its remnants when dragged back behind the lines for her attention. The night of 8/9 September was livid with gunfire, and by dawn most of Sevastopol appeared to be ablaze. When the smoke had cleared, it became apparent that the city had finally fallen to the allies, and that the siege was at an end. In reality, the French had won, which hardly delighted Mary. She was only able to forget her resentment when someone reminded her of a bet that had been made back at the British Hotel, 'that I would not only be the first woman to enter Sevastopol from the English lines, but that I would be the first to carry refreshments into the fallen city.' If she could win this personal Crimean campaign, she would dedicate her victory to those valiant soldiers she considered her less fortunate brothers-in-arms.

Rushing home to the British Hotel, Mary swiftly appropriated some mules from her neighbours, the Land Transport Corps; loaded them with panniers full of 'good things'; collected a dazed Mr Day and a few other supporters, and set off for her own assault on Sevastopol.

8

Proud and Unprotected

*. . . it was from a confidence in my own powers, and not at all
from necessity, that I remained an unprotected female.*

Mary's triumphal entry into Sevastopol on the morning of Sunday 9
September was not quite as pompous as she might have hoped.
Seductive visions of riding through the grateful streets on her flour-
caked horse like a vicarious Victoria, hailed by her 'sons' and
crowned with a coronet of herbs and late roses soon evaporated
when she and her attendants trotted past the sentries (thanks to a
specially issued pass), through the heaps of bizarrely assorted
trophies confiscated from hopeful soldiers on their way out of
the plundered city, and into hell. The Russians had retreated, after
a 349-day siege, to the distant northern portion of Sevastopol
beyond the harbour, but they continued firing intermittent shells
and round-shot from there, and unexploded mines still simmered
beneath the surface of the streets. There was hardly a building left
intact, and many were still blazing or sullenly smouldering. The
British were dizzy with looted wine, leering and capering about

dressed in Russian women's skirts and bonnets. Those still sober were famished, and snatched Mary's food and raspberry vinegar away. William Howard Russell, visiting the Redan as Mary did, described the scene in uncompromising detail.

> All the houses behind it [were] a mass of broken stones – a clock turret, with a shot right through the clock; a pagoda in ruins; another clock-tower, with all the clock destroyed save the dial, with the words, 'Barwise, London', thereon; cook-houses, where human blood was running among the utensils; in one place a shell had lodged in the boiler and blown it and its contents, and probably its attendants, to pieces. Everywhere wreck and destruction. This evidently was a *beau quartier* once. Climbing up to the Redan, which was fearfully cumbered with the dead, we witnessed the scene of the desperate attack and defence which cost both sides so much blood. The ditch outside made one sick – it was piled up with English dead, some of them scorched and blackened by the explosion, and others lacerated beyond recognition. The quantity of broken gabions[1] and gun-carriages here was extra-ordinary; the ground was covered with them. The bomb-proofs [shelters] were the same as in the Malakoff, and in one of them a music-book was found with a woman's name in it, and a canary-bird and vase of flowers were outside the entrance.[2]

The Russian hospital down by the docks, in which Mary took a professional interest, was too obscene for her to describe in print. Russell, however, readily obliged:

> In a long, low room, supported by square pillars arched at the top, and dimly lighted through shattered and unglazed window-frames, lay . . . the dead – the rotten and festering corpses of the soldiers, who were left to die in extreme agony, untended, uncared-for, packed as close as they could be stowed on the floor, others on wretched trestles and bedsteads or pallets of

straw, sopped and saturated with blood which oozed and trickled through upon the floor, mingling with the droppings of corruption . . . Many lay, yet alive, with maggots crawling about inside their wounds. Many, nearly mad by the scene around them, or seeking escape from it in their extremest agony, had rolled away under the beds and glared out on the heart-stricken spectator.[3]

All Mary could say of the hospital was that she would have given much not to have seen it at all, and would never, ever, forget it.

Having rapidly dispensed all the refreshments she had brought with her, and done her grisly sightseeing, Mary followed her party through the newly French quarter of Sevastopol before riding the 11km (seven miles) home to Spring Hill. The French, along with the Turks and Sardinians, had been allowed by their authorities to keep whatever booty they found, and so engrossed did Mary become in watching their skill and speed when stripping a house of its contents that she fell behind the others. Apparently somebody whispered to one of the French looters, while she obliviously looked on, that the bizarre-looking foreign woman over there was a Russian spy, and before she knew what had happened, she was under arrest. Predictably, Mary was outraged. When a French soldier tried to pull her from her horse, she set about him with a church bell she'd appropriated, until an officer, hearing the commotion, came up and rescued her (and the soldier). Luckily, the officer had been one of her patients in the aftermath of the Battle of the Tchernaya three weeks ago. Meanwhile Mr Day arrived back on the scene – a little late for gallantry – and proceeded to whip the poor, dazed soldier with a riding crop while Mary gave him a few more clangs of the bell for good measure.

A certain Lady Hodgson, involved in an African uprising some fifty years after this Crimean experience of Mary's, was responsible for what must be one of the most bemusing ladies' travel tips ever offered. 'Skirts are an impediment', she warned gravely, 'when fleeing for your life in Ashantiland.'[4] In less extreme circumstances, however, they could come in surprisingly handy. I suspect Mary found her all-enveloping petticoats invaluable on this occasion: besides the church bell, she managed to smuggle past the Sevastopol sentries a china teapot, a parasol, a hunk of brown bread retrieved from an oven on the Redan (how thoroughly she must have looked), a gilded altar candle which she presented to Sir William Codrington, commander-in-chief of the British Army, and – her pièce-de-résistance – a 3m (10-foot) long painting of the Madonna. The latter was cut from a church altarpiece by a 'little French soldier': Mary bought it, and eventually took it back to London where its air of 'divine calmness and heavenly love' helped inspire one of the most significant decisions of her life. Sadly, she couldn't carry everything she'd have liked to, and had to reject a portion of grand piano, a velvet settee and a stupendously vast armchair.

Mary may have been the first woman from the English lines to enter Sevastopol – thus winning her bet – but she fails to mention that she wasn't the only one. During the days that followed its fall, tourists of all sorts travelled in her wake. Fanny Duberly took the first possible opportunity to visit, on Thursday 13 September, once British restrictions on entering the city were lifted. She considered a table-leg, but in the end only managed some buttons, scraps of ammunition and weaponry, a glass salt-cellar, and her own little crust of bread (found initially by someone else). Soon, a British tour company was offering £5 holidays in the Crimea to include a fortnight's accommodation – although not, it appears, at the British Hotel – and guided trips to the battlefields with Sevastopol as the highlight, once the city had been somewhat sanitized.[5] Mary was proud to have seen it on the first day, in all its ghastly glory.

It's sometimes easy to forget, especially when reading *Wonderful Adventures of Mrs Seacole*, how many other women there were in the Crimea, both at this late stage and earlier on. Some of those wives lucky enough to draw the 'to go' ticket in the non-commissioned officers' ballots worked as laundrywomen, cooks, or seamstresses, and others – notably Elizabeth Evans and Nell Butler – cared for the sick. Mrs Evans's husband was the servant to an infantry officer in the

4th King's Own Royal Lancasters. She cut her teeth at the Battle of Alma back in September 1854, and had become so experienced and skilful a nurse by the following spring that Florence Nightingale head-hunted her for official duties. Nell was a private's wife in the 95th Foot, whose nursing career began when her husband Michael fell sick with fever at Balaklava. Again, her natural aptitude for the job ensured she was never without work.[6]

Most of the women involved in the war were engaged, of sheer necessity, in medical work of one kind or another. The vivandieres dutifully comforted the wounded, although this was not their primary task, and French Sisters of Charity were called up as nurses. Russian soldiers were attended by the Community of the Cross, a company of 140 lay volunteers organized by the Grand Duchess Elena Pavlovna in St Petersburg, all working with the sick and wounded in Sevastopol from November 1854. One Russian woman in particular is celebrated today: Ekaterina Bakunina, chosen to assist the surgeon Nikolai Pirogov in the makeshift hospital that had so horrified Mary.[7] While the siege was still in progress, Pirogov and Bakunina presided over hundreds of hurried but ground-breaking operations, pioneering the use of chloroform, plaster casts to mend breaks, and introducing to the wards a strict and methodical hospital routine. Despite Billy Russell's disgust at the conditions immediately after the fall of the city, this was, in many ways, a far more modern hospital than any British one, at home or abroad.

Heroic as Bakunina undoubtedly was, the person regarded as the Russian Nightingale – as Mary is dubbed 'the black Nightingale' – was Darya Michailova, fondly remembered as Dasha Sevasto-pol'skaya. She was a teenager, the daughter of one of the few Russian sailors killed during the attack on the Turks at Sinope. The legend goes that on her father's death she sold everything she (and he) had to buy a wagon, on which she rode – dressed in her father's uniform – to the banks of the river Alma. There she set up her own first aid station, and followed the Russian army through every battle and skirmish, basing herself at Sevastopol. When a doctor needed her help, she gave it; otherwise she worked, like

Mary, on her own initiative and with native skill and tenderness. Her devotion and personal history made her a celebrity after the war (again, like Mary). She was awarded decorations and a dowry, and lived out the rest of her days in Sevastopol, where she died aged sixty-five in 1901.[8]

Darya and Mary had much in common. Darya seems to have been rather less *large* than Mary, less proud and worldly, but they were both determined to help their fathers' countrymen, and shared the rare distinction of being 'unprotected' women at war: without an organization, patron or male appendage to take responsibility for them. How much that meant to Darya we don't know; to Mary it was crucial to her independence and self-esteem.

It has been convenient for history to call most of these women 'nurses' – i.e. conforming to the image of a professional hospital assistant subsequently popularized by Nightingale herself at her training school in London – and to judge them accordingly. In reality, they were a less manageable mixture, but after the war Florence was able to distil an abstract of the ideal nurse from the choicest qualities (sometimes more theoretical than practical) of them all. To that extent, the Crimean War was responsible for defining the modern nurse. Some of Florence's original recruits, although called nurses and drawn from hospital wards, were according to her merely specimens of 'the slipperiest race on earth'.[9] It was only when the most promising of them learned from Florence herself, and from the best their lay colleagues could offer, that their medical expertise began to assume an integrity of its own. The pattern for all of them, professional and amateur alike, was of course Nightingale herself. She was utterly dedicated to her cause, and a brilliant administrator, activist and politician. Some of her companions, like Selina Bracebridge and Lady Alicia Blackwood, were social ornaments who (newly liberated from the strictures of the drawing-room) helped where they could with humility, efficiency and high moral tone. Others were from religious orders with slight medical training, or none, but with devotion and selflessness, and the best of the soldiers' wives 'on the strength' worked hard and obediently wherever they were needed. Nightingale's perfect nurse would combine the strengths of all these women. But she'd lack the qualities that made Mary Seacole so popular: spontaneity, uninhibited warmth and the freedom to follow her instincts.

Mary Seacole could never be a model Nightingale nurse, even though she is often regarded as a black pioneer of the profession. She was a mixture of doctor and apothecary, surrogate death-bed mother (or even wife, on occasions), practitioner, comforter and – always – entrepreneur. She insisted on being useful to the sick and the healthy, with, if possible, mutual profit, both spiritual and material. Had she been successful in her interview back in London in the autumn of 1854, and accepted as one of Florence's angels, she might possibly have managed for a while. But I very much doubt it: her skills and needs reached beyond what Florence sought, and her temperament was utterly incompatible with the necessary constraints of being an employee. Especially Florence Nightingale's employee. It does both women a disservice when modern commentators on the war compare Mary's medical skills with Florence's: they approached those whom they wished to help quite differently, and relied on their own considerable but idiosyncratic gifts to try, with all their might, to treat their patients with dignity and compassion.

Florence's work in the Crimea spawned reams of documentary evidence. She wrote hundreds of letters between 1854 and 1856, and there is a mass of objective material in archives around the world.[10] With Mary, as usual, one must rely on her own testimony, on hearsay, and on the subjective evidence of those of her acquaintance who wrote books or newspaper columns. But Mary's reputation was widely appreciated both during the war and afterwards. Being an elderly, assertive, Jamaican tradeswoman, polite Victorian society could hardly build her up as the sentimental role-model Florence became, but credit was nevertheless given where credit was thought to be due. And people loved her.

Mary's influence over those high-ranking officers and social bigwigs who set up a subscription fund for her after the war was obvious, and they'll play their part a little later in her story. But humbler souls were just as ready to sing her praises, usually with a tang of patronization distasteful to the modern reader, yet with genuine admiration. Her greatest public champion was Billy Russell:

> I have seen her go down, under fire, with her little store of creature comforts for our wounded men; and a more tender or skilful hand about a wound or broken limb could not be found among our best surgeons. I saw her at the assault on the Redan, at the Tchernaya, at the fall of Sebastopol, laden, not with plunder [how hard did he look?], good old soul! But with wine, bandages, and food for the wounded or the prisoners.[11]

Lord William Paulet, the adjutant-general of the British Army in 1856, remembered her as an 'excellent woman' who 'frequently exerted herself in the most praiseworthy manner in attending wounded men, even in positions of great danger, and in assisting sick soldiers by all means in her power'.[12] Dr John Hall was the inspector-general of Hospitals in the East; he and Florence Nightingale regarded one another with mutual distrust and resentment, while his relationship with Mary was almost cordial. He sanctioned her unsupervised practice of medicine in the Crimea, having carefully inspected her medicine box with approval.[13] (Florence took Hall's public support of Mary as a personal insult.) The war artist William Simpson was particularly fond of Mary. He drew her looking for all the world like someone's favourite fluffy aunt, in lace, beribboned and bejewelled, but with a face of great tenderness and pity. He remembered her obvious pride in her Scottish genealogy, and commended her for wearing her usual bright colours on the otherwise utterly mournful occasion of the commander-in-chief Lord Raglan's funeral in the summer of 1855.[14]

Wonderful Adventures of Mrs Seacole cites plenty of (untraceable) testimonials to her good character and peculiar gifts, but we don't need to resort to those for evidence: there are plenty to choose from elsewhere. Perhaps the Crimean correspondent of the *Morning Advertiser* best summed up the attitude of Mary's supporters, in an

Mrs Seacole's hut   Major Cox's hut   Sebra Vicarage

From Sketches by
Lady Alicia Blackwood

INTERIOR OF ZEBRA VICARAGE   From a Sketch by Lady Alicia Blackwood

GILBERT SMITH & COMPY LITHO LONDON

A sketch by Florence Nightingale's friend, Lady Alicia Blackwood, showing the position of the British Hotel ('Mrs Seacole's Hut').

The site of the British Hotel as it looks today.

OUR OWN VIVANDIÈRE.

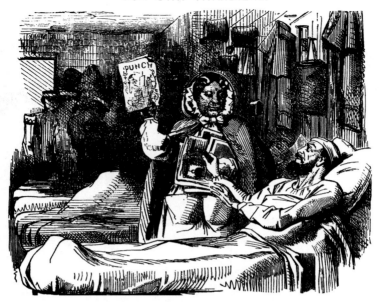

Mary featured in *Punch*, 30 May 1857, dispensing copies of the magazine
to cheer her patients at the Land Transport Corps Hospital.

The celebrated Chef Alexis Soyer visiting the British Hotel.

The Royal Surrey Gardens Music Hall on London's South Bank.

THE SEACOLE FUND.—ROYAL SURREY

GARDENS.—GRAND MILITARY FESTIVAL, for the BENEFIT of Mrs. SEACOLE, at the Royal Surrey Gardens, to commence on MONDAY, July 27, 1857. and continue four days. 1000 performers, including Eleven Military Bands.

Under the immediate Patronage of

His Royal Highness the General Commanding-in-Chief.
His Grace the Duke of Wellington.
Her Grace the Duchess of Wellington.
His Grace the Duke of Newcastle.
The Most Noble the Marchioness of Ely.
The Most Noble the Marchioness of Winchester.
The Right Hon. the Earl of Westmoreland.
The Right Hon. the Countess of Westmoreland.
The Right Hon. the Earl of Euston.
The Right Hon. Lord Rokeby.
The Right Hon. Lady Rokeby.
Lieutenant-General Sir W Codrington, M.P.
Major-General Sir W. Fenwick Williams. M.P.
The Hon. Mrs. Dawson Damer.

The Colonels of the following regiments have most kindly forwarded the object the Committee have in view, by granting the assistance of the Bands of their distinguished corps, which will be united in one Colossal Orchestra, viz :—the First Life Guards, the Second Life Guards. the Royal Horse Guards Blue, the Grenadier Guards, the Coldstream Guards, the Scots Fusilier Guards. the Royal Engineers, the Royal Artillery, the Royal Marines (Woolwich), the Royal Marines (Chatham), and the 11th Hussars.

These bands will be supported by M. Jullien's renowned Orchestra, strengthened by leading performers from the Philharmonic Society, Her Majesty's Theatre, and the Royal Italian Opera. The Royal Surrey Choral Society will also lend its aid, assisted by deputations from the principal Choral Societies in the country. The whole will form an ensemble of upwards of 1000 performers.

The Festival will commence on Monday, the 27th of July, and will continue four days. On the inauguration day (the 27th) will take place a Grand Concert, with eleven military bands, M. Jullien's orchestra, the Choral Societies, and several other distinguished artistes, the whole forming an ensemble of upwards of 1000 performers. On this occasion the price of admission will be 5s.: stalls and reserved seats, in the first, second, and third galleries. 2s. 6d. extra.

On the second day, 28th inst., a Grand Evening Concert will take place, with the same performers. Admission to the gardens, 2s. 6d.; stalls and reserved seats, in first, second, and third galleries, 2s. 6d. extra.

On the third day, 29th inst., a Grand Evening Concert, with six military bands, M. Jullien's orchestra, chorus, &c.. forming an ensemble of 600 performers. Admission to the gardens. 1s.; stalls and reserved seats, in first. second, and third galleries, 2s. 6d. extra.

On the fourth day, a Grand Evening Concert, with six military bands, forming an ensemble of 600 performers. Admission to the gardens, 1s.; stalls and reserved seats in the first, second, and third galleries. 2s. 6d. extra.

Tickets for the Inauguration Festival and for the following days to be procured at Jullien and Co.'s, 214, Regent-street; Cramer, Beale, and Co.'s, 201, Regent-street; Mr. Sams', Royal Library, 1, St. James's-street; Keith, Prowse, and Co.'s, Cheapside; and at the Office of the Gardens.

The Concert will commence each evening at half-past 7 o'clock.

An announcement of Mary's benefit festival at the Royal Surrey Gardens in the summer of 1857.

A bust of Mary Seacole sculpted by her friend Count Gleichen,
Queen Victoria's nephew, in 1871.

The only known photograph of Mary Seacole. A *carte de visite*, taken in about 1873, when Mary was nearing seventy.

article appearing on 19 July 1855. I quote it, as the final paean for the moment, in full.

> We have at present a lady of colour in Balaklava, and occasionally in camp, who is quite an original in her way; and an amusing specimen of the adaptability to circumstances of the darker specimens of the genus *homo*. She is both a Miss Nightingale and a Soyer in her way. A native of Jamaica, she has travelled extensively on the American continent [one wonders whether this was Mary's exaggeration, or the reporter's], and has acquired great experience in the treatment of cases of cholera and diarrhoea. Her powders for the latter epidemic are now so renowned, that she is constantly beset with applications, and it must be stated, to her honour, that she makes no charge for her powders. She is often seen riding out to the front with baskets of medicines of her own preparation, and this is particularly the case after an engagement with the enemy. Her culinary powers are also so great, that even Soyer told her the other day she knew as much about cooking as himself. Mrs Seacole is, moreover, a highly intelligent woman, and a further proof that the race from which she sprang is one capable of high intellectual development. She may well exclaim, with *Othello* –
> 'Mistake me not for my complexion,
> The burnish'd livery of the golden sun' . . .

After (a little wearily) making the usual allowances for chauvinism and prejudice, Mary must have been well pleased with that.

Following the fall of Sevastopol, Mary inevitably used her medicine chest less frequently than before. She remained on call to those with stomach upsets and the odd case of dysentery, but the devastatingly high incidence of fever and disease which characterized the first nine months of the campaign was now, thank God, long past. The odd, rather half-hearted, Russian shell still found its way into southern Sevastopol streets from the north, and accidents with ordnance and ammunition were apt to happen to those too relaxed to concentrate, but apart from one awful incident on 15 November, the urgency of battle was over.[15] That afternoon an ammunition magazine in the French siege train was accidentally detonated; the resulting explosions and fire caused scores of casualties, mostly French. Some were killed instantly, others more slowly, and many who survived were horribly burned and maimed. So violent was the force of the blasts that a horse was said to have been killed by a splinter of shell at Kadikoi, some 6km (four miles) away, and Mary herself was alerted by a rock hurling itself against the hotel door. An eye-witness remembered her rush to help, once word had come through of the extent of the damage.

> Returning from the scene of the disaster, I met hastening thither in her cart, a very well-known woman. This was Mrs Seacole who lived near the railway [near] Kadikoi, and kept a sort of general store. She was a wonderful woman, a native of the West Indies who had travelled over half the world. All the men swore by her, and in case of any malady would seek her advice and use her herbal medicines in preference to reporting themselves to their own doctors. That she did effect some cures is beyond doubt, and her never failing presence among the wounded after a battle and assisting them made her beloved by the rank and file of the whole army.[16]

This tragedy changed the way Mary felt about the French. Instead of resenting them for their victory at Sevastopol, she pitied and admired them. In an ill-deserved reversal of fortune they were suffering far more than the British this season, from illness and a degree of administrative mismanagement, which offended Mary's sense of natural justice. This awful accident was the last straw.

What everyone needed now, thought Mary, was a lift of spirits – cheering up. The authorities agreed: given the extra time and energy available, a whole range of unlikely Crimean activities was introduced during the winter of 1855–6, each as far removed from the wretchedness of the previous year and a half as possible. Sternly disciplined officers and men metamorphosed into gadfly party-goers, actors, picnickers, cricketers, diners, shoppers, jockeys and highly enthusiastic hunters – even if, as Mary witnessed on the odd lean occasion, their quarry was reduced to rats (too easy) or a fellow soldier trailing a paper bag from his horse, which was somewhat less than thrilling.

This new mood of gaiety suited the firm of Seacole and Day very well. They began to extend the hotel, building additional store-rooms, ordering an even wider variety of stock, and running what Mary described as a horse and mule stud (Thomas's venture), but which was surely more of a livery stable. Further staff were engaged to join the partners, Jew Johnny, Francis and the cooks. At some stage one of Edwin Seacole's young relations from Black River arrived to help Mary: Sarah Seacole, aged about fourteen, and fondly known to an admiring Alexis Soyer as Sally. She was possibly the daughter of C.W. Seacole, listed in the Jamaican Almanac of 1839 as being a Captain of the local Militia, and would hardly have remembered 'Mammy Mary', being only about three when the Seacoles left Black River for Kingston in 1843, but she seems to have settled into her temporary new home quite happily. As was the West Indian custom, she still called Mary 'Mammy', which led to a fair amount of innocent confusion on Soyer's part and later on – less innocently – on Florence Nightingale's.

Soyer himself had a coloured secretary by the name of Thomas Garfield. One wonders whether Mary sought him out as a comrade in arms. It's difficult to decide: on the one hand, she was a welcoming soul, with an instinct to make people feel at ease. But as an intense anglophile, and sharing a fair amount of the imperial bigotry of the age, she'd be loath to align herself with an obvious minority. Besides, Garfield was better educated than she, and moved habitually in higher circles. She was proud of her eccentricity, depended on it, and would hardly be likely to dilute it by inviting comparisons with Garfield. Sarah was different: she was young, she was family, and attractive enough to be a credit to Mary. The cook

Francis, of course, was 'black', according to Mary, and therefore – like the 'dark' vivandieres Soyer noticed in the Crimea – quite apart.[17] I think, on balance, Garfield probably forwent the pleasure of Mrs Seacole's company on social occasions. And for all I know, was happy to, for exactly the same reasons as she. There was no lack of more obviously elevated and gratifying company for Mary at the British Hotel.

As the Christmas of 1855 beckoned, and politicians were busy with their peace plans, numerous banquets were booked to celebrate military anniversaries or honour certain regiments and officers. It became the custom to drink a toast to Mrs Seacole on these occasions, and Mary would reply with panache. Her cuisine became more and more inventive and prodigious: 'course after course made its appearance, and to soup and fish succeeded turkeys, saddle of mutton, fowls, ham, tongue, curry, pastry of many sorts, custards, jelly, blanc-mange, and olives.' She developed a speciality plum-pudding for the festive season, in demand at mess dinners through-out the British Camp. Someone invited to a friend's table for Christmas lunch remembered the disappointment all round when the Seacole pudding ordered by his host was sent 'by mistake to a major with the same name . . .'. They had to make do with a 'good rolly-polly made with jam' instead: no way would the happy recipient of the surprise pudding relinquish it.[18] The *Daily News* reported that she was offering a bustard for sale – the flavour of which 'partakes both of that of the woodcock and wild duck' – weighing a stupen-dous 9kg (19.5 lbs).[19] An even larger one, at 10kg (22 lbs), she kept for her own Christmas dinner.

The British Hotel's busiest months were between September 1855 and April 1856, by which time the Armistice and the Treaty of Paris, which signalled the end of the war, had been signed. The allied armies stayed put until the formalities were done, which meant a constant clientele, and buoyed by the relief of survival and the promise of a comparatively imminent return home, that clientele was ready to spend. Unfortunately, Mary wasn't firm (or vulgar) enough to refuse credit, and too many people were taking advantage of her generosity. But this was neither the time nor the place for debt-collecting. Mary had suffered with her sons; now she felt perfectly entitled, with them, to kick up her heels a little. She would worry about the balance sheet later. At the Sevastopol spring race meeting on Easter Monday (4 March) she set up an outside catering enterprise in a bell-tent decorated with the British Hotel's banner (with a sick-bed behind it for the treatment of injured jockeys), and served sandwiches and fancies, wines and champagne to the Crimea's new hedonists. The young Duke of Cambridge, Commander of the First Division, Queen Victoria's cousin and son of Soyer's erstwhile employer, had lent Mary a covered wagon in which to transport her stock from Spring Hill to the racecourse by the banks of the river Tchernaya, and business was beautifully brisk. The *News of the World*'s reporter noticed Mary's booth and the merry chaos surrounding it:

> Corks were flying on all sides from bottles of champagne. French beer was selling at three francs a bottle, and even Highlanders were content to take it instead of their darling whiskey, which Camp regulations had sternly prohibited. Ham-sandwiches were devoured with a ferocity well becoming the big beards and mustachios of the military; and crowds upon crowds swayed to and fro, before and behind the tents of the suttlers, holding up French and English coin, and clamorously endeavouring to fight their way close up to the dainties they desired, but could not, without a long delay, hope to obtain.[20]

'Good humour,' he said, 'prevailed everywhere.' It was a chance for everyone in and around the British Camp to come together and recapture something of the old world before the war. According to one officer present some 50,000 men were there, and a dozen or so English ladies, together with the same number of French ladies 'and a score or two of French women who were *not ladies* but vivandieres . . . and such style of people who rode astride their ponies and dressed themselves in eccentric costumes with trousers *à la* Bloomer . . .'[21] Apart from these unfortunate females, and the general tendency towards drunkenness, the day at the races was completely magnificent.

For further entertainment several 'theatricals' were staged during that winter and early spring: revues and sketches put on in huts and storerooms grandly dubbed for the occasion the 'Theatre Royal' or suchlike, and with alluringly oblique titles like 'A Most Unwarrantable Intrusion' or 'Moustache Movement!'. Actresses to play the parts of suitably trenchant or twittery heroines were rather hard to come by, and although Mary resisted the invitation to tread the boards herself (a comedy turn?) and must have forbidden Sarah to do the same, she was more than happy to help make up for the lack of ladies in other ways.

> . . . I lent [those officers playing women's parts] plenty of dresses; indeed, it was the only airing which a great many gay-coloured muslins had in the Crimea. How was I to know when I bought them what camp-life was? And in addition to this, I found it necessary to convert my kitchen into a temporary green-room, where, to the wonderment, and perhaps scandal, of the black cook, the ladies of the company of the 1st Royals were taught to manage their petticoats with becoming grace, and neither to show their awkward booted ankles, nor trip themselves up on their trains . . . Although I laced them in [to their stays] until they grew blue in the face, their waists were a disgrace to the sex; while – crinoline being unknown then – my struggles to give them a becoming *embonpoint* may be imagined . . . The hair was another difficulty. To be sure, there was plenty in the camp, but it was in the wrong place . . .[22]

Resourceful as ever, Mary overcame the age-old problems of a theatre dresser on tour: the shows went on, and proved a riotous success.

Back in Scutari, Florence Nightingale and her colleagues were engaged in rather more earnest attempts to keep their patients occupied: there, a reading room was stocked with gifts from home, schoolrooms were fitted up in which illiterate soldiers could be taught the basics of reading and writing, while others, already educated, could listen to the occasional lecture. Convalescents could attend singing lessons, or go down to the Inkerman Coffee-house.[23] But all this was poor stuff compared with the excessive exuberance going on behind Sevastopol.

For those of a more sober or contemplative disposition, the flora of the local countryside provided a fruitful distraction from the tedium of ordinary Camp life. Several officers went plant-hunting during March and April (spring came late that year), their saddle-bags bulging with roots, bulbs and cuttings on their return. One thought he'd discovered a new species of violet, not retiring like the English ones but growing right out in the open with 'unblushing effrontery'. Its scent was almost overpoweringly strong. Another collected snow-drops, including a particularly large and late-blooming one which he introduced to his garden at home in memory of fallen friends.[24] The Crimean soil was particularly rich, of course, with the rot of hundreds of men and their horses buried hastily just beneath the surface; sometimes there blossomed a crop of bloated flesh and stained bone amongst the flowers to spoil the view.

As the spring of 1856 relaxed into summer, and the landscape began to recover from the combined onslaughts of winter and war, Mary found herself looking apprehensively towards the future. She was aware, with Thomas Day, that their financial partnership was in trouble. Goods they had ordered last winter – speculatively relying on the British being garrisoned in the Crimea for a reasonable time to come – were likely to cross at sea with the first of the veterans returning home to Britain. The evacuation of the peninsula started at the beginning of May 1856, and lasted for two months, during which time most of the survivors marched for the coast past Mary's door, without the time to stop. Orders to sail came unpredictably and at short notice, so that there was hardly a chance to say farewell to friends, let alone arrange the settlement of accounts. But incoming consignments of horses, saddlery, foods and wines, stock for the stores, and medicines still had to be paid for. George Ponsonby, one of Seacole and Day's shippers, was clamouring for payment.[25] So, less urgently, was Mary. Billy Russell owed her five shillings and ninepence: that was nothing. But there were a hundred others similarly in debt to her by the time she left the Crimea in July: mostly officers, from generals to lieutenants, and she hadn't the heart, or confidence, to chase them.[26] She resolved to wait, and trust in their good breeding and decency. Whether Thomas Day upbraided Mary for her past liberality to all those poor souls to whom she'd dispensed free tea and cake or medicines in times of need, is not clear. Her generosity must have been exasperating. Goodwill is a valuable asset to a business, but can't be relied upon to pay the bills. So it may have been Day who suggested a move from Spring Hill back to Balaklava at the end of June, to coax a few last shillings out of the British contingent before it finally disappeared from the Crimea altogether by the middle of July. For three weeks Mary and Thomas kept a shop down by the embarkation quay, but it didn't profit them much.

Closing down the British Hotel was a miserable business. Physically, it had to be dismantled piece by piece in order to salvage the iron. Can it really have been worth packing up the main building and shipping it home? That's what Seacole and Day decided to do with it, but surely more for the sake of pride than expedience. Such a gesture smacks of rather desperate romanticism. The sheds and outhouses were reluctantly abandoned to the old enemy (locals returning to what used to be their homes, and needing shelter). They stripped them of the kitchen equipment Mary couldn't sell, moved into the more substantial structures, and burned the rest for firewood. An auction was held at which the hotel and store's stock was disposed of for what seemed to be a fraction of its cost or true worth – again, mostly to Russians – and it was during this travesty of a sale that Mary, at last, broke down. It was now nearly two years since she'd left Navy Bay on her mission, and ever since she had been working flat-out for its success. No one could have been more useful to her sons than she, and she considered her decision to abandon friends and family in Jamaica had been utterly vindicated. She had helped whomsoever she could to the best of her native abilities, and found the fulfilment she'd always sought, amidst the horrors of the Crimea. Unlike Florence Nightingale, Mary never felt guilty about those she couldn't help, or those who died. She would rather be glad for those whose lives (or deaths) she had enhanced. Best of all, not only had the British establishment acknowledged her – even welcomed her – it was now *grateful*, and literally in her debt. She was, at last, where she belonged.

But it was all so temporary. That wretched auction emphasized how ephemeral the microcosmic world of the British Army in the East had been. The Crimean War was an episode, concentrated and enclosed and closely shared, but real life was about to reclaim the surviving play-actors. Mary didn't want to leave the stage.

> . . . I felt that I could not sympathise with the glad faces and happy hearts of those who were looking forward to the delights of home . . . Had I not been happy through the months of toil and danger, never knowing what fear or depression was, finding every moment of the day mortgaged hours in advance, and earning sound sleep and contentment by sheer hard work? What better or happier lot could possibly befall me? And alas! How likely it was that my present occupation gone, I might long in vain for another so stirring and so useful. Besides which, it was pretty sure that I should go to England poorer than I left it, and although I was not ashamed of poverty; beginning life again in the autumn – I mean late in the summer of life – is hard up-hill work. [27]

When the contents of Mary's cellar came up at the auction, including bottles of the finest wine for which she'd paid £4 a case (perhaps £170 now) knocked down for a mere 4d a bottle, the famously unassailable Seacole spirit finally gave way. She took up a hammer, bellowing incoherently at the Russian bidders, and blindly smashed it down around her until the red wine ran like blood.

People held their hands out to try to catch the flow before it was absorbed into the thirsty soil.

Once all the cases had been destroyed, Mary, sobbing, turned away and left. She went to tend for the last time the young shrubs and lilac saplings she had planted – 'obtained with no small trouble' – over the graves of the British fallen, and to pick flowers or even grass from the killing fields by which to remember her favourite sons. When I visited the Crimea, I did the same. And from the slopes of Spring Hill I uprooted a sprig of the pungent, bittersweet herb, locally called polyn, to plant by her grave in London as a souvenir of her happiest home. Of course, it never grew.

9

A Bold Front to Fortune

I have always turned a bold front to fortune, and taken, and shall
continue to take . . . 'my hurts before'.

On 9 July 1856 a ceremony was held at the ordnance wharf in
Balaklava to mark the formal evacuation of allied troops from the
Crimean theatre of war. It was an important occasion, attended by
the remaining officers, and watched by an assorted group of civilian
spectators, including Monsieur Soyer looking particularly dandy in
white. 'Conspicuous in the foreground,' according to a report in the
Illustrated London News, was 'Mrs Seacole, dressed in a plaid riding-
habit, and the smartest of hats, calling everybody her son. She was
very much liked . . .'[1] Her dress must have been stitched on
comparatively idle Sunday evenings in the rancid candlelight of
the British Hotel, perhaps from the tartan effects of a dead High-
lander acquired at auction at the British Camp. She wore it with a
frothy white lace fichu and a sort of prototype bowler hat stuck with
an impressive plume, and stood chatting not to the handful of other
ladies present, but to a group of the tallest, broadest-shouldered men

there. Despite the threat of financial ruin, and mourning the loss of her sons, Mary wasn't cowed. Just brave, and ineffably sad.

Before she and Thomas Day left Balaklava themselves, they made plans for the immediate future. The rationale behind salvaging the structure of the British Hotel becomes a little clearer when one reads an announcement in *The Times* of 5 July declaring that the 'celebrated proprietress of the provisions store in the Crimea' intended, with her partner, to open a similar business in the new garrison town of Aldershot, in Hampshire. At the beginning of the 1850s, Aldershot was a small village by the railway line between Southampton and London; now, six years later, it had been chosen as a base for Britain's standing army. It was already sprawling with a rapidly expanding population of military and auxiliary personnel. A haphazard hinterland of service industries was emerging, peopled by traditional camp followers ranging from prostitutes to professional provisioners like Seacole and Day. In fact the hasty establishment of the place, and its unpolished promise to opportunists, must have reminded Mary a little of old haunts in New Granada.

Mary forwarded this efficient advance notice to *The Times* from Spring Hill, with the same marketing expertise she'd used to advertise her arrival in the Crimea back in the winter of 1854–5. It would have been sensible to hurry straight to Aldershot by train on her return to prospect for a likely site (particularly convenient from Portsmouth or Southampton Docks), while Thomas bolted back to London to collate the names and addresses of their debtors and start pushing for payment. She might be the right woman for this Aldershot adventure, but the right time was running out. Passages out of Balaklava were secured not only for Mary and Thomas but for Francis the cook (who hereafter disappears from history), the loyal Jew Johnny, probably dropped off in Constantinople, and lovely young Sally Seacole, Soyer's 'Egyptian beauty', his 'Dark Maid of the Eastern War' (the chef got rather carried away) with her black hair, blue eyes and exotic bronze complexion.[2]

Mary never mentioned Sally. The girl obviously fascinated the Frenchman and Florence Nightingale; to the latter she offered gratifying evidence of Mrs Seacole's blatant immorality. Years after the war Florence assured her sister Parthenope that Sally was Mary's illegitimate daughter by an officer in the 23rd, whom Florence named as Colonel Bunbury.[3] Why? The facts that Sally was of mixed race (as were many of the Black River Seacoles) and called Mary 'mother' (like Soyer and most of the army) prove nothing. Mary was nursing the ailing Edwin in 1840, the date around which Sally was born; she was living with his relations in Black River in south-western Jamaica, loyally struggling to keep husband and business alive. There would have been neither the time nor the inclination for adultery with anyone, let alone an army officer, then with the 33rd, who – according to his letters, to regimental histories, and as far as his family is aware – never visited Jamaica at all.[4]

Henry Bunbury, later Sir Henry, while sharing certain fashionable prejudices towards foreigners, appears from his personal papers to have been a fastidious, honest and uncomplicated man. He was posted to Barbados in 1841, where he kept his distance from Creoles whom he regarded in the politically correct idiom of the day as somewhat less than civilized. Less than human, even. He also spent time in Dominica. Maybe it was this Caribbean connection that helped persuade Florence the rumour was true? And because Mary was so relaxed, so openly loving, so *very* unlike the anguished and emotionally retentive Miss Nightingale, it must have been easy for Florence to imagine Mary embracing easy virtue. Perhaps we should ascribe the invention or recycling of the Bunbury rumour on Florence's part to an over-enthusiastic readiness to believe the worst of Mary. At least it was never repeated in public.

If, as Nightingale suggested, Sally was about fourteen in 1855, it makes sense that she should have accompanied Mary back to England after the war, before taking onward passage home to Jamaica. She would have been useful in Aldershot as a maid and companion to her tired and harassed Mammy. No record of Sally's subsequent life or death in Black River has come to light: as in the case of black Francis, the trail runs cold after 1855. I suspect she stayed with Mary until the two were able to travel to Jamaica together

when Mary returned around 1860, and then settled back with closer
family there.

This time there was no prestigious *Hollander* waiting to meet Mary
at Constantinople and whisk her home. She couldn't afford the
luxury. Instead, she cobbled together a voyage with a number of
stopovers, which to some might have meant frustration and inconvenience, but to Mary in her reduced circumstances presented 'the
opportunity of seeing more men and manners in yet other lands'. By
the end of August she was back in England, most likely in temporary
accommodation in Aldershot.

On Monday 25 August she travelled up to London to attend a
public banquet held in the splendid Surrey Gardens down by the
Thames at Kennington. It was to be a huge celebration to honour
the non-commissioned officers and privates of the three battalions of
Guards who'd seen action in the Crimea. Over 2,000 troops attended, and in the galleries above the main dining area (set out in
the brand new music hall) members of the public were allowed to sit
and watch the speeches and toasts. Thousands more gathered outside to cheer the men as they came and went. The *News of the World*'s
correspondent was there:

> Immediately behind the chair in front of the orchestra was a
> very handsome trophy of flags and laurel wreaths, with Redan
> and Malakoff inscribed on each side and Miss Nightingale's
> name in the centre . . . among the fair visitors in the upper side
> gallery [i.e. where the uninvited guests sat] was Mrs Seacole,
> whose dark features were quite radiant with delight and good
> humour as she gazed on the pleasant scene below.[5]

Later on, according to *The Times*, things got a little less seemly:

> . . . among the illustrious [onlookers] was Mrs Seacole, whose
> appearance awakened the most rapturous enthusiasm. The
> soldiers not only cheered her, but chaired her around
> the gardens, and she really might have suffered from the

oppressive attentions of her admirers, were it not that two sergeants of extraordinary stature gallantly undertook to protect her from the pressure of the crowd.[6]

While Mary, complete with minders, was cavorting around the Surrey Gardens (which used to be a zoo), shrieking with laughter and being loudly and probably rather vulgarly acclaimed by her public, the *other* Crimean heroine's name reposed with sacred dignity on the wreathed altar inside the music hall. Florence Nightingale informed the Queen of 'a great objection to being lionised, and . . . a desire for seclusion',[7] and soon after returning to England, took to her bed. From there, it must be said, she wielded more influence over the British psyche than Mary ever could. Mary's effect on those who admired her was much less refined and lasting than Florence's. Her gregariousness and impulsiveness warmed grateful hearts like a cheerful flame or a slug of rum. But her social and cultural background prevented her from being cherished in the spiritual and sentimental fashion Florence enjoyed. Enjoyed is the wrong word: Florence *suffered* the public's adulation, dreading publicity, while Mary thrived on it, and wished it would last for ever.

With the cheers of the troops still ringing in her ears, Mary returned to Aldershot. It should have been the perfect place for Seacole and Day to prosper, as they might have with some capital behind them. Their creditors were pressing harder and harder for settlement, however, and one doubts whether the British Hotel arrived on English soil in any fit state for re-erection; beset by the practicalities of buying in stock, finding premises, and competing with established army sutlers, the new business failed within weeks. It was the most short-lived and disastrous venture Mary ever risked, and boded ill for the future. That shop in Aldershot was the last she ever kept.

By October 1856, Mary was back in London. She rented a room at 1 Tavistock Street, on the corner of Drury Lane and close to the piazza of Covent Garden Market. It felt like a reward, being back at the hub of things, with the scent of the flowers and the earthier smell of the vegetables and fruit so familiar from the Kingston Sunday market of her youth (and so desperately scarce in the Crimea), and there was a certain sense of security in the constant noise and bustle of a relaxed and rather bohemian neighbourhood. The market opened before dawn at that time of year, and was packed from 6 a.m. with customers. A little later in the day labourers would begin work rebuilding the Royal Opera House after a sensational fire the previous March; omnibuses and carriages would rumble along the nearby Strand all day, and the area's theatres would be shimmering with life and incident until the wee small hours. After the lean delights of Aldershot, it was both welcome and invigorating to be back at the heart of the Empire.

Often she would meet fellow Crimean veterans, by accident or design. Billy Russell paid calls on her,[8] and former patrons gave her as warm a greeting to their Mayfair homes as she had offered them under the rusting iron roof of the British Hotel. In these straitened times, their moral support meant a lot.

> Where, indeed, do I not find friends? In . . . river steamboats, in places of public amusement, in quiet streets and courts, where taking short cuts I lose my way oft-times, spring up old familiar faces to remind me of the months spent on Spring Hill. The sentries at Whitehall relax from the discharge of their important duty of guarding nothing to give me a smile of recognition . . . Now, would all this have happened if I had returned to England a rich woman? Surely not.[9]

Guarding *nothing*? It's evident that a thin trickle of bitterness had begun to seep into Mary's customarily cheerful demeanour after the war. She saw Florence revered for her work in the Crimea, invited to Balmoral to stay with the Queen, offered royal jewels and virtually canonized by the press, and that was all fine. She deserved it. But Mary deserved something too. She acknowledged that she'd not exactly been 'flung aside like – like some of the brave men for whose blood there is no further need', but didn't she warrant a better reward for her patriotism, her time, money and energy, than a stack of unpaid bills and the threat of bankruptcy? That's what faced Seacole and Day now, and it was a bleak prospect. Their business partnership had been dissolved, the mariner Gordon Ponsonby and others refused to wait any longer for settlement, and a good proportion of the hotel's patrons (men Mary had been proud to serve, and had trusted) remained obstinately in debt.

No single factor appears to have been responsible for the mess. Scores of people still owed Mary and Thomas money; one character, a war correspondent for the *Morning Herald* by the name of William Knight, had run up an account of over £40 (some £1,600 now).[10] It was suggested in *The Times* that Day, behind Mary's back, had rashly been operating an unofficial banking service, cashing IOUs which were never honoured.[11] His livery and horse-trading business certainly lost substantial amounts of money. Thomas himself rather verbosely ascribed their troubles to 'losses by the elements and by robbery, and the depreciation of stock-in-trade and buildings consequent on the unexpectedly rapid evacuation of the Crimea on the conclusion of the war'.[12] Their neighbour at Spring Hill, Lady Alicia Blackwood, tended to agree:

Mrs Seacole kept a perfect Omnibus Shop, which was greatly frequented; and one must appreciate the wisdom exhibited by the good old lady not only in providing every variety of article, both edible and otherwise, but likewise the tact and never varying good-nature she exhibited to all her customers; and notwithstanding the heavy prices at which her goods were sold, no-one grumbled [because, presumably, they could rely on Mary's 'tact', or snobbery, to allow them to pay later – or not at all]. No doubt she paid heavy prices herself . . . [I]t was always remembered that she had, during the time of battle, and in the time of fearful distress, personally spared no pains and no exertion to visit the field of woe, and minister with her own hands such things as could comfort or alleviate the sufferings of those around her; freely giving to such as could not pay, and to many whose eyes were closing in death, from whom payment could never be expected. That she did not make her fortune by her merchandise . . . was no doubt in consequence of the termination of the war being far sooner and more sudden than was expected.[13]

Unlike many of her supporters, when her predicament became public Mary steadfastly refused to blame her clientele or her partner. Billy Russell was convinced she had been the victim of deception, implying that Day had bled her dry.[14] But she wouldn't rise: pride and loyalty forbade her. Circumstances had mutinied against the success of the business, that's all.

On 28 October 1856, a small, dry notice appeared in the columns of the *London Gazette*:

> Whereas a Petition for adjudication of Bankruptcy, filed the 27th day of October, 1856, hath been presented against Mary Seacole and Thomas Day the younger of no. 1, Tavistock-street, Covent-garden, and of no. 17, Ratcliff-terrace, Goswell-road, both in the County of Middlesex, and late of Spring-hill and Balaklava, both in the Crimea, Provision Merchants, Traders, Dealers and Chapmen [brokers].

Mary felt no shame at the declaration: she was pragmatic enough to realize its inevitability. Though thoroughly exhausted by the last two years' exertions, Mary was too proud of herself and of those she had served in the Crimea to think of recrimination or regret.

For the next nine months, culminating in the publication of her autobiography, Mary was rarely out of the news. For once it's easy to trace her progress through the columns of the press and official papers, beginning with the report of the official hearing in the Bankruptcy Court in London's Basinghall Street on 7 November. It describes Mary as 'a lady of colour', whose presence in court – defiantly sporting her usual shouting colours – 'attracted much attention'.

After several proofs had been admitted, and Mr Day had stated that he had sustained great loss by horses at Balaklava . . . an allowance of three guineas per week was suggested for Mrs Seacole, and two guineas a week for the other bankrupt. A creditor, however, dissented to the proposed three guineas. He thought two guineas per week sufficient for each bankrupt.

Mrs Seacole, – 'I have got my washing to pay.'

(Great laughter)

His Honour [the judge] thought two guineas sufficient.[15]

Just over a fortnight later, the first of several letters of support was published in *The Times*. It was signed simply 'Da Meritis', or a friend to merit, and addressed – perhaps significantly – from Alexis Soyer's haunt, the Reform Club.

Sir. That good old soul whose generous hospitality has warmed up many a gallant spirit on the chilly heights of Balaklava has now in her turn been caught in the worst storm of all – the gale of adversity.

Where are the Crimeans? Have a few months erased from their memories those many acts of comfort and kindness which made the name of the old mother venerated throughout the camp? While the benevolent deeds of Florence Nightingale are being handed down to posterity with blessings and an imperishable renown, are the humbler actions of Mrs Seacole to be entirely forgotten, and will none now substantially testify to the worth of those services of the late Mistress of Spring-hill?

[This is a] favourable opportunity of showing an appreciation of those . . . acts of benevolence which were characteristic of Mrs Seacole.[16]

He'll forward a donation of £20, says the writer, to start a subscription fund for Mary. Who will join him?

A running correspondence was soon established, involving Major-General Lord Rokeby (an officer in the Scots Fusilier Guards who commanded the 1st Division in the war), Billy Russell, Captain the Hon. Hussey Fane Keane of the Royal Engineers, a few anonymous admirers, Thomas Day, and even Mary herself. It began on 25 November with a note from Rokeby reporting that Mrs Seacole had called on him since the court proceedings 'requesting advice and assistance', and that he and Sir Henry Barnard, a fellow officer, had already taken steps to establish a fund 'with a view to presenting her with some testimonial'. Any donations could be sent to the official army agents, Messrs Cox, in Whitehall (where Mary had gone at the beginning of the campaign to find the home address of Sidney Herbert).

Two days later, another letter appeared, suggesting Mary's needs might be faster served if people sent money straight to her, avoiding the inevitable bureaucratic delay at Coxes.

Sir. If you would spare a corner in the Times publishing the residence of Mrs Seacole, I have no doubt that many who profited by her energy and success in importing the good things of this life to the Crimea, to say nothing of her attention in sickness to numbers who had only thanks to give in return, would now forward their mite to relieve her from embarrassment.[17]

On 28 November, a further plea on behalf of the Mistress of Spring Hill informed the British public that all monies collected by the fund would be used 'to re-establish her in business' as soon as the Bankruptcy Court allowed. Its author had known Mrs Seacole for some months in the Crimea, he said.

I am able to testify to her self-sacrificing and bountiful kindness to all sick and wounded who came under her notice. In addition to the numerous diseases she had to contend with she has been several times under fire, and I am assured she rendered considerable assistance on the memorable 8th of September [i.e. the final allied assault on Sevastopol].

Mary must have glowed: her sons were coming good, just as she knew they would. One or two of them had been rascals, it was true, but the rest – the finest – were striding to the breach to defend their mother's honour and her livelihood. She wrote to Lord Rokeby (there seems to have been a mutual fondness there), giving him permission to forward her letter to *The Times*.

I am fully aware of the kind feelings yourself and the army have towards me, and this knowledge tends to sustain me in my present difficulties; and, far from regretting my visit to the Crimea, I feel proud indeed that I have had an opportunity to gain the esteem of your Lordship, along with that of many others in the army; and indeed I would much rather suffer my present poverty, with the knowledge that the Almighty permitted me to be useful in my small sphere, than have returned wealthy without the esteem and regard of the brave defenders of our country.[18]

Pledges of money, of course, came rattling in. Mary knew how to milk an audience: she was charismatic, fulsome, flirtatious, genuinely well-meaning, and adept at public relations. But she wasn't officially allowed to receive a penny herself until all creditors were paid. That didn't discourage her champions from keeping her cause in the public eye. Mark Lemon, the editor of the hugely popular satirical periodical *Punch*, delighted Mary just before Christmas by publishing 'A Stir for Seacole', to be sung to the nursery-rhyme tune of 'Old King Cole'.

Dame Seacole was a kindly old soul,
And a kindly old soul was she:
You might call for your pot, you might call for your pipe,
In her tent on 'the Col' so free.

Her tent on 'the Col', where a welcome toll
She took of the passing throng,
That from Balaklava to the front
Toiled wearily along.

That berry-brown face, with a kind heart's trace
Impressed in each wrinkle sly,
Was a sight to behold, through the snow-clouds rolled
Across that iron sky.

The cold without gave zest, no doubt,
To the welcome warmth within:
But her smile, good old soul, lent heat to the coal,
And power to the pannikin.

No store she set by the epaulette [really?],
Be it worsted or gold-lace;
For K.C.B., or plain private Smith,
She still had one pleasant face.

But not alone was her kindness shown
To the hale and hungry lot,
Who drank her grog and ate her prog [food],
And paid their honest shot [share].

The sick and sorry can tell the story
Of her nursing and dosing deeds.
Regimental M.D. never worked as she
In helping sick men's needs.

Of such work, God knows, was as much as she chose,
That dreary winter-tide,
When death hung o'er the damp and pestilent camp,
And his scythe swung far and wide.

And when winter [passed], and spring at last
Made the mud-sea a sea of flowers,
Doghunt, race and review her brown face knew,
Still pleasant in sunshine or showers.

Still she'd take her stand, as blithe and bland,
With her stores, the jolly old soul –
And – be the right man in the right place who can –
The right woman was Dame Seacole.

She gave her aid to all who prayed,
To hungry, sick, and cold:
Open hand and heart, alike ready to [im]part
Kind words, and acts, and gold.

And now the good soul is 'in the hole,'
What red-coat in all the land,
But to set her on her legs again
Will not lend a willing hand?[19]

Had there been room, Mary would have liked all that on her tombstone: especially the bit about the right woman in the right place, which was a phrase she stole for her autobiography to sum up her usefulness in life. She loved *Punch* after this, and was even pictured by one of its cartoonists as an alternative Florence Nightingale, standing stout and black-faced at the bedside of a sickly looking soldier with not a lamp in her hand – nor even a tea-mug – but a revitalizing copy of *Punch*.[20]

On 1 January 1857 newspapers published an account of the Examination Meeting *in re* Seacole and Day, held by the Court of Bankruptcy to determine how efficiently the company's financial affairs were being settled. Lists of debtors were given: 'good' debtors, whose money could be relied upon, and 'doubtful' ones, like William Knight. Thanks, perhaps, to the cheques that had bypassed official channels by arriving directly at Tavistock Street, it seemed as though outstanding creditors would soon be satisfied, and Mary and Thomas would be awarded their 'ticket', or certificate of conformity, and discharged.

> Mrs Seacole asked His Honour if he could kindly give her her ticket of leave [now]?
>
> (A laugh).
>
> The Commissioner enquired what she meant; and Mrs Seacole answered that she meant her certificate. Money was very scarce just now, and her friends in the army would not pay their subscriptions until she had got her ticket of leave. She had no intention to 'garotte' anybody [or force them to pay] but 'the ticket' . . . would be desirable for the reason stated.
>
> His Honour said the certificate meeting would be in about three weeks, and she had better wait.[21]

She did wait, until 30 January, when Seacole and Day were formally and publicly granted 'certificates of the first class' (the normal designation). 'A spectator: Of what class are the certificates? Mrs Seacole: What class? First, to be sure! Am I not a first-class woman? (Great laughter).'[22]

Now that she was free to begin again, in what she optimistically called the 'late summer' of her life (her early fifties), Mary felt re-energized. Most women would not have survived so long: the average life expectancy in London was about thirty-five at the time. Ladies living sheltered lives might hope to last a little longer, but living a sheltered life had never been a desire – nor an option – for Mary. Ever since her first voyage to London as a teenager, she had embraced risk and refused to be circumscribed in any way by precedent. At least she was her own woman again now, and assured of the support of the English establishment. Voluntary support, that is: she never received an official pension, even though Prime Minister Lord Palmerston is said to have considered her 'a treasure to the army'.[23] And despite the repeated assumptions of her own contemporaries and almost every commentator since, she was never formally awarded any campaign medals for her part in the war.

So where did the medals she indubitably possessed come from? The first mention of them is in newspaper reports of the November court appearance.[24] Friends and journalists who met her thereafter often mentioned the decorations perched so proudly on her bosom. A terracotta bust, modelled in 1871 by the Queen's nephew Count Gleichen, one of the hotel's patrons and an erstwhile patient of Mary, shows her with four of them above her left breast: apparently the British Crimea medal, a Sardinian award, the French Légion d'Honneur and the star-shaped Turkish Order of the Mejidie. They're rather small, though. A recently discovered photograph of Mary, taken at about the same time, only shows three decorations. And, judging by their size, they're all miniatures, or 'dress' medals. There is no notice in the *London Gazette* or the War Office archives to suggest that Mary was offered an award; nor does she enlighten us (which surely she would have done if formally honoured) in *Wonderful Adventures*. None of her medals can be found now (although the Institute of Jamaica thinks it might have the French and Turkish ones, at the moment, at least, they are lost). In Mary's will, amongst the bedsteads and linen, pearls and diamond rings, there is mention of 'jewellery, trinkets, and ornaments of the person' left to her sister Louisa – but nothing else. Indeed, a review of her book in the *Athenaeum* specifically bewailed their absence: 'the war did not bring her fortune,' it said, 'and peace has not distinguished the soldiers' friend with a medal . . .'.[25]

It is more likely that Mary 'distinguished' herself. Miniatures were obtained for her by army friends, or bought on the open market, and with the full support of her military admirers – perhaps even a suitable private ceremony – she resolved to wear them, by right, to commemorate the fallen and in recognition of her commitment to the British cause. Miniatures are not *real* medals: they're items of jewellery. But what they signified to Mary went far beyond vain ornament.

Perhaps unwilling entirely to forfeit her financial independence, Mary decided at the end of 1856 to attempt another business venture. It was somewhat more conventional (though no less ambitious) than most of her others: to launch herself on the frenetic waters of London's literary scene and write her memoirs concentrating, naturally, on the Crimea. Scores of military and civilian veterans planned to do the same, including the odd officer's lady or nurse, but even so, the public appetite for eye-witness accounts of the late victory was not expected to be sated for a few years. Mary was fortunate to be commissioned by James Blackwood, publisher of the pioneering 'London Library' series of popular (and cheap) board-backed books: her story would be guaranteed a wide readership. By the same token Blackwood was assured of sensational publicity, so famous, eccentric and unprecedented was his new author. Mary was assigned an editor, and with the promise of a foreword by Billy Russell, permission to dedicate the book to her kind and influential friend Lord Rokeby, and carte blanche from the publisher to write whatever she wanted however she wished, she set to work.

The editor, acknowledged in Mary's book merely by his initials W.J.S., was possibly W.J. Stewart, the translator of another book in the 'London Library' series which includes mention of the Crimean campaign.[26] It was his job, I think, to take dictation of the whole book from Mary, sympathetically advising her when a little extra information might help, and rearranging any impenetrable syntax, but otherwise keeping quiet. Of course Mary could read and write, although she can't have had much practice at anything other than the odd letter since her schooldays in the home of her Kingston patroness. She never kept a diary, and friends and family in Jamaica used to complain that she rarely wrote home. She could physically have produced *Wonderful Adventures of Mrs Seacole in Many Lands* (after some deliberation), but it reads so like the spoken word, and has such natural fluency, that one doubts she did. Stewart looked after the grammar and orthography for her, and spared her the laborious mechanics of the manuscript, leaving Mary free to express herself with the immediacy and wit which hallmark the book.

Sometime between the end of January and the beginning of May 1857, Mary moved from Tavistock Street to a boarding-house room in the slightly calmer – and cheaper – environs of Soho.[27] Donations had been diminishing lately for want of publicity, and on 2 May *Punch* printed an appeal for extra funds to keep 'the Mother of the Regiment' in the comfort she deserved. Mary replied, cannily thanking *Punch* for cheering her up with his good humour and reminding her sons that although saved from dishonour and destitution by their recent generosity, times were still dangerously hard for their old Mama. She reminisced about walking through the wards of the Land Transport Hospital at Spring Hill distributing copies of the magazine donated by officers to the men, and asked for public support in finding some more 'women's work' for her to do, 'perhaps in China, perhaps on some other distant shore to which Englishmen go to serve their country'. (It's ironic that the letter was dated only two days before the Mutiny broke out in British India on 10 May, instigating a military campaign that would eclipse the Crimean War.) Meanwhile, she wrote, she was hanging on to her top-floor room at 14 Soho Square in the hope that circumstances wouldn't force her up, in penury, to the attic.

Punch responded most satisfactorily:

> It will be evident, from the foregoing, that Mother Seacole has sunk much lower in the world, and is also in danger of rising much higher in it, than is consistent with the honour of the British army, and the generosity of the British public. Both will be disgraced if Mother Seacole, by reason of declining circumstances, should have to ascend into a garret. Although she has a heart and hands left to help herself, in case of opportunity, the opportunity may never arrive; in the meantime, has England no heart left to help her?[28]

The plea for Mary's welfare continued with reference to Donizetti's *La Figlia del Reggimente*, an opera playing to full houses in London at the time, featuring 'a mimic sutler-woman, and a foreigner'; why pay to see that, asked *Punch*, when you might far more usefully 'bestow money on a genuine English one' instead? The 'genuine English' bit was particularly thrilling for Mary: what a breakthrough. (Even she, like the majority of the population then and now, regarded the Scots, along with the British, merely as different-flavoured Englishmen.)

By now the subscription fund for Mary had been put on an official footing with the establishment of a committee of trustees. It asked for contributions in recognition not only of her work in the Crimea, but of valuable services rendered 'as a nurse and medical attendant in Jamaica in 1850 and 1853 when the yellow-fever and cholera committed such ravages'. The committee comprised officers and gentlemen – even royalty – who had served in the Crimea, together (of course) with friend Billy, and its simple purpose was to raise as much money as possible for Mrs Seacole, described in the Trust literature rather disingenuously as a 'poor old soul, late in life'.[29] After some humming and hah-ing, it was decided that the best way to achieve this noble object was to hold an outrageous party, back in the Surrey Gardens, to coincide with the publication of *Wonderful Adventures* and set her up, financially, for good. For Mary – one of life's natural extroverts – it was the perfect plan: high-profile, original and flamboyant.

10

The Crimean Heroine

I shall make no excuse to my readers for giving them a pretty full history of my struggles to become a Crimean heroine!

Wonderful Adventures of Mrs Seacole in Many Lands came out at the beginning of July 1857, at 1s 6d a copy. Its 200-odd pages were bound in appropriately bright boards of scarlet and yellow, with a swashbuckling sketch of Mary on the front looking like a cross between Prince Rupert of the Rhine and a black Britannia. She's dressed in a wide-brimmed, floppy hat with a plume and ribbons, and is wearing a military-looking bodice with horizontal braiding, epaulettes and big brass buttons. Her sleeves are still rolled up ready for work, as they were when that first portrait was taken six or seven years ago in Jamaica, and she's just taken some lint (or – as likely – a bouquet garni) from the satchel that hangs heavily from her stocky shoulders. She looks resolute, and utterly confident. There's another illustration inside, a wide, wood-engraved frontispiece showing the interior of the British Hotel. Boots, strings of onions, and hams hang from nails in the wooden wall, and the shelves are lined with bottles and tins. There are barrels and flagons on the floor, along with the discarded helmets of relaxing officers sitting at (or on) her table smoking and drinking wine. Mary herself is welcoming the decorative figure of Monsieur Soyer, while his horse waits, with an adventurous glint in its eye, ready to be stolen at the door. Mr Day is elsewhere, probably outside and very near the horse. Everyone looks happy and at home.

Twelve of the book's nineteen chapters deal with Mary's Crimean experiences. Of the remaining seven, six are about New Granada, and the rest of her life is done with in a single six-page chapter elliptically entitled 'My Birth and Parentage – Early Tastes and Travels – Marriage, and Widowhood'. It may have been her editor who advised skipping over the first forty-five years of her life. It's more likely, however, that the decision to cut to the chase was entirely Mary's. The publication of *Wonderful Adventures* was principally a money-making enterprise, and Mary's target English audience was unlikely to be wooed by lingering over the Jamaican connection. Mentioning Up-Park and Newcastle was sensible, but too many details of Mary Grant's domestic circumstances in Kingston might make her seem a little too foreign for comfort (culturally as well as geographically), and distance her from those she not only wished to impress, but with whom she liked to identify.

Numerous lengthy papers have been written since its first modern reprint in 1984 by academics slightly troubled by *Wonderful Adventures*.[1] Like its author, the book has become an icon of feminist and/or Afro-Caribbean literature. Some of its critics can't understand why Mary was not as politically correct as they are, or as such an icon *should* be. After all, it's the first published autobiography to have been written by a black (i.e. non-white) woman in Britain, and arguably only the second in the world (not that many white women had written autobiographies by 1857, either).[2] It's an early example of women's travel writing.[3] It's robust and witty, deftly manipulative of its readers' responses and emotions, and remarkably assured: in fact, more like a professional gentleman's piece of work than a lady's. It celebrates the life of an unprotected, self-sufficient tradeswoman with the blood of slaves in her veins, yet still managed to become a bestseller in what was perceived as the most civilized country on earth. So why didn't Mary thump the political tub more vigorously, and challenge her imperialist Victorian audience to change their assumptions about illegitimate/unconventional/ lone/female/black travellers/writers-with-attitude, like her? The answer is easy: because she shared so many of those assumptions herself.

One of Mary's proudest boasts was that she was unique and unclassifiable. The assumption she challenges, in both her contemporary and her modern audience is that people can be pigeonholed according to their race, their gender and their circumstances. She wrote *Wonderful Adventures*, part autobiography, part travelogue, not to raise the profile of Afro-Caribbeans or women, but of herself. It is neither a political statement nor an artistic exercise; it's a glorious advertisement, written by a celebrity fully in control of her own image.

What disturbs many modern readers most about the book is Mary's refusal to identify more fully with her African heritage. She acknowledged and respected her mother's gift of healing, and once (in the face of abuse) claimed pride in the colour of her skin, but otherwise she chose to ignore her black ancestry, even going so far on several occasions as to share in print British and American society's pervasive prejudice towards 'niggers', as well as towards the Americans themselves, Spaniards, Greeks, Turks and Catholics. She mentioned the odd occasion – on the streets of London during her first visit in the 1820s, for example, or during Mrs Herbert's interview on behalf of Florence Nightingale – when her personal feelings were hurt by the bigotry of others, and picked the best Creole characteristic of tender-heartedness for herself, while repudiating their supposed laziness and lack of energy. But she was a child enough of her time and chosen place to want to avoid identification with any 'inferior' people, and used prejudice as a weapon of self-defence where necessary.

In reality, off the printed page, she treated her Jamaican family with loyalty and generosity;[4] she chose for her early travels the new republics of Haiti and New Granada, practised traditional rather than 'modern' medicine, and actually came to embrace the religion she so ridiculed by privately converting to Roman Catholicism in her mid-fifties. Publicly, however, everything she said and everything she wrote was designed to increase her standing in the society she prized above all others: that of her adopted sons in the British military. She needed their money. I don't doubt she savoured the delicious irony (given her background) of being feted as their heroine, being needed by them, respected, admired, and called their mother. But she would consider such celebrity and mutual dependence as nothing less than she – and they – deserved.

The book went down well. The first print-run sold out within eight months, and another was issued in March 1858. One review praised Mary for the friendly and confidential air of her writing, calling *Wonderful Adventures* an 'unpretending' and affecting volume and commending its author to her readers' prayers, blessings and charity.[5] It might have done even better, had it not been for the Indian Mutiny. A few weeks before its publication, news reached London of a horrifying uprising against the British military and civil authorities which had erupted in Meerut, a town some 64km (40 miles) north of Delhi. It was spreading to other garrisons with ferocious rapidity: all over British India white officers were being turned on by their Indian soldiers and killed, along with their wives and children. Some Crimean veterans were already stationed out there; having survived Sevastopol, they were now faced not by a foreign enemy but – even more shockingly – by massacre and insurrection at the hands of those they had supposed to be on their side. The Mutiny (now called India's First War of Independence) only lasted for six months, but its brutality resulted in hundreds of British men – and in many cases their families – losing their lives. Countless Indian lives were squandered too, in the name of right-eous retribution.

The perceived treachery of the mutineers shocked the compla-cent British to the core, although had they looked, they might have noticed that the rebels' discontent had been building up for years. It also engendered a nervous distrust of those who, like Mary, possessed 'a somewhat duskier skin than theirs'. It may have impacted on the long-term success of *Wonderful Adventures*, and on Mary's image as a British heroine. In 1857 she was well enough known to avoid confusion as a West Indian with any other sort of Indian, and her loyalty to the army was legendary already. But the long Crimean slog quickly became consumed in the British consciousness by the fiery sensationalism of the Mutiny. From 1858 onwards, if the public felt moved to buy a book about a woman at war, it could choose from an ever-widening choice of hair-raising accounts being written by white memsahibs suffering at the hands of those savage black men in Delhi or Lucknow.

In the short term, however, Mary timed *Wonderful Adventures* just right. Before the book had been out a month, the committee's promised party was held to celebrate (and promote) its heroine. And what a party: not quite as riotous as those New-Year junkets Lady Nugent used to write about in Jamaica, but as close as polite British society was going to get. Lord Rokeby and his colleagues on the Seacole Fund had been working hard behind the scenes, and as the opening night grew closer, produced a tempting advertisement:

GRAND MILITARY FESTIVAL, for the BENEFIT of Mrs SEACOLE, at the Royal Surrey Gardens, to commence on MONDAY July 27, 1857, and continue four days. 1000 performers, including Eleven Military Bands.

Under the Immediate Patronage of
His Royal Highness the General Commanding-in-Chief [Duke of Cambridge]
His Grace the Duke of Wellington
Her Grace the Duchess of Wellington
His Grace the Duke of Newcastle
The Most Noble the Marchioness of Ely
The Most Noble the Marchioness of Winchester

The Right Hon. The Earl of Westmoreland
The Right Hon. The Countess of Westmoreland
The Right Hon. The Earl of Euston
The Right Hon. Lord Rokeby
The Right Hon. Lady Rokeby
Lieutenant-General Sir W. Codrington, M.P.
Major-General Sir W. Fenwick Williams, M.P.
The Hon. Mrs Dawson Damer.

The Colonels of the following regiments have kindly forwarded
the object the Committee have in view, by granting the assistance of the Bands of their distinguished corps. Which will be
united in a Colossal Orchestra, viz: – the First Life Guards, the
Royal Engineers, the Royal Artillery, the Royal Marines (Woolwich), the Royal Marines (Chatham), and the 11th Hussars.

These bands will be supported by M. Jullien's renowned
Orchestra, strengthened by leading performers from the Philharmonic Society, Her Majesty's Theatre, and the Royal Italian
Opera. The Royal Surrey Choral Society will also lend its aid,
assisted by deputations from the principal Choral Societies in
the country. The whole will form an ensemble of upwards of
1000 performers . . .

On the inauguration day (the 27th) will take place a Grand
Concert, with eleven military bands, M. Jullien's orchestra, the
Choral Societies, and several other distinguished artistes . . .
The Concert will commence each evening at half-past 7
o'clock.[6]

Louis Jullien was a flamboyant foreigner whose celebrity was
coupled with severe cashflow difficulties – like Soyer, at times,
and even Mary herself. He was a vastly popular French musician
exiled from his homeland by bankruptcy, who had made his home in
London. He had shares in the new Royal Surrey Gardens Music Hall,
and toured with his light-entertainment orchestra both in Britain
and in America. He admired Mary's spirit, and was delighted from a

business point of view to accept the commission to be musical director of the festival: it was bound to be a resounding success. And so it appeared, particularly on the first night: 'on no previous occasion,' wrote *The Times* correspondent, 'have the Royal Surrey Gardens been thronged by a greater multitude.'

> Nothing could have been more triumphantly successful. The entertainment had evidently been organised *con amore* by the directors, and the talent and indomitable energy of M. Jullien, as usual, surmounted all obstacles. Notwithstanding that the charge for admission was quintupled, there was an immense concourse in the hall, and it need scarcely be said the audience was of a character more 'exclusive' than is customary at transpontine musical performances [i.e. in the unaristocratic environs south of the Thames]. The hall was tastefully decorated with English, French, Sardinian, and Turkish flags, a magnificent transparency being conspicuous above the orchestra. Mrs Seacole sat in state in front of the centre gallery [I wonder what she chose to wear for this most auspicious of occasions?], supported by Lord Rokeby on one side, by Lord George Paget[7] on the other, and surrounded by the members of her committee . . .
> Mrs Seacole is not inclined to lead an idle life, and if the exertions now making on her behalf prove successful it is, we understand, her intention to start at once for India, where she will be enabled to resume those self-imposed duties which earned for her at the recent seat of war the title of 'mother' of our soldiers.[8]

The evening's delights opened with a massed rendition of the National Anthem; there followed a couple of Jullien's own compositions, the 'British Army Quadrille' and the 'English Quadrille'. Then guest artists Monsieur and Madame Edouard and Pepita Gassier performed excerpts from Mozart's *Don Giovanni* before the orchestra played the last two movements of Beethoven's 5th Symphony.

The famous English tenor John Sims Reeves sang Purcell's air 'Come if you Dare'; and to close the first half the soprano Madame Erminia Rudersdorff sang a solo from Mendelssohn's *Lorelei* (modern music, composed ten years ago). There was no let-up during the interval: Handel's 'Hallelujah' chorus accompanied that, and the second half included more Jullien, more Sims Reeves, and a hefty chunk of Haydn's *Creation*. It is unlikely that Mary chose the programme. No matter: it certainly suited the audience.

> At the ends of both the first and the second parts the name of Mrs Seacole was shouted by a thousand voices. The genial old lady rose from her place and smiled benignantly on the assembled multitude, amid a tremendous and continued cheering. Never did woman seem happier, and never was hearty and kindly greeting bestowed upon a worthier object.[9]

The concert was repeated on Tuesday evening, at half price (2s 6d); on Wednesday and Thursday the number of military bands dropped from eleven to six, and the total number of performers shrank to six hundred. The ordinary Surrey Gardens admission fee of one shilling was charged for those two nights. In all, thousands of people patronized the festival: Mary Seacole was truly, by now, a Victorian celebrity of the very first water. One can imagine her feeling at once utterly overwhelmed by the sheer improbability of little Mary Grant from Kingston's East Street being feted by the greatest men in the greatest country on earth, and quite at home, recognizing yet again that here was the right woman in the right place. For all four evenings she sat at the centre of everything, radiant and as proud of herself and her country as could be. This, surely, marked the zenith of her career? The squeeze of a thankful soldier's hand as he lay on a saturated pallet of straw on Cathcart's Hill might have been reward enough for her work at Sevastopol. A comradely clap on the back from Sir John Campbell as she poured his champagne at the British Hotel, or a kiss on the hand from an admiring Alexis Soyer in her kitchens, must both have been extremely gratifying. The letter that reached Spring Hill during the campaign from the family in New Blundell Hall congratulating Mary on her work stirred her heart with pride. But nothing could have bettered the last week in July 1857, when so many people came to pay their respects to the heroine of the British Army and to say thank-you to the mother of all its Crimean sons. How proud Jane and James would have been of the daughter who, by complementing her mother's heritage as a healer with her father's as a builder of Empire, had bridged their separate, distant worlds so well.

The idea of the festival was, of course, to raise money. Once Jullien and all the musicians had been paid their unexpectedly high expenses, and various auxiliary costs had been met, it was estimated by the committee that £228 – about £9,000 today – would remain for Mary.[10] This was perhaps a little disappointing, given the crowds who came, but still a tidy sum: quite enough, if well invested, to sustain a modestly comfortable lifestyle in London, especially when funds from the sale of the book were added. Rokeby was satisfied with his efforts.

He shouldn't have been. Had the committee done their home-work properly, they would have realized that all was far from well at the Royal Surrey Gardens. A number of its directors had resigned during the three weeks leading up to the Seacole festival, sensing impending financial disaster, and on 3 August – just four days after Mary's final performance – Jullien served a writ on the Company, forcing them on the 27th of that month into the Bankruptcy Court, and Mary with them – but this time, as a creditor. Represented by her solicitor, Mr George, she asked in court to be allowed to examine the Company's accounts: '[s]he wanted to go to India,' reported George, 'but was prevented by the position of her affairs with the Company.'[11] On 29 July – the third day of the benefit festival – she had made an appointment with the Secretary-at-War, successfully this time, and asked for permission to leave for the site of the mutiny as soon as possible: 'Give me my needle and thread, my medicine chest, my bandage, my probe and scissors,' she said, 'and I'm off.' The secretary, Lord Panmure, Sidney Herbert's successor, didn't offer any official help, but nor did he forbid Mary to go. This Indian campaign was of quite a different nature from the Crimean one, though: it was being fought in a rapidly shifting theatre of war and against an unpredictable and unconventional enemy specifically targeting British women. There were no centralized hospitals (except in the case of Lucknow, where the besieged banqueting hall in the residency compound was being used) and only in Calcutta, away from the action, was there any sort of organized welfare system for survivors. That was being run by the Viceroy's wife, Charlotte Canning, who might not have welcomed Mary's eccentricity any more than Miss Nightingale had.

Nevertheless, Mary might be forgiven for expecting a more generous response from Panmure (who was closely associated with the Crimean campaign) than she'd had from Herbert in 1854. She failed to understand why sponsorship wasn't available to send her to India, now the army knew what she could do. She had no capital to finance her own expedition, having only just paid off her debts, and Mr Day, similarly broke, had already left an ungrateful Britain for the Antipodes.[12] She needed her £228 to comfort her sons: the Mutiny was already three months old and, by all accounts, as brutal a business as anyone could imagine.

James Coppock, director of the Royal Surrey Gardens Company, assured Mr George that a cheque had already been sent to Cox's bank in settlement of Mrs Seacole's benefit, and proceedings were adjourned until October. The cheque bounced. Mary's friend and Fund Committee member the Duke of Cambridge was so outraged (and embarrassed, no doubt) that he took Mary's case straight to Lord Palmerston, the Prime Minister, who sent a directive to Coppock to pay Mrs Seacole's dues immediately.[13] But by October Mary was still waiting. In fact nothing was settled until 21 December, when payment to the Company's creditors of five shillings in the pound was finally agreed. Coppock died the same month, and by the time the case was wound up in March 1858, the Indian Mutiny was over. Mary netted £57 from the whole affair.

She was uncertain, now, what to do. The book had reprinted: that was good. Her Crimean friends still kept her company, from the loftiest rank in the drawing-rooms of Mayfair to the lowliest file on the London streets, and she valued their esteem and affection. For a while she was content to freewheel a little, relying on the heady momentum of her celebrity to keep her life moving along satisfactorily. In May 1858 she volunteered, with her dear friend Soyer, to help with a 'Fancy Bazaar' held at Wellington Barracks in the heart of London for the benefit of 'the wives and families of soldiers and sailors, and for relieving the frightful distress consequent on the departure of so many of our troops for the East' (i.e. India, where reinforcements were being sent out in great number to quash any further uprising).[14] It was a three-day affair, with stalls selling gifts donated – even personally embroidered or watercoloured – by 'many titled ladies'. Mary manned a stall every day. Three months later, in the fetid midst of what Londoners came to know as 'the big stink', a particularly hot and dry summer which turned the over-loaded Thames solid with sewage, Mary learned of the death of Soyer at the age of forty-nine.

Soyer was buried beneath a memorial he'd designed for his wife in St Mary's Catholic cemetery off the Harrow Road in London. The cemetery had only been open a year, and adjoined the very fashionable Anglican acres of Kensal Green in which luminaries of the social and artistic hierarchy lay in leafy repose. Mary must have been at the funeral: not only had she admired the Frenchman, but she recognized his benign eccentricity and passionate philosophy of practical compassion as characteristics she possessed herself. I think it more than likely that his death was the catalyst for Mary's spiritual conversion to Catholicism.

Given her strident ridicule of the 'superstitious' papists she'd met in New Granada, it's probably safe to assume that she was not a Catholic when she wrote *Wonderful Adventures* in 1857. But she did cherish that strangely affecting picture of the Madonna salvaged from Sevastopol, and her extended family tree in Jamaica included the odd Catholic branch.[15] Although married as an Anglican, and obviously a godly woman, she was never evangelical. She responded to the spiritual purity of the Protestant Hedley Vicars just as much as the humanistic philanthropy of the Catholic Soyer. But the latter suited her better, as a practical woman. An uncomplicated but conscientious woman, she saw religion in terms of instinct rather than intellect. Eschewing the elaborate theology of an increasing number of High Anglican converts during the 1850s (amongst whom Florence Nightingale almost numbered herself), she must have been inspired on a very human level by a man she admired and loved, and by the only woman (save her mother) she'd wish to emulate. After all, that woman – the Blessed Virgin Mary – had sons too. Far more than her namesake Mary Seacole, and she loved and mourned them all. When she quietly converted to Roman Catholicism sometime between 1858 and 1860, Mary became the Blessed Virgin's proud daughter, and possibly for the first time in her life, felt spiritually at home. Not that she'd ever felt exiled by her Anglicanism: it's just that she'd never had occasion to consider it at length before. At comparative leisure for the first time since she'd left the care of her patroness in Kingston, cumulatively inspired by witnessing the deaths of so many throughout her life and perhaps, in her mid-fifties, approaching her own demise, religious affinity suddenly became an urgent matter.

It hasn't been possible to find a record of Mary's reception into the Catholic Church either in London or in Jamaica. It's most probable that she was baptized in England, but registers weren't collated and centralized in the dioceses of Westminster and Southwark during the nineteenth century. The Catholic church nearest her home in 14 Soho Square was St Patrick's, at number 21. But she doesn't appear in any entry there.

The first evidence we have of Mary's new religious affiliation is in the registers of Catholic baptisms in Kingston, Jamaica. There, in a column dated 16 May 1860, she appears as the sponsor for candidate Christopher Henricks Seacole, aged thirteen, and two months later, on 1 July, for Edward Ambleton Seacoll [sic], aged ten.[16] It was common for baptism candidates to be recorded with their sponsor's surname: these two lads were not 'real' Seacoles. Mary was related to members of the Henricks or Henriques family in Kingston: the now-famous 'Mammy' Mary may have agreed to become young Christopher's ward or patron and stipulated his baptism (with the fervency of a new convert) as part of the bargain. Edward Ambleton was her brother Edward's child, born in 1850. Maybe his mother Ann was dead now, too.

These entries suggest that by 1860, Mary was back in Jamaica. That would make sense: £57 wasn't going to go far for long in London, even supplemented by receipts from James Blackwood, her publisher. Her health was not as robust now as it had been before the Crimean winter of 1855–6 and, for the first time in her life, she admitted to being tired. The campaign had wounded her constitution, she said, and she felt too old to recover. London had lost its glamour, too. In summer the heavy stench of sludge and soot cloyed your lungs and made you retch; the winters were sour with smog and that chill she had found so novel and exciting as a young girl. She also lacked company. Not only was Soyer dead, but Jullien, her musical champion, had returned to Paris where, in 1859, he was arrested for debt and was reported to be incarcerated and losing his reason. In fact he died in prison in March 1860. Billy Russell had been to the first night of the festival, complimenting Mary for looking so splendid and 'great in her fine dress', but he, along with many of her army friends, had left for India soon afterwards.

A little low-spirited, Mary began to crave some warmth and the love of those who had known her all her life. It would be cheaper to live with Louisa in Kingston than here in Soho Square, and she had enough money for the passage home. There she would be feted all over again, and be able to stretch out in the Jamaican sunshine and bask, for a while, in family life.

When the English novelist Anthony Trollope visited Jamaica in late 1858, he was not particularly pleased by what he saw. Kingston was a 'disgrace to the country that owns it', he declared, with unpaved streets, rotting wooden houses, and no gas lamps at night.[17] There was one bright spot, however: the realization that his hotel landlady's sister was none other than 'good Mrs Seacole'. Louisa

Grant boasted to Trollope of Mary's celebrity, and chattered of her royal connections while serving up a decidedly untropical menu of oxtail soup, roast beef and beer. She didn't mention Mary's imminent arrival, but there can be little doubt that when Mary eventually disembarked at the familiar quay – minutes down the road from New Blundell Hall – sometime during late 1859 or early 1860, she was clasped to the capacious bosom of her family with just as much warmth as ever Mary herself hugged her sons. By now cousin Amelia had become a 'sick nurse' in Kingston, like her illustrious aunt Jane and even more illustrious cousin Mary.[18]

Since her last residence in Kingston in early 1854, things had changed. Edward Jordan, whom Mary knew as a journalist and politician dangerously outspoken in support of Afro-Caribbean rights, was now the mayor, and in 1861 became the first black Jamaican to receive a knighthood. Her own renown had given her mulatto peers confidence, and there was an invigorating air of assertiveness discernible amongst the emancipated classes. Correspondingly, however, white British concerns were in even greater decline than they had been a decade or two ago. The Civil War prevented business with America, and fewer planters than ever were managing viable livelihoods for themselves – let alone their servants – in this expensive post-slavery era. These were precarious times, which culminated in 1865 in a sort of West Indian Mutiny, when a political demonstration in Morant Bay (on the south-eastern corner of the island) was dispersed by the local militia firing into the crowds and killing twenty-eight. Riots followed, with brutality on both sides of a widening racial divide. The greatest outrage of all was the hanging by British Governor Edward Eyre of the leader of the initial demonstration, a black Baptist minister called Paul Bogle, and his principal supporter in the island's House of Assembly, the mulatto politician George Gordon. Four hundred and thirty other rebels were also put to death, and a bitter and uneasy calm ensued. When news of the uprising reached London, the papers screamed their indignation at the crass and barbarous behaviour of Eyre (who had forced the militia, mostly Afro-Caribbeans, to shoot their own people), and the British Government summarily recalled him home, dissolved the island's Assembly or parliament, and embraced Jamaica as a Crown Colony.

This move may have meant the revocation of a certain political independence, but in newly liberal and enlightened times, it also resulted in the island's economic recovery. British money was invested in building local roads, in laying an electric telegraph line to England, and subsidizing the reclamation of farming land from the post-plantation wilderness. By 1872, Kingston was smart and integrated enough to assume the role, from Spanish Town, of Jamaica's capital city. A city, indeed, to make Mary proud.

She became a political figure by default, seen in some circles as a sort of ambassadress from the mother-country, and as such, became allied in the public consciousness with Eyre. A legend even survives in Jamaica that Eyre, too 'busy' carousing at his country residence, Flamstead, during the visit of Queen Emma of the Sandwich Islands (Hawaii) in the early 1860s, deputized Mary Seacole to arrange a royal reception and meet the Queen on his behalf.[19]

The ferocity of the Morant Bay rebellion must have shaken Mary, and made her question where her loyalties lay. It very soon became apparent that Jamaica was to benefit by Eyre's removal, and that Britain, shocked into action, meant not so much to control the island and its people as to empower them. It was about time: a whole generation had grown up unsustained since emancipation in the early 1830s.

Mary became a direct beneficiary of this new liberal spirit of generosity towards the country of her birth, when the Seacole Fund was resurrected in London in the January of 1867. No doubt she had delicately let it be known to Rokeby and her old Crimean champions (those who had survived) that her money had run out, and that she felt a burden on her younger sister who was too busy trying to keep New Blundell Hall in profit to worry about maintaining Mary in the manner to which she had become accustomed. Mary was over sixty now, and facing an unsuitably frugal old age. Rokeby, predictably, was ashamed that the heroine he had so publicly patronized ten years ago should find herself in such embarrassing circumstances, and stirred up the old gang – with some illustrious new additions – to give the old lady one last chance of prosperity. There were no fancy concerts arranged this time, nor any dubious agents like the Royal Surrey Gardens Company: the new committee just asked for money, and got it, as they say, in spades. What made all the difference was the involvement of Queen Victoria – a widow too, now – joining her sons the Prince of Wales (the future King Edward VII) and his brother the Duke of Edinburgh, their cousin the Duke of Cambridge, an admiral, and a clutch of colonels.

Sadly there is no record of the Queen's personal attitude to Mrs Seacole. But there is a series of letters in the Royal Archives from the royal residence at Osborne on the Isle of Wight, to her nephew, Mary's friend, Count Gleichen (a Naval officer during the Crimean War).[20] The Queen is asked by Gleichen to subscribe publicly to the Fund, but refuses, citing a lack of precedent. She subscribed to charities, but never to an individual. She suggests the committee should send her a list of other subscribers, and when she has studied that (to see how much has been given, and by whom) she'll decide whether to add a donation of her own. She will only give money if she considers enough has been raised already to be of 'permanent benefit' to Mrs Seacole – to buy her a house, perhaps, or settle a respectable annuity on her. And any sum she might choose to give (probably, she said, about £50) must always remain anonymous.

Two weeks after the new fundraising effort was announced, a list was duly forwarded to the Queen. The amount pledged already was impressive: two shillings short of £138 (over £5,000 today), including a massive £25 from the Prince of Wales. Whether the Queen added to the sum is not recorded, but we may assume she did: Mary Seacole died a rich woman.

At the least she allowed her name to appear somewhere on the official literature of the Fund:

The disinterested services of Mrs SEACOLE in the Crimea, Panama, and England, being considered by the undermentioned Gentlemen as deserving of recognition and reward from the Army, Navy, and British Nation, they have formed themselves into a Committee to carry out a scheme to ensure for Mrs SEACOLE in her declining years, the means of obtaining remunerative employment, whereby competence [or financial self-sufficiency] would, to her, be secured.

The Committee feel the more emboldened to solicit aid to carry out this good work, from the circumstance of THE QUEEN having been graciously pleased to express her appro-bation of Mrs SEACOLE'S services, and HER MAJESTY'S kind interest in her future welfare.[21]

That must have encouraged subscribers, who may in turn have encouraged Victoria to dip into the royal purse.

There was no delay, this time, in forwarding the funds raised to Mary: according to a Mrs Stewart, a Kingston acquaintance, soon after the Morant Bay rebellion Mary bought for herself a parcel of land on Duke Street (a couple of blocks from New Blundell Hall, and fashionably further inland). There she built 'a charming little bungalow', her new Jamaican home, together with another dwelling she promptly let (her 'remunerative employment'). Mrs Stewart remembered Mary well during this period.

She was a valued friend of Capt. Cooper R.N., and his sister, and one afternoon she was at their home when a carriage drove up with a 'Big Gun' resplendent in gold lace and a string of medals – on his way from some function at King's House he had called in for a chat with his old comrade. As he entered the drawing room the old lady sprang up, 'Oh, my dear!' holding out her hands. In a moment the big man's arms were round her and he was hugging and kissing her like his long-lost mother. When their excitement quietened down a little he told us 'But for this little woman I would not be here today. Her nursing saved my life in the Crimea.' . . . This must have been about '68 or '69.[22]

History was to repeat itself somewhat when, in 1870, Mary read of the outbreak of the Franco-Prussian War. Her immediate instinct then, as it had been in 1854, was to rush back to England and offer her help to those of her sons who might be involved. And I think that's exactly what she did. She could hardly pretend in her mid-sixties to be lingering still in the 'late summer' of her life, but the autumn was a mild one, and she was proud to offer a stout and tender heart in the service, once again, of her country. So for the fourth time in her life, she left the Kingston quays for London (no doubt enjoying the voyage every bit as 'amazingly' as before), and prepared herself for war.

11

Age and Consequence

I do not mind confessing that the century and myself were both young together and that we have grown side by side into age and consequence.

Mary was sixty-five in 1870. She'd been affectionately known as an 'old woman' for the past fifteen years at least; now she was positively venerable. But her hair still gleamed black, and her fine, stout figure was still biddable when sternly disciplined with whalebone. Her purse and her health were robust enough to stand travelling, and she pined for the heady days of her heroism. The time was ripe for more adventure.

Just as before, it was probably *The Times* that gave Mary the inspiration to launch her latest campaign. On 19 July 1870 an irresistible notice appeared about the military victims (on both sides) of the Franco-Prussian War,[1] inviting applications from

> . . . [a] number of gentlemen and gentlewomen possessing sufficient surgical knowledge to enable them to temporarily

bind a wound and move, or attend to, the wounded until the military surgeons can apply proper treatment, possessing also such a knowledge of French or German, or both, as would enable them to read, write, and converse fluently with the wounded; also to endure much fatigue and hardship and to spare the time and the expense of thus employing themselves . . .[2]

Closely involved with a growing movement to provide non-partisan first aid to the casualties of war (the forerunner of the British Red Cross) was the Member of Parliament for Buckingham, Sir Harry Verney.[3] As well as qualified volunteers, the so-called 'British National Society for the Relief of the Sick and Wounded in War' encouraged lay women, to whom 'the privilege of taking up arms for the defence of the honour and independence of their country has been denied'.[4] Another 'even more sacred' possibility was available to them: nursing. Queen Victoria's eldest daughter Vicky, married to the Prussian Crown Prince, had already set up a hospital in Frankfurt (after having consulted Florence Nightingale), and her mother-in-law organized bands of gracious ladies to dispense cigars and refreshments to the French enemy; England, though not militarily involved in the conflict, felt morally bound to do its humanitarian duty.

It's not difficult to imagine Mary's response to this piece in *The Times*. She was an honorary gentlewoman, possessing more than 'sufficient surgical knowledge' to make a difference; what she lacked in linguistic accomplishment she surely made up for in readiness to spend time, energy and money to help the cause. The non-partisan nature of the enterprise would have appealed to her, too: after all, she had cared for wounded Russians as well as Britons in the Crimea. Convinced, again, that she was the right woman for the job, it's likely she applied directly to Sir Harry, and started bustling about making plans to leave for Europe without delay.

Mary's letter to Verney has not survived; nor has a letter Verney subsequently wrote to his sister-in-law Florence Nightingale, asking her opinion of Mary's suitability. Florence's reply, however, makes horribly fascinating reading. Dated 5 August 1870 it is ominously headed by a single word: 'Burn'.

Mrs Seacole

I dare say you know more about her than I do.

She kept – I will not call it a 'bad house' but something not very unlike it – in the Crimean War.

She was very kind to the men &, what is more, to the Officers – & did some good – & made many drunk.

(A shameful ignorant imposture was practised on the Queen who subscribed to the 'Seacole Testimonial').

I had the greatest difficulty in repelling Mrs Seacole's advances, & in preventing association between her & my nurses (absolutely out of the question) when we established 2 hospitals nursed by us between Kadikoi & the 'Seacole Establishment' in the Crimea. But I was successful. Without any open collision with Mrs Seacole – which I was anxious to avoid – (You will understand that any 'rivalry' between the 'Seacole' & the 'Nightingale' 'Establishments' was very much to be averted.)

Anyone who employs Mrs Seacole will introduce much kindness – also much drunkenness & improper conduct, wherever she is.

She had then, however, one or more 'persons' with her, whom (I conclude) she has not now. I conclude (& believe) that respectable Officers were entirely ignorant of what I . . . could not help knowing, as a Matron & Chaperone & Mother of the Army.[5]

Mary wasn't, of course, appointed.

Florence must genuinely have believed Mary to be a pernicious influence on her guests and patients. Once more it's difficult to understand why Florence should have judged Mary so harshly – unless, unflatteringly, one puts it down to jealousy.

Verney may have used the same excuse on this occasion as Lord Panmure had when declining to dispatch Mary to India in 1857: she was 'too precious' to lose, and should go home quietly and enjoy the prosperous old age so generously provided for her by the trustees of the Seacole Fund. She could conceivably have financed her own expedition to the Franco-Prussian War, but it would have been much harder for her to operate independently there than in the Crimea. She could speak neither French nor German, and the area around Alsace, where the Prussians and Germans invaded France, was bristling with high-minded ladies under the aegis of various societies for the succour of the sick. Food, drink and tobacco were being provided free to the combatants, so there would be no call for another British Hotel. She accepted Verney's decision with reluctant resignation, and quietly unpacked her travelling medicine chest.

Finding herself back in London gave Mary the chance to renew old friendships. The loftiness of her social circle proves her lasting celebrity. Those black secrets cherished by Florence had – amazingly – failed to seep out and stain Mary's reputation (as celebrities' secrets have a nasty habit of doing), and by the time she was seventy, she had become a royal favourite. First, her Crimean 'son' Prince Viktor (later Count Gleichen) had honoured her by sculpting a bust of his fond Jamaican Mammy. When he retired from the navy he devoted himself to his art, and although he appears to have specialized (wisely) in figures of his illustrious aunt Queen Victoria, he did attempt other members of the royal family, but only the occasional commoner. His bust of Mary wears the same irrepressible smile as that portrait the Up-Park officer had drawn back in 1850. She has a string of fat, blueberry-sized pearls around her neck, draping heftily over her lace collar; four medals are pinned to her chest,[6] and she looks noble, kind and comfortable. The bust was sculpted in 1871, and exhibited the following year at the Royal Academy's Summer Exhibition.[7] It lacks the slightly saccharine romanticism of a marble bust carved by Henry Weekes in 1859, which has Mary as a swan-necked beauty of Grecian cast – but then Weekes didn't know her as Gleichen did.

Gleichen's cousin was Bertie, Prince of Wales (later King Edward VII), who had been such a generous donor to the resurrected Seacole Fund in 1867 and whose wife Alexandra appears to have enjoyed a particularly close relationship with Mary. The royal family tended to talk of Alexandra as 'poor Alix'. She was deaf, was afflicted by 'white leg' (oedema of the legs due to thrombosis) and rheumatic fever, and was considered by the Queen to be 'dear and good and gentle' – but somewhat stupid. 'I know she is not brilliant in mind or conversation,' wrote Alix's sister-in-law Crown Princess Victoria in 1866, 'but I respect her and look to her as she is so thoroughly good, straightforward and unaffected, so equal in temper, so pure in mind.'[8] Alix was famously unpompous and jolly, delighting in the company of similarly down-to-earth souls. Where she and Mary met is unknown (as most of Alexandra's personal papers have been destroyed, and Mary kept no record of her later life), but the Prince and Princess of Wales had made a visit to the Crimean battlefields in 1869, chronicled by Mary's old friend Billy Russell, so perhaps he introduced them. By 1873, while Alix was still in her twenties, they were on remarkably familiar terms. One source suggested Mary was the Princess's masseuse, easing her rheumatism with strong and sympathetic hands, and making her laugh.[9] Another, someone who knew Mary, had them as family friends:

In '73 [Mrs Seacole] was in England . . . Hearing Captain Cooper [a friend in Kingston] would be going over on furlough in the summer she wrote asking him to bring her a basket of mangoes 'on the ice' as she wanted them for her 'dear Princess' (the then Princess of Wales, Alexandra). The Princess wished to taste Jamaica mangoes and she had promised to get some for her. As Superintendent of the Royal Mail Company Capt. Cooper easily got them 'on the ice' and on his arrival in London sent her the basket.

I was with him when she called a few days later to 'report' and thank him. She had taken them to Marlborough House [the Prince and Princess's London residence] and delivered them 'personally' to her old friend, 'the dear Princess', who was so pleased with them that she had at once eaten one and said she enjoyed it! I impertinently enquired of Mrs Seacole if she had made a nice curtsy when she entered the reception room.

'Oh, my dear child, I don't go there. When I go to see the Princess, I go up to her private sitting room and we sit and talk like the old friends we are.'[10]

Even allowing for Mary's tendency to overstate familiarity with famous 'friends', this relationship seems extraordinarily warm. The person who reported it added that later, 'a gentleman connected with the Court told Capt. Cooper that Mrs Seacole was a privileged guest at Marlborough House and highly thought of there.'

The last picture – and only known photograph – we have of Mary Seacole dates from around the same time as the royal mango delivery. It's a carte-de-visite, taken by the highly respected photographers Maull & Company, and features Mary still very much playing the Crimean heroine. Smarting, perhaps, from Verney's refusal, she has chosen – probably designed and sewn – a military-looking outfit of dark, brass-buttoned silk, with faux epaulettes, cuffs and a sort of crenellated frill at the hem like a castle battlement or the tabbed canopy of a medieval tent, all trimmed in a chequered braid reminiscent of the Argyll and Sutherland Highlanders' uniform. Unusually for a carte-de-visite, Mary appears to have brought her own props into the studio. Against the painted backdrop of a wide valley in which the wheels of a cannon can just be discerned, she is seated beside a tent, with a table to her left loaded with bottles of medicine. There's a camp-stool to her right, and on her lap is a bowl in which she's mixing some fragrant herbal elixir. Her little medals cling to a vertiginous bosom, while her waist strains under creaking stays, the buttons of her bodice threatening to burst off like musket balls. Her neatly dressed hair shines without a hint of grey, and her contemplative face, looking down at the bowl, has lost none of its tenderness or resolution.

If the photograph had been taken two or three years earlier, it would have been the perfect advertisement to Sir Harry Verney of all that Mary perceived herself to be. The fact that she commissioned it around 1873,[11] when there was no obvious reason to do so, suggests how deeply her own identity was rooted in the slopes of Spring Hill. The sixteen months she spent between Balaklava and Sevastopol made sense of her past, and shaped her future. Most of all, they proved to the world (or to Britain, for her the same thing) what Mary had known all along, that she was a uniquely *useful* person, born to succeed, and still very much her own woman.

By the autumn of 1876, Mary was living at 26 Upper George Street, off Portman Square, in what is now (and to a lesser extent was then) a smart area of London. She considered this to be a propitious time to make her will, having safely achieved her three score years and ten. Upper George Street was just around the corner from Upper Berkeley Street, where Mary's kinsman Amos Henriques lived with his wife Julia. The Henriques' had been in London for at least thirty years; their eldest son Ernest was born there.[12] As well as bequeathing Amos and Julia 19 guineas each – the same rather mystic sum she left to most other legatees – she directed her executors, Amos and an esteemed friend from Black River, William Neilson Farquharson, to invest £300 for the benefit of Ernest Henriques, his brother Edward and sister Josephine.[13] To her cousin David Henriques – which might suggest Amos was also her cousin – she left the usual 19 guineas. Her other cousins, Amelia Kennedy (the nurse), Matilda Simmett (or Simmonett), and Louisa Cochrane, each got 19 guineas, as did two of Edwin Seacole's great-nieces resident in London, Ada and Florence Kent.[14] The Hon. John Salmon, erstwhile President of the Legislative Council in Jamaica, got £50, and his daughter Elizabeth £200, to be paid from the sale of the larger of the two houses Mary owned – and was presently leasing out – in Kingston. Thomas Day, now back from the

Antipodes and living in Gracechurch Street in the City of London, only received the standard 19 guineas, and of Sally Seacole, the apple of Alexis Soyer's eye, there's no mention at all. That disposed of most of her Jamaican friends and family. She also left £100 to the Cambridge Institution for Soldiers' Orphans, but that was the only charity to benefit.

Lord Rokeby, who had masterminded the foundation of the Seacole Fund, was bequeathed £50 'as a slight mark of my gratitude for his many kindnesses to me . . . to purchase a ring if he so pleases'. Colonel Hussey Fane Keane, another of Mary's high-ranking champions, was left the same sum 'which I hope (but without imposing any obligation in respect thereof) will be laid out by him in the purchase of some ornament or jewel'. His Serene Highness Count Gleichen was honoured with Nelson's diamond ring *and* £50. His eldest daughter Fedora was to receive Mary's 'best set of pearl ornaments' – possibly those she wore when modelling for the Count in 1871 – and his other children each got the 19 guinea package.

When Mary died, rumours of her liberality to those who already had much (and to whom she wasn't even related) caused some disquiet. 'The sum raised [by the Fund] for Mrs Seacole,' reported *The Times*, 'enabled her to end her days in comfortable ease. Strange to say, she has bequeathed all her property to persons of title.'[15] A correspondent to the paper thought it an outrage that Mary had left nothing to Louisa Grant of New Blundell Hall, currently (apparently) in financial difficulties after a life spent, like her sister's, in being over-generous to others.

When the will was actually published, however, all qualms were forgotten. Mary looked after her nearest and dearest best of all. To her brother's son Edward Ambleton, who was living in the smaller of Mary's houses in Duke Street, Kingston, she left £100 and the house for life, to devolve on his heirs and if he had none, to his aunt Louisa Grant and hers. Louisa inherited £300, her sister's household linen, watch, jewellery and ornaments, and anything else that remained. The stocks and shares managed for Mary by Rokeby, Fane Keane and

Count Gleichen (under the terms of the Trust) were to go to Louisa, with most of the proceeds of the larger Kingston house, moneys from the sale of Mary's household effects, in fact the whole of Mary's now considerable estate, minus the named bequests and funeral expenses.

According to a local newspaper report – and implied by Mary's will – New Blundell Hall already belonged to Louisa. Whether Jane wished her younger daughter to inherit it, or whether Mary relinquished it when she left Kingston for the Crimea (with no guarantee of a safe return) is unclear, but one suspects the latter. Their brother Edward was probably already dead by then (definitely so by 1857), and Mary had her eye on greater glory; it would make sense to consign the local family business to the capable and unambitious hands of Louisa Grant.

By 1881, Mary had made her final house move. She rented lodgings at 3 Cambridge Street, off the Edgware Road, where she lived with her landlady, a cook and another female lodger. Early that year Mary also had a visitor staying with her, Rose Boydon from Kingston.[16] It was a companionable life. Amos Henriques had recently died, but Mary could rely on the company and care of Sarah Kent, the sixty-three-year-old wife of Edwin Seacole's nephew William. Sarah lived with her adult children in Brixton, an hour or so's walk from Cambridge Street, and when Mary fell ill of 'apoplexy', or a stroke, at the end of April, it was Sarah who was called to her side.

Mary refused to die meekly. She hung on for over a fortnight before falling into a coma on 11 May and finally surrendering three days later. She was seventy-six. Sarah Kent went to register the death herself.[17] When Mary's will was proved in July, Sarah found herself the proud possessor not only of Mary's 'best bedding and bedstead and also two pairs of linen sheets and one pair of calico sheets and one white counterpane', but of her choice of Mary's furniture. And when the Seacole estate was finally totted up, it came to the magnificent sum of £2,615 11s 7d. Once the specified disbursements had been made, Louisa Grant was left with about £850 (worth over

£37,000 today). Mary's trustees had obviously invested wisely; she enjoyed the income from her big house in Kingston, let to a Mr Levy, and was probably spending reasonably frugally at the time of her death, saving for a rainy day, a voyage, or best of all, another war.

Mary Seacole was buried, according to her own instructions, in St Mary's Roman Catholic Cemetery in Kensal Green. Next door, in the fashionable Anglican enclosure, lay British noblemen and women. Closer to Mary's grave was her old friend Alexis Soyer, who no doubt gave Mother Seacole the hearty welcome she expected on her well-attended entrance into heaven.

Goodness knows what parties there would have been had Mary died in Kingston. The wake would have lasted till the rum-soaked dawn; everyone would have worn their brightest colours and sung their loudest hymns, in extravagant celebration of a life well lived. Victorian north London was less exotic. Those friends and relations who remembered Mary paid their respects in dull clothes and with hushed voices as her worn-out body was laid to rest on the slope facing south, by the railway line to Paddington.

Obituaries appeared in British and Jamaican newspapers during the weeks after Mary's death, and in 1903 a book was published by the Religious Tract Society in London called *Noble Deeds of the World's Heroines*, which recalled Mary piously as 'the soldiers' friend'. 'England seems to have forgotten her,' wrote the author, 'but it is hoped that this account of her life may help to remove the reproach.'[18] It didn't. Hardly anything else was heard in England of Mary for nigh on eighty years – except for a small and rather pathetic notice tucked into a corner of the *Sunday Times* on 9 January 1938:

> I am desirous of identifying a hand-coloured print or photograph of a lady with some military decorations on the left side, signed 'Mrs Seacole, 1859'. Can any of your readers supply information as to who this lady was?

Surprisingly, the memory of Mary didn't fare that much better in Jamaica. It stirred a little when Louisa died in 1905, at the age of

ninety, after enduring a ghastly cocktail of illness and disease
including erysipelas, gangrene and asthma; there was some correspondence about 'Mother Seacole' in the national paper, the *Daily
Gleaner* during the 1930s,[19] and on the anniversary of the outbreak of
the Crimean War in 1954, a decision was taken to name the Kingston
mother-house of the Jamaican General Trained Nurses' Association
in her honour. A hall of residence for women in the University of the
West Indies at Mona was also given her name and portrait.

It is a shame that Mary was so quickly forgotten, but not inexplic-
able. Her own strength of character (together with considerable skill
in marketing and public relations) kept her profile high during her
lifetime, and that profile was arresting enough to catch attention.
She burned brightly. But when she was gone, and the context in
which she'd made her mark had evaporated into distant history,
there was nothing left to fuel the flame. Towards the end of her life
she was famous for being Mary Seacole, and that slightly hollow sort
of celebrity never lasts. Despite the efforts of the Seacole Fund
trustees, and those veterans of the Crimean War who loved and
admired her, she could never, in the nineteenth and early twentieth
centuries, be extolled as a true British heroine: she was too black.
And despite the (quiet) pride she had in her homeland and her
Afro-Caribbean roots, she couldn't fully identify or be identified with
black Jamaicans: she had become too white.

Only within the last thirty-odd years has Mary's memory been
resurrected with any real vigour. Her gravestone was lovingly
restored in the early 1970s by a group of Jamaican women,[20]
and in 1981 a service was held there in May to celebrate the
centenary of her death. It has now become an annual event. A
touring exhibition about British black history – *Roots in Britain* –
featured her unfamiliar story and drew much curiosity from visitors
and historians in 1980. *Wonderful Adventures of Mrs Seacole in Many
Lands* was reprinted with useful biographical notes in 1984; further
editions have followed, together with a host of children's books
about her (since she's now on the National Curriculum, alongside
Florence Nightingale, in British primary schools). In 1990 Jamaica's

'third highest honour', the Order of Merit, was bestowed on her, and now there are Mary Seacole nurseries across Britain, Mary Seacole roads and streets, Mary Seacole Houses, and a Mary Seacole Award.[21] Reams of academic ponderings on her literary, cultural, medical, even political, significance are piling up in libraries around the world, and she's fast becoming a heroine again, voted in 2004 the 'greatest black Briton in history'.

The problem is that the real Mary Seacole is in danger of being obscured by all this modern gloss. It is too easy to stick labels on dead heroines and claim them for some modern cause. She deserves more than mere iconology. Mary was not a political figure, no freedom-fighter, nor even a pioneer of hospital or battlefield nursing. She never held back from expressing her opinions, certainly, but those opinions were the orthodox opinions of any imperialist Briton at the time. She believed in the inherent nobility of the African people and cherished her kinship with them, but perceived herself to be unique, not representative. And she nursed as her mother had done, to make people feel better, not to change the system. Her true heroism lies not in her colour, nor even in her extraordinary career, but in her self-belief. She believed she had a right to follow her own instincts, to be respected by others for doing so, to be useful (on her own terms) and to be happy. History teaches us that ambitions like these, acted upon with such energy and success, were probably unprecedented in a person of her time, place, gender, race and class. To Mary, though, the necessary drive, self-confidence and cheerful eccentricity to go out and conquer the world came natu-rally.

One of the letters I came across whilst researching the Crimean section of this book was written by a keen botanist, an officer in the 23rd, who used to spend his spare time hunting plants.[22] His favourite find was the shockingly unsubtle Crimean violet he dis-covered flowering with 'unblushing effrontery' in the spring of 1856. He was, of course, familiar with those nice, demure little blossoms which cower beneath English hedgerows, but this one bloomed shamelessly out in the open. It was robust and richly tinted, almost overpoweringly fragrant, and kept its own company, the better to show itself off. It was large, strong and singular, he wrote: utterly original, and as true to itself as it's possible to be. Its self-possession and joie-de-vivre exhilarated him.

It reminds me, irresistibly, of Mary.

Notes and References

All unattributed quotations throughout the text are taken from Mary Seacole's *Wonderful Adventures of Mrs Seacole in Many Lands*.

1 A Female Ulysses

1. Anna Maria Falconbridge, *Two Voyages to Sierra Leone*, p. 240.
2. Christopher Baker, *Jamaica*, p. 580.
3. Lady Maria Nugent , *Lady Nugent's Journal of her Residence in Jamaica*, (ed. Philip Wright) p. 219.
4. Ibid.
5. Edward Long, *The History of Jamaica*, p. 484.
6. Anna Maria Falconbridge, op. cit., p. 236.
7. Every male over the age of sixteen and resident in the island for a minimum of a month was automatically enlisted into the militia (founded in 1662). None but the white commissioned officers was paid.
8. Noted in Gretchen Gerzina, *Black England*, p. 68.
9. Edward Brathwaite, *The Development of Creole Society in Jamaica*, p. 152.
10. The Saint-Domingue uprising of 1791–2 was brutal: its genesis was hidden in the outbreak of guerrilla warfare between renegade slaves (dubbed 'marrons', known in Jamaica as Maroons) and white French landowners in the 1750s. It culminated in a political agreement between local mulattos, or 'gens de couleur', and the French Government. More than 10,000 blacks died, and 2,000 whites; over 1,000 plantations were ruined. But what resulted was a new

society, with the black activist François-Dominique Toussaint L'Ouverture as its hero, which blossomed into independence in 1804 as Haiti.

11. Christopher Baker, op. cit., p. 23.

12. Edward Brathwaite, op. cit., p. 167.

13. Mary Seacole's letter to *Punch* was published on 30 May 1857, and a letter written by her to Lord Rokeby was reproduced in *The Times* of 29 November 1856.

14. Thanks to the exigencies of earthquake, hurricane and fire, Jamaican registers, particularly relating to non-whites, are notoriously incomplete. Births and deaths were not required to be notified at the time in question; records of baptisms and burials were kept by some parishes from 1688 onwards; after 1824 they were centrally collated and are now located in the official Archives in Spanish Town, as well as in individual church registers. Exhaustive searches have failed to produce unequivocal evidence of the date of Mary's baptism. Although several Mary Grants, of varying status (or colour) and ages, were baptized in Jamaica between 1800 and 1850, only one might have a claim to be our Mary Grant. She was a quadroon, baptized on 18 December 1813 aged eight years (Registration B1224000/I/171) – but in the Jamaican county of Westmoreland, at the other end of the island from Kingston. Sadly (and predictably) no details of this Mary's family are entered in the Register.

15. Thomas Dancer, *The Medical Assistant*, p. v.

16. Mary Seacole, *Wonderful Adventures* (1984 edition), p. 109.

17. Sir Harris Nicolas (ed.), *Dispatches and Letters of Vice-Admiral Lord Viscount Nelson*, vol. 1, p. 34. See also Christopher Hibbert, *Nelson, A Personal History*, p. 28, and John Bigelow, *Jamaica in 1850*, p. 58.

18. See Paulette Kerr, 'Victims or Strategists? Female Lodging-house Keepers in Jamaica', in Verene Shepherd et al. (eds), *Engendering History*, p. 197.

19. Lady Maria Nugent, op. cit., p. 68.

20. Ref. AA5224 (1905 Kingston Register of Deaths).

21. Anthony Trollope, *West Indies and the Spanish Main*, p. 21.

22. From the Baptismal Register of the Holy Trinity Roman Catholic Church, Kingston (1852–65), p. 337, dated 1 July 1860. Edward was aged ten at his baptism.

23. British soldiers' personal papers are usually held by the Public Record Office in London, and duplicated or augmented in regimental archives. Many records were lost, however, during the Second World War – amongst them, most probably, Mary's father's.

24. Mary named the numerous family of Amos Henriques in her will, which included her cousin David, resident in Dundrum, now in Northern Ireland, in 1876. British census indices for 1881 mention other members of the family, including the retired Jamaican merchant Jacob, living not far from Mary at the time of her death in the parish of St Marylebone in London.

25. Mary Seacole, op. cit., p. 56.

26. Lady Maria Nugent, op. cit., p. 234.

27. Merchantmen only sailed when fully laden, whereas 'packets', or mailships, provided a scheduled service. It is natural to assume that Mary used any contacts she had amongst the merchants of Kingston to cadge as cheap a passage as possible. Time was hardly of the essence.

28. William Cobbett, *The Emigrant's Guide*, p. 110.

29. See Ben Weinreb and Christopher Hibbert, *The London Encyclopaedia*, p. 938, for a fuller description of this acknowledged modern wonder of the world.

30. *Gentleman's Magazine*, vol. 34 (1764), p. 493; James Walvin, *Black and White*, p. 46.
31. James Walvin, op. cit., p. 47.
32. Poor Sara was sold on to a Frenchman in 1814, and died in Paris two years later. Her famous organs were preserved and displayed in a bottle in a French museum where they stayed until 2002, when her remains were sent home to Africa for a dignified funeral and burial.
33. Christopher Hibbert, *London*, p. 179.
34. Arthur Bryant, *The Age of Elegance*, p. 150.
35. Jane Austen, *Works* (ed. J. Bailey), pp. 424–5.
36. Mary Seacole, op. cit., p. 58.

2 Daughter and Doctress

1. Amelia Kennedy, Matilda Simmet (or Simmonett) and Louisa Cochrane were beneficiaries of Mary's will. Amelia Kennedy became a nurse in Kingston, and died in 1878 (two years after Mary made her will) aged fifty-four. Her sister Matilda (who was illiterate) registered her death (Kingston Parish Registers no. 732, November 1878).
2. Edward Brathwaite, *The Development of Creole Society in Jamaica*, p. 284. See also Richard Sheridan, *Doctors and Slaves*; Aleric Josephs, 'Mary Seacole: Jamaican Nurse and Doctress' in *Jamaican Historical Review*, vol. 17 (1991), p. 48.
3. Florence Nightingale visited Kaiserwerth first, briefly, in 1850. She returned the following year, this time staying with the Protestant Deaconesses for three months.
4. Kingston Common Council Minutes, dated 23 September 1816. See Edward Brathwaite, op. cit., p. 288.
5. Lady Maria Nugent, (ed. Philip Wright), *Lady Nugent's Journal of her Residence in Jamaica*, p. 124.
6. Noted in Edward Brathwaite, op. cit., p. 282.
7. The ten regiments represented at Up-Park (for varying lengths of time) between 1826 and 1836 were the 22nd, 33rd, 37th, 50th, 56th, 77th, 84th, 91st, 92nd, and the 2nd West India Regiment.
8. J. Stewart, *A View of the Past and Present State of the Island of Jamaica*, pp. 46–7.
9. Cynric Williams, *A Tour through Jamaica*, p. 27.
10. Ref. B1291727/I/065 (Jamaica Parish Registers, Marriage, vol. 1 (1826–39). They were married in a Church of England service by the Reverend John Magrath.
11. John Bigelow, *Jamaica in 1850*, p. 21.
12. Cynric Williams, op. cit., p. 10.
13. Mary Seacole, *Wonderful Adventures* (1984 edition), p. 59.
14. A John Gordon Seacole, a mustee child, was baptized in the parish of St Elizabeth (which includes Black River) on 24 March 1824, aged eight months (ref. B1368561/II/258). His father was possibly the C.W. Seacole who appears in the Jamaican Almanac for 1824 as Harbour-Master, and in 1839 as a captain in the militia; Seacole and Miller are listed in the Almanac for 1833.
15. Edwin's baptism appears in the Register of Prittlewell Parish Church on 18 September 1803, together with that of a sister, Elizabeth Caroline Lind Seacole,

implying that they were twins, or else that Elizabeth was an older child whose baptism was delayed for some reason. Alternatively, Edwin Nelson may have conveniently been slipped into the Seacole family under the pretence that he was Elizabeth's twin.

16. Admiral Lord Horatio Nelson, *The Letters of Lord Nelson to Lady Hamilton,* vol. 1, p. 124.
17. For all the information I have about Edwin Seacole's family circumstances I am indebted to a report researched by his kinsman Len Matthews (whose wife was Thomas Seacole's great-great-granddaughter), published in the *Essex Review* of 1950, and brought to my attention by his daughter Jenny Lightstone.
18. Mary Seacole, op. cit., p. 59.
19. Mary confuses the timing of Edwin's and Jane's deaths, and the great fire, in her autobiography. She remembered both husband and mother dying before 1843 (the date of the fire), whereas Edwin's burial record is dated 26 October 1844.
20. The *Jamaican Times* ran a report of the fire, which was reprinted in the London *Times* on 7 October 1843.
21. Edwin was described (as 'Edward') in the record of his burial in Kingston Burial Ground (Kingston Parish Register, vol. 4 (1837–48) p. 350) as being of the parish of St Elizabeth – i.e. Black River – but currently resident at East Queen Street, which may have been mistaken by the clerk for East Street. Either that, or Edwin and Mary lodged at East Queen Street, some three blocks north of Blundell Hall, on their return from Black River until his death.
22. Mary Seacole, op. cit., pp. 59–60.
23. Ibid., p. 60.
24. Sir William Gomm, *The Story of Newcastle,* p. 6.
25. *The Iron Duke,* p. 207. This is Captain Henry Bunbury.
26. John Bigelow, op. cit., p. 12.

3 Up and Doing

1. Madame Moustache and Kitty, along with 'Poker Alice', were notorious professional gamblers who preyed on unsuspecting punters in mid-nineteenth-century western America.
2. The black writer and army officer Martin Robson Delany (1812–85) recommended New Granada as the perfect destination for black and coloured emigrants: it was a land of opportunity, both politically and financially. Only the climate and impenetrable landscape mitigated against it.
3. Mary Seacole, *Wonderful Adventures* (1984 edition), p. 64.
4. See specifically C.D. Griswold, *The Isthmus of Panama;* Joseph Fabens, *A Story of Life on the Isthmus;* H. Hussey, *The Australian Colonies; together with notes of a Voyage from Australia to Panama.*
5. Mary Seacole, *Wonderful Adventures* (1984 edition) p. 67.
6. Mary Kingsley surveyed the upper reaches of the Ogowe river, West Africa, from her canoe in the mid-1890s, before making an ascent (still immaculately dressed) of Mount Cameroon. See Jane Robinson, *Wayward Women,* pp. 137–8.
7. Darien was the name of the neck of land between North and South America now known as the Isthmus of Panama.

8. Muriatic – or hydrochloric – acid is a highly poisonous and corrosive substance (a mixture of sulphuric acid and salt) which produces a rusty appearance in certain metals. Astonishingly it has been used as an ingredient of homeopathic remedies for sore throats, when mixed with bark infusions and laudanum: perhaps that's where Mary's familiarity with the chemical originated. See H. Hartshorne, *Household Cyclopedia of General Information* (1881).
9. H. Hussey, op. cit., p. 94.
10. Mary Seacole, op. cit., pp. 71–2.
11. Frank Soule, et al., *The Annals of San Francisco*, p. 723.
12. Joseph Fabens, op. cit., p. 42.
13. Mary Seacole, op. cit., p. 77.
14. Ibid., pp. 78–9.

4 An Inclination to Rove

1. Lady Emmeline Stuart Wortley, *Travels in the United States*, p. 27.
2. Mary rarely dignifies black people with names (her servants Mac and Francis are the only exceptions), and is often dismissive of them in her autobiography. Her lip curls most, however, in the presence of those unfortunate Yankees.
3. A Mr L. Levy, whose letter to a friend describing a visit to Cruces at the beginning of July 1851 was published in the *Panama Star* newspaper.
4. Mary Seacole, *Wonderful Adventures* (1984 edition), pp. 95–6.
5. Ibid., pp. 97–8.
6. The first mention I can find of a women-only hotel is an advertisement in a 1913 Thomas Cook publication, describing Miss Davies's 'Private Hotel for Ladies, very quiet and refined' in Westminster, London.
7. See Basil Walsh, *Catherine Hayes, the Hibernian Prima Donna*, p. 219.
8. Lola recorded her opinion of the alleged meeting in her *Autobiography and Lectures* (1858).
9. Lola Montez, op. cit., pp. 49–50.
10. According to Bruce Seymour, author of *Lola Montez: A Life*.
11. Quinine, derived from the bark of the chinchona tree native to Peru and Ecuador, was – and is – used to relax muscle cramps and reduce fever; powdered cedron seeds from a small tree peculiar to New Granada were thought to eradicate poison from the system. Both tasted extremely bitter.
12. Mary Seacole, op. cit., pp. 106–7.
13. According to the records of the Women in Military Service for America Memorial Foundation in Washington, DC, George Washington mustered untrained nurses for service in the American Revolution, paying them $2 per month, plus their rations, in 1776. By 1777 their wages had grown to $8 per month. Washington's preferred ratio of nurses to sick or wounded men was one to ten.
14. Public Record Office, London, ref. WO 25/264.
15. Nellie Cashman (c.1850–1925) was an Irish Catholic who joined the gold-rush in Nevada in 1869, and became a lodging-house keeper and restaurateur (like Mary) both there and elsewhere in America. Her affectionate care and concern for the bodily and spiritual comfort of her fellow (male) miners endeared her

to them all. They called her the 'Saint of the Sourdoughs', the 'Miners' Angel', and her hardy and gentle spirit made her a heroine of the old Wild West.

5 Pomp, Pride and Circumstance

1. The best books to explain the origins and progress of the war are Christopher Hibbert, *The Destruction of Lord Raglan*; Trevor Royle, *Crimea: The Great Crimean War 1854–1856*, and Ian Fletcher and Natalia Ischenko, *The Crimean War*.
2. The phrase is attributed to Tsar Nicholas I; what he actually said was that the Ottoman Empire was 'a sick man – a very sick man'. See the letter by Christopher de Bellaigue in the *New York Review of Books*, vol. 48, no. 11 (July 2001).
3. Mary Seacole, *Wonderful Adventures* (1984 edition), p. 120.
4. See Jane Robinson, *Pandora's Daughters*, pp. 66, 100 and 105.
5. According to the 1854 Lloyd's Registers in the National Maritime Museum, the *La Plata* would fit most neatly with Mary's timetable. Another possibility, the *Tamar*, wasn't due in from New Granada until 16 November.
6. *The Times*, 9 October 1854.
7. Ibid.
8. The other two interviewers were Mary Stanley, a highly religious friend of Florence's (though they grew apart after Mary Stanley brought more nurses out to Scutari unbidden by Florence) and Selina Bracebridge, perhaps Florence's closest non-family friend of all.
9. From the rules and regulations for nurses in London's Public Record Office, ref. WO 43/963.
10. Mary proudly transcribed the letter in *Wonderful Adventures* (1984 edition, p. 123):

     I became acquainted with Mrs Seacole through the instrumentality of T.B. Cowan, Esq., H.B.M. Consul at Colon [Navy Bay], on the Isthmus of Panama, and have had many opportunities of witnessing her professional zeal and ability in the treatment of aggravated forms of tropical diseases.

     I am myself personally much indebted for her indefatigable kindness and skill at a time when I am apt to believe the advice of a practitioner qualified in the North would have little availed.

     Her peculiar fitness, in a constitutional point of view, for the duties of medical attendant, needs no comment.
11. Mary Seacole, op. cit., p. 124.
12. See note 8.
13. Mary Seacole, op. cit., p. 125.
14. Public Record Office, London, ref. WO 25/264.
15. Mary Seacole, op. cit., pp. 125–6.
16. The archive of the Crimea Fund is held at the Essex Record Office, ref. D/DGg/7 1854–5.
17. This was Sir John Campbell, whose wife had stayed at New Blundell Hall in the past, and of whom Mary was particularly fond.
18. Mary Seacole, op. cit., pp. 126–7.
19. Ibid., p. 127.

20. I am indebted to Ron Brand, librarian of the Maritime Museum in Rotterdam, for the information that the *Hollander* was built in Chester in 1854; she was a state-of-the-art 487-ton iron screw-steamer belonging to the Dutch shipping firm of J.P. van Hoey Smith.

6 Enjoying it Amazingly

1. Nelson must have made provision for his 'godson' early on – perhaps even at Edwin's baptism. By the time the infant was two years old, Nelson was dead. What the connection was between the Essex midwife Thomas Seacole and the most illustrious celebrity of the age (if one assumes the Seacole family legend to be unfounded) remains a tantalizing mystery. Emma, Lady Hamilton, does not appear to have had anything to do with Edwin at all: she died, in debt and disgrace, when he was twelve. There is no mention of Seacole in Nelson's last will and its codicils (Public Record Office, PROB 11/1435 and 11/1446), despite Mary's claim that Edwin had his diamond ring.
2. Henry Swinburne, *Courts of Europe*, p. 172.
3. Emily Lowe, *Unprotected Females in Norway*, p. 3.
4. No mothers were allowed to accompany their husbands 'on the strength'; they had to survive with their children on their own independent wages, on money spasmodically and uncertainly sent home from the Front or on charity.
5. Public Record Office, London, ref. WO 25/264 (Bundle N).
6. Piers Compton, *Colonel's Lady and Camp-Follower*, p. 26.
7. Fanny Duberly, in a letter to her sister Selina; quoted by E.E.P. Tisdall in *Mrs Duberly's Campaigns*, p. 61.
8. Ethel Berry, in Frances Backhouse (ed.), *Women of the Klondike*, p. 40.
9. Mary Seacole, *Wonderful Adventures* (1984 edition), pp. 131–2.
10. See John Shepherd, *The Crimean Doctors*, for exhaustive details of hospitals and medical staff in the Crimean region during the war.
11. Cecil Woodham Smith, *Florence Nightingale 1820–1910*, p. 151.
12. Ibid., p. 152.
13. Mary Seacole, op. cit., pp. 132–3.
14. Selina Bracebridge had been one of the three women originally responsible for interviewing Florence's first nursing staff in London.
15. Mary Seacole, op. cit., p. 136.
16. Mary recognized Florence's influence in Scutari, admiring her for 'evoking order out of confusion, and bravely resisting the despotism of death'. However, that is exactly what Mary would consider she herself was doing at the Front.
17. I found this unacknowledged quotation at the Florence Nightingale Museum in London, in a teacher's resource pack on Florence in the Crimea.
18. Cecil Woodham Smith, op. cit., p. 161.
19. In E.E.P. Tisdall, op. cit., p. 115.
20. Douglas Arthur Reid, *Memories of the Crimean War*, pp. 13–14.
21. 'Mrs Seacole's Hut' is clearly marked on Captain Frederic Brine's *Map of Sebastopol and Surrounding Country* (1857); Public Record Office, London, ref. WO 78/4982.
22. Mary Seacole, op. cit., p. 153.

23. Alexis Soyer, *A Culinary Campaign*, p. 142.
24. Ibid., p. 143.
25. Mary Seacole, op. cit., pp. 156–7.

7 Comfort and Order

1. For information on Alexis Soyer I am grateful to his biographer Frank Clement-Lorford.
2. The ingredients for Famine Soup were as follows: 2 gallons of water, 2 oz dripping, 2 onions 'and other vegetables', ½ lb of second-quality flour and of pearl barley, 3 oz salt, ½ oz of brown sugar, and some maize as a thickener. It saved people's lives.
3. George Cruchley, *Cruchley's Picture of London*, p. 46.
4. Alexis Soyer, *A Culinary Campaign*, pp. 325-6.
5. Alan Palmer, *The Banner of Battle*, p. 182.
6. Claydon House Trust collection, MS Nightingale 110.
7. Alexis Soyer, op. cit., p. 143.
8. Mary Seacole, *Wonderful Adventures* (1984 edition), pp. 178–9.
9. Anon., *A Story of Active Service*, p. 126.
10. Mary Seacole, op. cit., p. 158.
11. Alexis Soyer, op. cit., p. 269.
12. Claydon House Trust collection, MS Nightingale 110.
13. Claydon House Trust collection, MS 9004/60.
14. Claydon House Trust collection, MS Nightingale 110.
15. Fanny Duberly daringly recounted the joke in a letter to her sister Selina; see E.E.P. Tisdall, *Mrs Duberly's Campaigns*, p. 125.
16. Colonel Henry Bunbury, MS letter dated 5 November 1855 (private collection).
17. Jane Williams (ed.), *The Autobiography of Elizabeth Davis. Besty Cadwalladyr. A Balaclava Nurse*, p. 154.
18. Claydon House Trust collection, MS Nightingale 110.
19. Lady Hornby, *Constantinople During the Crimean War*, p. 311.
20. George Buchanan, *Camp Life. As Seen by a Civilian*, p. 217.
21. Ibid., p. 177.
22. Sir John Astley, *Fifty Years of My Life*, vol. 1, p. 268.
23. Colin Robins (ed.), *Captain Dunscombe's Diary*, p. 207.
24. Mary Seacole, op. cit., pp. 161–2.
25. Captain Frederick Savage, MS Diary, 11 August 1855. Courtesy of John Bilcliffe.
26. Thomas Buzzard, *With the Turkish Army in the Crimea and Asia Minor*, p. 179.
27. Mrs Henry Duberly's MS journal (British Library Add. MSS 47218), parenthesized in E.E.P. Tisdall, op. cit., pp. 158–9.

8 Proud and Unprotected

1. A gabion is a large wickerwork cylinder, like an open-ended basket, which when filled with earth was used as fortification against enemy fire.

2. William Howard Russell *Russell's Despatches from the Crimea* (ed. N. Bentley), p. 262.

3. Ibid., p. 264.

4. See Jane Robinson, *Wayward Women*, p. 264.

5. Piers Compton, *Colonel's Lady and Camp Follower*, p. 137. The tours were run by Inman's Travel Company.

6. Ibid., pp. 26, 29, 190, 195.

7. Igor Klishevich, 'Unknown Pirogov' (a paper given at the International Scientific Conference on The Eastern War of 1853–1856, Sevastopol, October 2003).

8. For information on Dasha I am indebted to Ludmilla Golikova of the Museum of the Heroic Defence and Liberation of Sevastopol. Dasha is the only female to feature in the famous panorama of the Siege of Sevastopol in the Crimea.

9. In a letter to Lady Cranworth dated 22 February 1856; British Library Add. MSS 43397 f 93b. See Anne Summers, *Angels and Citizens*, for a history of British women in military nursing.

10. The principal collections of personal papers of Florence Nightingale are to be found in the British Library, the London Metropolitan Archive, the Wellcome Institute, and at Claydon House in Buckinghamshire, the home of her sister Parthenope. The National Register of Archives indicates various other collections. See Sue Goldie's excellent *Calendar of the Letters of Florence Nightingale* for a near-exhaustive index of Florence's (copious) correspondence.

11. Quoted by Mary Seacole (*Wonderful Adventures*, 1984 edition, p. 208) from *The Times* of 11 April 1857.

12. Mary Seacole, op. cit., p. 172.

13. Claydon House Trust collection, MS Nightingale 110.

14. William Simpson, *The Autobiography* (ed. George Eyre-Todd), p. 57.

15. There was still action centred in the Kinburn peninsula at the mouth of the river Dnieper north of the Crimea, and in Kars, down on the mainland of Turkey near the Russian border, but the main body of the campaign was now over.

16. Frederick Hans D. Vieth, *Recollections of the Crimean Campaign*, p. 74.

17. Alexis Soyer, *A Culinary Campaign*, p. 130.

18. Edwin Galt, *The Camp and the Cutter*, p. 75.

19. *Daily News*, 15 January 1856 (the report was filed on New Year's Day).

20. *News of the World*, 13 April 1856.

21. Colonel Henry Bunbury, MS letter dated 24 March 1856 (private collection).

22. Mary Seacole, op. cit., p. 216.

23. Cecil Woodham Smith, *Florence Nightingale 1820–1910*, p. 238.

24. Colonel Henry Bunbury, MS letter dated 21 April 1856 (private collection). Mrs Amoret Tanner tells me the snowdrop is now known as Warham's Seedling, after the soldier who brought it home from the Crimea.

25. According to the general docket book in the Public Record Office in London (ref. B6/100) George Ponsonby of 47 Mark Lane, London, was the principal petitioning creditor against Seacole and Day.

26. *The Times*, 9 January 1857.

27. Mary Seacole, op. cit., p. 227.

9 A Bold Front to Fortune

1. *Illustrated London News*, 30 August 1856.
2. Alexis Soyer, *A Culinary Campaign*, pp. 164, 267.
3. Claydon House Trust collection, MS Nightingale 110.
4. The family of Colonel Bunbury has been unstintingly generous in allowing me access to their illustrious forebear's letters and personal papers, for which I am heartily grateful.
5. *News of the World*, 31 August 1856.
6. *The Times*, 26 August 1856.
7. *Punch*, 25 October 1856.
8. Russell's manuscript diaries record his contacts with Mary after the war; they are held by the Archives of News International (who own *The Times*) in London, unfortunately with certain passages irrevocably excised by members of his family.
9. Mary Seacole, *Wonderful Adventures* (1984 edition), pp. 232–3.
10. *The Times*, 9 January 1857.
11. Ibid., 15 April 1857.
12. Ibid., 14 April 1857.
13. Lady Alicia Blackwood, *A Narrative of Personal Experiences . . . Throughout the Crimean War*, pp. 262–3.
14. *The Times*, 15 April 1857.
15. Ibid., 7 November 1856.
16. Ibid., 24 November 1856.
17. Ibid., 27 November 1856.
18. Ibid., 29 November 1856.
19. *Punch*, 6 December 1856.
20. Ibid., 30 May 1857.
21. *The Times*, 9 January 1857.
22. Ibid., 31 January 1857.
23. *Punch*, 5 September 1857.
24. The *News of the World* reported on 9 November 1856 that on Mrs Seacole's appearance in the Court of Bankruptcy 'the gaily-coloured decorations on her breast' were 'in perfect harmony with the rest of her attire'.
25. *Athenaeum Journal*, 25 July 1857, p. 936.
26. W.J. Stewart translated *Debtor and Creditor: A Romance* from the German of Gustav Freytag (published by Blackwood in 1857).
27. Mary's address by 8 May 1857 was 14 Soho Square; it was published in *Punch* on 30 May.
28. *Punch*, 30 May 1857.
29. Literature regarding the subscription fund is held in the Royal Archives (ref. PP Vic/1867/23078).

10 The Crimean Heroine

1. The starting-point for anyone interested in the life and work of Mary Seacole has to be Ziggi Alexander and Audrey Dewjee's excellent edition of *Wonderful Adventures* (1984).

2. The first autobiography by a black woman writer is arguably *A Narrative of the Life and Travels of Mrs Nancy Prince* (Boston, 1850); Nancy was a free Afro-American, born in 1799, who shook off her heritage of slavery to become a missionary. Three of her grandparents were 'stolen from Africa' and the other was a native American. Mary left home in Massachusetts at fourteen to work as a servant for a succession of cruel employers; in 1824 she married a black servant in the household of the Tsar and sailed with her husband to St Petersburg, returning after nearly ten years. As a widow, she travelled within America and twice to Jamaica, before publishing her autobiography. In 1831, rather confusingly, *The History of Mary Prince A West Indian Slave* was published, but this is more likely to be a biography by Susanna Strickland of a woman who escaped slavery in Antigua and joined the abolitionists in London.

3. Travel accounts by women were few and far between before the Austrian globe-trotter Ida Pfeiffer's highly popular books appeared in English in the early 1850s. See Jane Robinson, *Wayward Women*.

4. Mary's will left numerous bequests in favour of her sister, nephew and cousins. Not only did she enjoy her friends' company when she visited Jamaica, but she also invited them over to London: one, Rose Boydon, was staying with her when Mary died.

5. *Athenaeum Journal*, 25 July 1857, p. 937.

6. Taken from a notice in the collection of Southwark Local History archive (ref. O/S 725.76 SUR).

7. Paget was the son of the Marquis of Anglesey, and was second-in-command to Lord Cardigan at the Charge of the Light Brigade.

8. *The Times*, 28 July 1857.

9. Ibid.

10. Ibid., 31 August 1857.

11. Ibid., 27 July 1857.

12. Mary mentions Thomas's departure in *Wonderful Adventures* (1984 edition, p. 231); by the time she wrote her will in 1876, however, he was back in London.

13. *The Times*, 26 August 1857; the meeting was satirized in *Punch*, 5 September 1857.

14. *Illustrated London News*, 29 May 1858 and 5 June 1858.

15. As well as members of the Henriques family, members of the Ambleton family are recorded in the Catholic Baptism Registers in Kingston (1837–46).

16. Baptism Register of Holy Trinity Catholic Church 1852–1865, pp. 333, 337.

17. Anthony Trollope, *The West Indies and the Spanish Main*, pp. 14, 20–21.

18. According to Amelia Kennedy's Registration of Death (Kingston Parish Registers no. 732, November 1878).

19. There is an unsubstantiated statement to this effect on the Flamstead Heritage Society's website (www.nvo.com/tradejamaica/scrapbook7); if true, it's an interesting sidelight on Mary's status at home in Jamaica after the war. Queen Emma was a friend of Queen Victoria.

20. Mary and Count Gleichen, otherwise known as Prince Victor of Hohenlohe-Langenburg, had a soft spot for each other. He was one of Mary's 'kindest customers' at the British Hotel, calling her Mammy, and Mary left him one of her most precious possessions – Nelson's diamond ring – on her death. Sadly, his children died without issue, and I have been unable to trace the whereabouts of the ring.

21. Royal Archives, ref. RA PP/VIC/1867/23078. This material is reprinted with permission of Her Majesty Queen Elizabeth II, for which I am most grateful.
22. *Daily Gleaner* (Kingston), 29 August 1938.

11 Age and Consequence

1. Spain had offered its throne to a member of the Prussian royal family (Prussia being an area of what is now Germany); this enraged Emperor Napoleon III of France, who challenged Prussia to refuse the Spanish. This they did, but tensions remained and grew (due to some spirited and malicious propaganda) until war was declared between France and Prussia – who had the support of southern Germany – on 19 July 1870. The Prussian forces invaded France a fortnight later.
2. *The Times*, 19 July 1870.
3. The British Red Cross was not called such until 1905; its predecessor in Britain was the society born of this conflict, the British National Society for the Relief of the Sick and Wounded. Sir Harry Verney – who is supposed to have been rejected by Florence Nightingale before wedding her sister Parthenope – had a lifelong interest in medical welfare, both in his Buckinghamshire constituency and beyond.
4. *The Times*, 2 August 1870.
5. Claydon House Trust collection, MS 9004/60.
6. I believe these medals were the miniatures Mary awarded to herself, as discussed in Chapter 9. By the time she had her photograph taken in 1873, one seems to have gone missing: it's impossible, unfortunately, to tell which one. Perhaps it was only lent to her by Gleichen for the purposes of the sitting.
7. According to the Royal Academy's records, Gleichen's terracotta bust was entitled 'Mary Seacole, the celebrated Crimean heroine'.
8. Roger Fulford (ed.), *Your Dear Letter*, p. 106. Reprinted by kind permission of Her Majesty Queen Elizabeth II.
9. Major A.C. Whitehorne writing in the *Daily Gleaner*, 16 January 1938; quoted by Ziggi Alexander and Audrey Dewjee in Mary Seacole, *Wonderful Adventures*, 1984 edition, p. 37 (original source unseen).
10. *Daily Gleaner*, 29 August 1938.
11. The carte-de-visite – kindly brought to my attention by Professor Simon Schama and Amoret Tanner of the Tanner Collection – is signed 'Maull & Co., 187a Piccadilly and 68 Cheapside'. Maull only used that colophon between 1873 and 1878. I am indebted to Ruth Kitchin of the National Museum of Photography, Film and Television for this information.
12. Recorded in the 1881 census return.
13. William Neilson Farquharson was an eminent gentleman, recorded in the 1861 Jamaican Almanac as being a magistrate in the parish of St Elizabeth (which included Black River). In 1876 he was staying at the Royal Navy Club, known as the 'Thatched House Club' after the name of the tavern where its meetings were held, in St James's, London; he was the only one of her executors to survive Mary, and was present at the proving of her will in July 1881.
14. Florence Seacole Kent (aged nineteen) is named in the 1881 census return, living with her mother Sarah, two elder sisters and brother Herbert. Perhaps Ada had married and left home by then, or died.

15. *The Times,* 21 May 1881.
16. Information from the 1881 census return, where Mary's age was noted erroneously as seventy-one.
17. Mary's death certificate, dated 17 May 1881, registered in the district of Kensington (sub-district of St John Paddington), no. 444.
18. Henry Charles Moore, *Noble Deeds of the World's Heroines,* p. 134.
19. *Daily Gleaner,* 19 and 29 August 1938.
20. Members of Lignum Vitae Club in London, and the British Commonwealth Nurses' War Memorial Fund, together with the Jamaican Nurses' Association, were responsible for this. The Mary Seacole Memorial Association organizes the annual service at her graveside.
21. The Mary Seacole Leadership Award is administered by the Department of Health in London, and offers a substantial annual grant to a black or minority ethnic nurse, midwife or health visitor.
22. This was Captain Henry Bunbury.

Bibliography

Agard, John (ed.), *Life Doesn't Frighten Me* (London: Heinemann, 1989).

Alexander, Ziggi and Dewjee, Audrey, *Mary Seacole. Jamaican National Heroine and 'Doctress' in the Crimean War* (London: Brent Library Service, 1982).

Anon., *Jamaica . . . A Series of Letters written from Jamaica to a friend in England* (London: Rayner and Hodges, 1842).

Anon. [Taylor, C.F.], *Eastern Hospitals and English Nurses; the Narrative of twelve months' experience in the hospitals of Koulali and Scutari by a Lady Volunteer* (London: Hurst and Blackett, 1856).

Anon. [Nicol, M.], *Ismeer, by a Lady* (London: James Madden, 1856).

Anon., *A Story of Active Service in Foreign Lands by An Edinburgh Boy* (Edinburgh: Blackwood, 1886).

Arthur, Sir George, *Queen Alexandra* (London: Chapman and Hall, 1934).

Astley, Sir John, *Fifty Years of My Life* (London: Hurst and Blackett, 1894).

Athenaeum Journal (London: James Holmes, 25 July 1857).

Austen, Jane *The Works* (ed. J. Bailey) (London: Nash and Grayson, 1927).

Ayensu, E., *Medicinal Plants of the West Indies* (Algonac: Reference Publications, 1981).

Backhouse, Frances (ed.), *Women of the Klondike* (Vancouver: White Cap, 1995).

Baker, Christopher, *Jamaica* (London: Lonely Planet, 2000).

Bamfield, Victoria, *On the Strength: The Story of the British Army Wife* (London: Charles Knight, 1974).

Bassett, C., *Mary Seacole* (*Nursing Standard*, vol. 6, 1992).

Battiscombe, Georgina, *Queen Alexandra* (London: Constable, 1969).

Bickell, R., *The West Indies as They Are* (London: Hatchard, 1825).

Bigelow, John, *Jamaica in 1850* (New York: Putnam, 1851).

Blackwood, Lady Alicia, *A Narrative of Personal Experiences . . . Throughout the Crimean War* (London: Hatchard, 1881).

Bolt, Christine, *Victorian Attitudes to Race* (London: Routledge and Kegan Paul, 1971).

Brathwaite, Edward, *The Development of Creole Society in Jamaica 1770–1820* (Oxford: Clarendon Press, 1971).

Briggs, Asa, *Victorian People 1851–67* (Chicago: Chicago University Press, 1970).

[British Army] *Local Regulations and Orders for the Troops, Serving in the West India Command, and Her Majesty's Colonies on the South American Continent* (London, 1843).

British Catalogue of Books June 15–30, 1857 (London: Sampson, Low, 1857).

Brooke, Elisabeth, *Women Healers Through History* (London: Women's Press, 1993).

Browning, Elizabeth Barrett, *Aurora Leigh* (London: Women's Press, 1978).

Bryant, A., *The Age of Elegance 1812–1822* (London: Reprint Society, 1954).

Buchanan, George, *Camp Life. As Seen by a Civilian* (Glasgow: Maclehose, 1871).

Buzzard, Thomas, *With the Turkish Army in the Crimea and Asia Minor* (London: John Murray, 1915).

Campbell, Colin Frederick, *Letters from Camp* (London: Bentley, 1894).

Carlyle, Thomas, *Occasional Discourse on The Nigger Question* (London: Bosworth, 1853).

Carmichael, Mrs., *Domestic Manners and Social Conditions of the White, Coloured, and Negro Population of the West Indies* (London: Whittaker and Treacher, 1833).

Carnegie, 'Black Nurses at the Front', *American Journal of Nursing*, vol. 84, (1984).

————, M., *The Path We Tread* (Philadelphia: Lippincott, 2000).

Carter, Violet Bonham (ed.), *Surgeon in the Crimea* (London: Constable, 1968).

Clifford, Henry, *His Letters and Sketches from the Crimea* (London: Michael Joseph, 1956).

Cobbett, William, *The Emigrant's Guide* (London: the author, 1829).

Coleman, Terry, *Nelson* (London: Bloomsbury, 2001).

Compton, Piers, *Colonel's Lady and Camp-Follower. The Story of Women in the Crimean War* (London: Hale, 1970).

Cook, E., *The Life of Florence Nightingale* (London: Macmillan, 1914).

Cooper, Helen, 'England: The Imagined Community of Aurora Leigh and Mrs Seacole', *Studies in Browning and his Circle*, vol. 20 (1993).

Crawford, P., 'The Other Lady with the Lamp', *Nursing Times*, vol. 88, no. 11 (1992).

Cruchley, George, *Cruchley's Picture of London* (London: Cruchley, 1865).

Dancer, Thomas, *The Medical Assistant; or Jamaican Practice of Physic. Designed Chiefly for the Use of Families and Plantations* (Kingston: Alexander Aikman, 1801).

Delany, A., *A History of the Catholic Church in Jamaica* (New York: Jesuit Press, 1930).

Duberly, Mrs Henry (Fanny), *Journal kept during the Russian War . . .* (London: Longman, 1855).

Duff, David, *Alexandra: Princess and Queen* (London: Collins, 1980).

Duperly, Adolphe, *Daguerian Excursions in Jamaica* (Kingston: A. Duperly [n.d.]).

Edgerton, Robert, *Death or Glory: The Legacy of the Crimean War* (Boulder: Westview, 1999).

Edwards, Paul and Dabydeen, David (eds.), *Black Writers in Britain 1760–1890* (Edinburgh: Edinburgh University Press, 1991).

Egan, Pierce, *Life in London* (London: Sherwood, Neely and Jones, 1820–1).

Equiano, Olaudah, *Equiano's Travels . . .* (ed. Paul Edwards) (London: Heinemann, 1967).

Fabens, Joseph W., *A Story of Life on the Isthmus* (New York: Putnam, 1853).

Falconbridge, Anna Maria, *Narrative of Two Voyages to the River Sierra Leone during the*

Years 1791–2–3 . . . Also the Present State of the Slave Trade in the West Indies and the Improbability of its Total Abolition (London: Higham, 1802).

Ferguson, Moira (ed.), *Nine Black Women. An Anthology of Nineteenth-Century Writers from the United States, Canada, Bermuda, and the Caribbean* (New York: Routledge, 1998).

Ffrench-Blake, R., *The Crimean War* (London: Cooper, 1971).

File, Nigel and Power, Chris, *Black Settlers in Britain 1555–1958* (London: Heinemann, 1981).

Fish, Cheryl, *Black and White Women's Travel Narratives* (Gainesville: University Press of Florida, 2004).

Fletcher, Ian and Ischenko, Natalia, *The Crimean War: A Clash of Empires* (Staplehurst: Spellmount, 2004).

Fraser, Flora, *Beloved Emma. The Life of Emma, Lady Hamilton* (London: Weidenfeld and Nicolson, 1994).

Frederick, Rhona, 'Creole Performance in *Wonderful Adventures of Mrs Seacole in Many Lands*', *Gender and History*, vol. 15, no. 3 (2003).

Fryer, Peter, *Staying Power* (London: Pluto, 1984).

Fulford, Roger (ed.), *Your Dear Letter. Private Correspondence of Queen Victoria and the Crown Princess of Prussia 1865-1871* (London: Evans, 1971).

Furst, L. (ed.), *Women Healers and Physicians: Climbing a Long Hill* (Lexington: University Press of Kentucky, 1997).

Galt, Edwin, *The Camp and the Cutter; or, A Cruise to the Crimea* (London: Hodgson, 1856).

Gernsheim, Helmut and Alison, *Roger Fenton Photographer of the Crimean War* (London: Secker and Warburg, 1954).

Gerzina, Gretchen, *Black England. Life Before Emancipation* (London: John Murray, 1995).

Gikandi, Simon, *Maps of Englishness. Writing Identity in the Culture of Colonialism* (New York: Columbia University Press, 1996).

Gilbert, O., *Narrative of Sojourner Truth* (New York: Arno Press, 1968).

Gilmore, John, *Faces of the Caribbean* (London: Latin America Bureau, 2000).

Golby, J.M., *Culture and Society in Britain 1850–90* (Oxford: OUP, 1986).

Goldie, Sue, *Calendar of the Letters of Florence Nightingale* (Oxford: Oxford Microforms, 1983).

———— (ed.), *'I have done my duty': Florence Nightingale in the Crimean War 1854–1856* (Manchester: Manchester University Press, 1987).

Gomm, W., *The Story of Newcastle* (Westminster: for private circulation, 1864).

Goodman, Margaret, *Experiences of an English Sister of Mercy* (London: Smith, Elder, 1862).

Gowing, Timothy, *A Soldier's Experience, or, A Voice from the Ranks; Showing the Cost of War in Blood and Treasure* (Norwich: for the author, 1884).

Griswold, C.D., *The Isthmus of Panama and What I Saw There* (New York: Dewitt and Davenport, 1852).

Gustafson, M., 'Mary Seacole, the Florence Nightingale of Jamaica', *Christian Nurse International*, vol. 12, no. 4 (1996).

Handbook of Jamaica . . . by Two Members of the Jamaica Civil Service (Kingston: Jamaica Government Printing Establishment, 1881).

Hartshorne, H. *Household Cyclopaedia of General Information* (Philadelphia: Zell, 1881).

Hawthorne, Evelyn, 'Self-Writing, Literary Traditions, and Post-emancipation Identity: the Case of Mary Seacole', *Biography*, vol. 23, no. 2 (2000).

Henriques, Fernando, *Children of Caliban: Miscegenation* (London: Secker and Warburg, 1974).

Hibbert, *The Destruction of Lord Raglan* (London: Longman, 1961).

————, Christopher, *London: The Biography of a City* (London: Allen Lane, 1977).

————, *Nelson. A Personal History* (London: Penguin, 1995).

Holmes, Rachel, *Scanty Particulars: The Life of Dr James Barry* (London: Viking, 2002).

Hornby, Lady, *Constantinople During the Crimean War* (London: Bentley, 1863).

Hume, Hamilton, *The Life of Edward John Eyre, Late Governor of Jamaica* (London: Bentley, 1867).

Hurwitz, Samuel and Edith, *Jamaica. A Historical Portrait* (London: Pall Mall Press, 1971).

Hussey, H., *The Australian Colonies; Together with notes of a Voyage from Australia to Panama in the 'Golden Age'* (London: Burt [n.d.]).

Innes, C.L., *A History of Black and Asian Writing in Britain 1700–2000* (Cambridge: CUP, 1992).

Iveson-Iveson, J. 'The Forgotten Heroine', *Nursing Mirror*, vol. 157 (1983).

Jacobs, Harriet, *Incidents in the Life of a Slave Girl* (ed. V. Smith) (New York: OUP, 1988).

Josephs, Aleric, 'Mary Seacole: Jamaican Nurse and "Doctress"', *Jamaican Historical Review*, vol. 17 (1991).

Judd, Catherine, *Bedside Seductions. Nursing and the Victorian Imagination 1830–1880* (London: Macmillan, 1998).

Kelly, Mrs Tom, *From the Fleet in the Fifties* (London: Hurst and Blackett, 1902).

Khan, H., 'Remembering Mary Seacole', *West Indian Digest* (June 1981).

Kilham, Hannah, *A Report on a Recent Visit to the Colony of Sierra Leone* (London: William Phillips, 1828).

King, A., 'Mary Seacole', *Essence*, vol. 4., nos 11 and 12 (1974).

Kinglake, A.W., *The Invasion of the Crimea* (Edinburgh: Blackwood, 1863–87).

Laguerre, Michel, *Afro-Caribbean Folk Medicine* (South Hadley: Bergin and Garvey, 1987).

Liot, W.B., *Panama, Nicaragua, and Tehuantepec* (London: Simpkin and Marshall, 1849).

Long, Edward, *The History of Jamaica* (London: Cass, 1970).

Lorimer, Douglas, *Colour, Class and the Victorians. English Attitudes to the Negro in the Mid Nineteenth Century* (Leicester: Leicester University Press, 1978).

Lowe, Emily [Anon.], *Unprotected Females in Norway* (London: Routledge, 1857).

Madol, H. *The Private Life of Queen Alexandra* (London: Hutchinson, 1940).

Malam, John, *Tell Me About Pioneers: Mary Seacole* (London: Evans, 1999).

Maryatt, F., *Mountains and Molehills or Recollections of a Burnt Journal* (London: Longman, 1855).

McKenna, Bernard, 'Fancies of Exclusive Possession: Validation and Dissociation in Mary Seacole's England and Caribbean', *Philological Quarterly*, vol. 76, no. 2 (1997).

Messmer, P.R. and Parchment, Y., 'Mary Grant Seacole: the First Nurse Practitioner', *Clinical Excellence for Nurse Practitioners*, vol. 2, no. 1 (1998).

Mills, Therese, *Great West Indians* (Kingston: Longman Caribbean, 1973).

Montez, Lola, *Autobiography and Lectures* (London: James Blackwood, 1858).

Moorcroft, Christine and Magnusson, Magnus, *Famous People: Mary Seacole 1805–1881* (London: Channel 4, 1998).

Moore, Henry Charles, *Noble Deeds of the World's Heroines* (London: Religious Tract Society [1903]).

Morris, Helen, *Portrait of a Chef* (Oxford: OUP, 1980).

Nelson, Admiral Lord Horatio, *The Letters of Lord Nelson to Lady Hamilton* (London: Thomas Lovewell, 1814).

Nicolas, Sir Harris (ed.), *Dispatches and Letters of Vice-Admiral Lord Viscount Nelson* (London: Colburn, 1844–6).

Norman, Edward, *Roman Catholicism in England* (Oxford: OUP, 1985).

Nugent, Lady Maria (ed. Philip Wright), *Lady Nugent's Journal of her Residence in Jamaica from 1801–1805* (Kingston: Institute of Jamaica, 1966).

Okokon, S., *Black Londoners 1880–1990* (Stroud: Sutton, 1998).

Oliver, Vere Langford, *Caribbeana* (London: Mitchell, Hughes and Clarke, 1909–19).

Osborne, Francis, *A History of the Catholic Church in Jamaica* (Chicago: Loyola University Press, 1988).

Palmer, Alan, *The Banner of Battle: The Story of the Crimean War* (London: Weidenfeld and Nicolson, 1987).

Paquet, Sandra Pouchon, 'Mary Seacole: The Enigma of Arrival', *African American Review*, vol. 26, no. 4 (1992).

Plato, Ann, *Essays* (ed. K.J. Williams) (New York: OUP, 1988).

Pollitt, N., 'Forgotten Heroine', *Times Educational Supplement*, no. 3965 (1992).

Porter, Roy, *London. A Social History* (London: Hamish Hamilton, 1994).

Prince, Mary, *The History of Mary Prince A West Indian Slave* (ed. S. Salih) (London: Penguin, 2000).

Prince, Nancy, *A Narrative of the Life and Travels* (ed. R.G. Walters) (Princeton: Weiner, 1995).

Pritchard, R.E. (ed.), *Dickens's England. Life in Victorian Times* (Stroud: Sutton, 2002).

Publishers' Circular and Booksellers' Record (London: 1837–1859).

Reid, Douglas Arthur, *Memories of the Crimean War* (London: St Catherine Press, 1911).

Rhys, Jean, *The Wide Sargasso Sea* (ed. H. Jenkins) (London: Penguin, 2001).

Robins, Major Colin, *Captain Dunscombe's Diary: The Real Crimean War* (Bowdon: Withycut House, 2003).

Robinson, Amy, 'Authority and the Public Display of Identity: *Wonderful Adventures of Mrs Seacole in Many Lands*', *Feminist Studies*, vol. 20, no. 3 (1994).

Robinson, Jane, *Wayward Women: A Guide to Women Travellers* (Oxford: OUP, 1990).

————, *Parrot Pie for Breakfast: An Anthology of Women Pioneers* (Oxford: OUP, 1999).

————, *Pandora's Daughters: The Secret History of Enterprising Women* (London: Constable and Robinson, 2002).

Rogers, J.A., *The World's Great Men of Colour* (New York: Macmillan, 1972).

Royle, Trevor, *Crimea: The Great Crimean War 1854–1856* (London: Little, Brown, 1999).

Russell, Sir William Howard, *Russell's Despatches from the Crimea 1854–1856* (ed. N. Bentley) (London: Deutsch, 1966).

————, *The War: from the landing at Gallipoli . . . to the evacuation of the Crimea* (London: Routledge, 1856).

Sala, G.A., *Twice Round the Clock* (London: Houlston and Wright, 1859).

Schaw, Janet, *Journal of a Lady of Quality; Being the Narrative of a Journey from Scotland to the West Indies . . .* (ed. E.W. Andrews) (New Haven: Yale University Press, 1939).

Seacole, Mary, *Wonderful Adventures of Mrs Seacole in Many Lands* (London: James Blackwood, 1857).

————, *Wonderful Adventures . . .* (ed. Z. Alexander and A. Dewjee) (Bristol: Falling Wall Press, 1984).

————, *Wonderful Adventures . . .* (ed. W. Andrews) (New York: OUP, 1988).

Seaman, L.C.B., *Life in Victorian London* (London: Batsford, 1973).

Seymour, Bruce, *Lola Montez. A Life* (New Haven: Yale University Press, 1996).

Shepherd, John, *The Crimean Doctors. A History of the British Medical Services in the Crimean War* (Liverpool: Liverpool University Press, 1991).

Shepherd, Verene, Brereton, Bridget and Bailey, Barbara (eds), *Engendering History* (London: J. Currey, 1995).

Sheridan, Richard, *Doctors and Slaves. A Medical and Demographic History of Slavery in the British West Indies 1680–1834* (Cambridge: CUP, 1985).

Simond, Louis, *Journal of a Tour and Residence in Great Britain During the Years 1810 and 1811* (London: John Murray, 1823).

Simpson, William, *The Seat of War in the East from Eighty-one Drawings made During the War in the Crimea* (London: Day and Son, 1902).

————, *The Autobiography of William Simpson RI* (ed. G. Eyre-Todd) (London: T. Fisher Unwin, 1903).

Small, Hugh, *Florence Nightingale: Avenging Angel* (London: Constable, 1998).

Smith, J.P., 'Mary Jane Seacole', *Journal of Advanced Nursing*, vol. 9, no. 5 (1984).

Soule, Frank, Gillon, John and Nisbet, James, *The Annals of San Francisco* (New York: Appleton, 1855).

Soyer, Alexis, *A Culinary Campaign* (eds M. Barthorp and E. Ray) (Lewes: Southover Press, 1995).

Stewart, J., *A View of the Past and Present State of the Island of Jamaica* (Edinburgh: Oliver and Boyd, 1823).

Stewart, William J. (trans.), *Debtor and Creditor: A Romance . . . from the German of Gustav Freytag* (London: James Blackwood, 1857).

Stuart Wortley, Lady Emmeline, *Travels in the United States, etc. during 1849 and 1850* (London: Bentley, 1851).

Stuart Wortley, Victoria, *A Young Traveller's Journal of a Tour in North and South America* (London: Bosworth, 1852).

Summers, Anne, *Angels and Citizens. British Women as Military Nurses 1854–1914* (London: Routledge and Kegan Paul, 1988).

Sweetman, John, *The Crimean War* (Oxford: Osprey, 2001).

Swinburne, Henry, *The Courts of Europe at the Close of the Last Century* (London: Colburn, 1841).

Taylor, George Cavendish, *Journal of Adventures with the British Army* (London: Hurst and Blackett, 1856).

Terrot, Sarah Anne, *Nurse Sarah Anne. With Florence Nightingale at Scutari* (ed. R. G. Richardson) (London: John Murray, 1977).

The Iron Duke: Journal of the Duke of Wellington's Regiment (Aldershot, 1925–).

Tisdall, E.E.P., *Mrs Duberly's Campaigns* (London: Jarrolds, 1963).

Tomes, R., *Panama in 1855* (New York: Harper, 1855).

Trollope, Anthony, *The West Indies and the Spanish Main* (London: Cass, 1968).

Tyrrell, Henry, *The History of the War* (London: Printing and Publishing Co., 1855–8).

Vernon, C., 'The Story of Mary Seacole', *Jamaican Nurse*, vol. 25 (1986).

Vicars, Capt. Hedley, *Memorials . . .* (ed. C. Marsh) (London: James Nisbet, 1856).

Vieth, Frederick, *Recollections of the Crimean Campaign* (Montreal: John Lovell, 1907).

Vulliamy, C., *Crimea. The Campaign of 1854–56* (London: Cape, 1939).

W., J., *Perils, Pastimes and Pleasures of an Emigrant in Australia, Vancouver Island and California* (London: Thomas Cautley Newby, 1849).

Walsh, B., *Catherine Hayes: The Hibernian Prima Donna* (Ballsbridge: Irish Academic Press, 2000).

Walvin, James, *The Black Presence. A Documentary History of the Negro in England 1555–1860* (London: Orbach and Chambers, 1971).

————— *Black and White. The Negro and English Society* (London: Allen Lane, 1973).

Weinreb, Ben and Hibbert, Christopher, *The London Encyclopaedia* (London: Macmillan, 1983).

Wheatley, Phillis, *Complete Writings* (ed. V. Carretta) (New York: Penguin, 2001).

White, Deborah Gray, *Ar'n't I a Woman? Female Slaves in the Plantation South* (New York: Norton, 1899).

Whiteley, Henry, *Three Months in Jamaica in 1832* (Newcastle: for the Anti-Slavery Society, 1833).

Williams, Cynric, *A Tour through Jamaica* (London: Thomas Hunt, 1826).

Williams, Jane (ed.), *The Autobiography of Elizabeth Davis. Betsy Cadwalladyr. A Balaclava Nurse* (London: Hurst and Blackett, 1857).

Wilson, Harriet E., *Our Nig, or Sketches from the Life of a Free Black* (ed. R.J. Ellis) (Nottingham: Trent Editions, 1998).

Woodham Smith, Cecil, *Florence Nightingale 1820–1910* (London: Constable, 1950).

Index

Abd Al-Majid   78, 79
ague   44
Albert, Prince of Wales (later,
    Edward VII)   186, 193
Aldershot   126, 154, 157
Alexandra, Princess (later,
    Queen Alexandra)   193–4
Alma, Battle of the   82, 113,
    139
Ambleton, Edward
        (brother)   10, 12, 21,
        68, 72
    death   197
    New Granadian hotel and
        stores   42, 47–8, 50, 51, 60,
        62, 63
Ambleton, Edward
        (nephew)   10, 182,
        183, 196
American War of
    Independence   6
army catering   116–17
army rations   116

Athenaeum   167
Austen, Jane   19

Baartman, Sara ('Hottentot
    Venus')   17, 124
Bakunina, Ekaterina   139
Balaklava   91, 101, 104–6, 114
    Battle of Balaklava   113
Barber, Francis   17
Barnard, Sir Henry   162
Beckford, Charlotte   29
Bigelow, Mr (visitor to
    Jamaica)   38–9
Bird, Isabella   49
Black River   32, 34, 155
Blackwood, Lady Alicia   109,
    140, 159–60
Blackwood, James   67–8,
    168, 183
Blundell Hall   9, 14, 22, 29, 30
Bogle, Paul   184
Boxer, Port-Admiral   106–7
Boydon, Rose   197

Bracebridge, Selina   102, 103, 104, 140
British Hotel, Cruces   55–6
British Hotel, Spring Hill   91, 171–2
  closing down   150–2
  creditors and debtors   146–7, 149–50, 154, 157, 159, 165
  description of   111–12
  establishment   11, 106–9, 110
  Florence Nightingale's allegations against   122–3, 124, 125
  menus and provisions   117–18, 119–20, 127–8, 146
  and the Sevastopol race meeting   147–8
  thieving from   129–30
British National Society for the Relief of the Sick and Wounded in War   190
British Red Cross   190
Buchanan, George   127–8
Bunbury, Sir Henry   155
Butler, Nell   138, 139

Calcutta   180
California Gold Rush   40–1
Cambridge, Duke of   115, 147, 180, 186
Cambridge Institution for Soldiers' Orphans   196
camp-followers   96, 101
Campbell, Major-General Sir John   108, 110, 132, 178
Canning, Charlotte   180
Caroline of Brunswick   15
Cashman, Nellie   72
Cathcart's Hill   131–2
cedron   68
Charge of the Light Brigade   1, 90, 105
Chelsea pensioners   84
Chenery, Thomas   83, 84

chloroform   139
cholera epidemics   50–5, 68
  Crimea   82
  Jamaica   36–7
  New Granada   50–5, 68
Christmas Rebellion (1831)   27–8, 29
Church Missionary Society   49
Church of the Nativity, Bethlehem   78, 80
Cochrane, Louisa   21, 195
Codrington, Sir William   138
Community of the Cross   139
Constantinople   99–100
Cook, Thomas   64
Cooper, Captain   187, 193
Coppock, James   180
Cornwallis, Couba   8
Covent Garden Market   157–8
Cox, Major Samuel   108
Creoles   7, 29, 37, 155, 173
Crimean Fund   90
Crimean War   1, 75–154
  administrative and military mismanagement   113–14, 123
  Armistice   146
  army catering   116–17
  army rations   116
  background to   78–80
  British campaign   113–14
  Charge of the Light Brigade   1, 90, 105
  Crimean nurses   71, 87, 100–1, 139–41
  evacuation of the peninsula   149, 153
  government-commissioned nursing service   85–6, 87
  Mary Seacole's nursing activities   102, 107–8, 131, 142, 143, 159–60, 162–3
  newspaper dispatches   76–7, 83, 84, 143

postwar celebrations 156–7
sightseers 127, 138
soldiers' wives 96–7, 138–9,
140–1
Cruces, New Granada 42,
47–63, 68
British Hotel 55–6, 57–8,
59–61
Independent Hotel 47,
48–50, 51, 60, 62, 63
Cuba 26–7
A Culinary Campaign
(Soyer) 116–17, 122

Dancer, Thomas 8
Darien 46
Date Tree Hall 22
Davis, Betsy 125–6
Day, Thomas 180
Aldershot business 126,
154, 157
bankruptcy 160–1, 165–6
business partnership with Mary
Seacole 91, 100, 105, 106,
120, 130, 137, 145, 150, 154,
157, 159
legacy to 195–6
livery and horse-trading
business 145, 159
mine superintendent 72, 73
Delany, Martin Robson 206n 2
doctresses 7–8, 11, 22–3, 24–5
Donizetti, Gaetano 169
dropsy 44
drunkenness 122, 125
Duberly, Fanny 105, 132, 138

Emma, Queen 185
Equiano, Olaudah 17
Escribanos, New Granada 72–4
Evans, Elizabeth 138–9
Eyre, Edward 184–5

Falconbridge, Anna Maria 4

Fane Keane, Colonel
Hussey 162, 196
Farquharson, William
Neilson 195
field stove 116
Fort Bowen Mine 72, 73
France
Franco-Prussian War 188,
189–90, 192
French Revolution 6
see also Crimean War
Francis (cook) 120, 145,
146, 154
Frankfurt 190
French, George and Edward 29

Garfield, Thomas 145, 146
Gentleman's Magazine 17
George IV 15
Gibraltar 94–5
Gleichen, Count 167, 186, 192,
196, 197
Gordon, George 184
Gorgona, New Granada 47, 61,
63–4
Grant, James (father) 11, 12,
14, 35
Grant, Louisa (sister) 10, 12,
21, 25, 43, 80, 183–4, 196
death 198–9
Mary Seacole's bequest
to 196, 197–8
Grant, Ulysses Simpson 54
Great Exhibition (1851) 115
Greek Orthodox Church 78
Grundy, Mrs (Crimean
nurse) 71

Hall, Dr John 121, 142
Hamilton, Lady 30, 31
Hayes, Catherine 64
Henriques family 11, 183
Henriques, Amos 195, 197
Henriques, David 195

Henriques, Edward 195
Henriques, Ernest 195
Henriques, Josephine 195
Henriques, Julia 195
herbal medicine 7–8, 12
Herbert, Elizabeth 86, 89,
 125, 173
Herbert, Sidney 85, 87
Hessel, Phoebe 81
History of Jamaica (Long) 4
Hodgson, Lady 137
Hollander 91, 92, 94
hospitals
 Balaklava 101
 Kingston naval hospital 8, 23
 Koulali 101
 Land Transport Hospital,
  Spring Hill 126, 169
 Renkioi 101
 Russian hospital,
  Sevastopol 136–7, 139
 Scutari 82–3, 84, 85, 100–4,
  148–9
 slave hospitals 4, 23
 Smyrna 101
 Up-Park military hospital 35,
  71
Hottentot Venus *see* Baartman,
 Sara

Illustrated London News 121, 153
Independent Hotel, Cruces 47,
 48–50, 51, 60, 62, 63
Indian Mutiny 169, 174–5,
 179–80
Industrial Revolution 15
Inkerman 101, 113
Institute of Jamaica 167
Irish famine 115

Jamaica 2–10
 Black River 32, 34, 155
 British Crown Colony 185
 cholera epidemic 36–7
 climate 3, 93
 doctresses 7–8, 11, 22–3,
  24–5
 earthquake (1692) 2
 economy 6
 emancipation, effect of 28
 Kingston 5, 8
 miscegenation 6, 9–10, 29
 Morant Bay rebellion
  (1865) 184–5
 Newcastle 35, 37, 172
 nurses 23–4
 Obeah and Myalism 22–3
 plantocracy 5–6, 28, 37
 Port Royal 2, 8
 slave trade 4–5, 6
 Up-Park Camp 22, 23, 35, 71,
  89, 172
 yellow fever 8, 25, 35,
  70–1, 72
James, Thomas 65
'Jane' (mother) 10, 11, 14,
  21–2, 26, 173
 death 33
 doctress 7, 11, 25
 lodging-housekeeper 8–9
Jew Johnny (Mary Seacole's
  servant) 99, 108, 145, 154
Johnson, Samuel 17
Jones, Elizabeth Emma 115
Jordan, Edward 184
Jose (New Granadian
  barber) 59
Jullien, Louis 176–7, 179, 183

Kadikoi 108–9, 119, 126,
  127, 144
 see also Spring Hill
Kaiserwerth 23, 86
Kalamita Bay 113
Kamiesch 119, 126
Kangaroo 83
Kennedy, Amelia 21, 184, 195,
  205n 1

Kent, Ada 195
Kent, Florence 195
Kent, Sarah 197
Kent, William 197
Kingsley, Mary 45–6, 49
Kingston, Jamaica 2–4, 5, 8, 183, 185
  Blundell Hall 9, 14, 22, 29, 30
  fire (1843) 32–3
  naval hospital 8, 23
  New Blundell Hall 33, 35, 37, 70, 185, 197
  Port Royal 2, 8
  public hospital 23
Kitty the Schemer (gambler) 41
Knight, William 159, 165
Koulali 101

Land Transport Hospital, Spring Hill 126, 169
Lemon, Mark 163
letters of introduction 98
London 15–16, 17–19, 183
  black population 17
  Covent Garden Market 157–8
  Great Exhibition (1851) 115
  St Mary's Catholic cemetery 181, 188
  Surrey Gardens 156–7
  West India Dock 15
London Gazette 160
Long, Edward 4
Lowe, Emily 95
Lucan, Lord 97
Lucknow 180
Ludwig of Bavaria, King 65

Mac (Mary Seacole's servant) 43, 45, 46, 47, 50, 59, 69
McAuley, Catherine 71
Madonna painting 138

Malta 96
Mapp, Mad Sally 121
Mary (Mary Seacole's maid) 43, 59, 69
Mary Seacole Award 200
Mary Seacole Memorial Association 215n 20
Maull & Company 194
Menshikov, Prince Alexander 78–9
Michailova, Darya 139–40
Moldavia 79
Montenegro 79
Montez, Lola 65–8, 122
Morant Bay rebellion (1865) 184–5
Morning Chronicle 121, 142
Morning Herald 159
Moustache, Madame (gambler) 41
Mrs Seacole's Wonderful Adventures in Many Lands xii-xiii, 6–7, 66, 67, 121, 171–5, 199
  composition 168
  extracts 19–20, 30, 32, 33, 34, 44, 45, 46, 48–9, 50, 51, 58, 61, 62–3, 69, 81, 87–8, 89–91, 100, 102, 109, 111–12, 129–30, 148, 151, 158
  illustrations 171–2
  popular success 174, 180–1
  publication 170, 171
mulattos 6, 7, 9, 10, 27, 28, 29
muriatic acid 46
mustees 6
mustiphinis 6
Myalism 22, 23

Nachimoff, Admiral 76
Napoleon Bonaparte 14, 15
Napoleon III 78
Nassau 26
Navy Bay 40, 44–5, 68, 70, 72
Nelson, Horatio 30

Nelson, Lord   8, 30–1, 32,
        94, 196
    and the Seacole family   30–1
New Blundell Hall   33, 35, 37,
        70, 185, 197
New Granada   40, 41–70, 72–4
    cholera epidemic   50–5
    Cruces   42, 47–63, 68
    Escribanos   72–4
    Gorgona   47, 61, 63–4
    Navy Bay   40, 44–5, 68, 70, 72
New Providence   26
Newcastle, Jamaica   35, 37, 172
News of the World   147, 156
Nicholas I, Tsar   78
Nightingale, Florence   23, 71,
        115, 139, 140, 182, 190
    at Scutari   100–4, 148–9
    authority and discipline   86–7,
        125–6
    class consciousness   86–7, 122
    illness   119, 123, 157
    London hospital
        superintendent   86
    meets Mary Seacole   103–4
    nursing training   23
    opinion of Mary
        Seacole   122–3, 124, 126,
        128, 155, 190–1
    public adulation   103, 157,
        158, 161
    qualities   140, 155
    on recruiting nurses   103
    requested to organize Crimean
        nursing service   85
    and Sally Seacole   154–5
97th Regiment   35–6, 77, 132–3
Noble Deeds of the World's Heroines
        (Religious Tract
        Society)   198
Norman, Matilda   96–7
Nugent, Lady Maria   3, 9–10,
        14, 24, 175
nurses

American nurses   71
Crimean nurses   71, 87,
        100–1, 139–41
    disreputable behavior   23–4
    early military nursing
        services   71
    Jamaican nurses   23–4
    professionalization   23, 140
    recruitment   89
    religious orders   23, 71, 86,
        125, 139, 140
    soldiers' wives   138–9

Obeah   22, 23, 24
octoroons   6
Ottoman Empire   78, 79, 80

Paget, Lord George   177
Paine, Tom   4
Palmerston, Lord   166, 180
Panama   40–1, 54, 75
    see also New Granada
Panama Railroad Company   44
Panmure, Lord   179–80, 192
patroness, Jamaican
        (unnamed)   12–13, 22, 26
Paulet, Lord William   121, 142
Pavlovna, Grand Duchess
        Elena   139
Pera   99
Pfeiffer, Ida   49
Pirogov, Nikolai   139
plant-hunting   149, 200–1
Ponsonby, George   150, 159
prejudice   13, 16, 37, 45, 58,
        90, 173
    American   41, 45
    Mary Seacole's experience
        of   16, 45, 62–3, 69, 90,
        173
Prince, Nancy   49
Prittlewell   30
Public Record Office   204n 23
Punch   121, 163, 165, 169

quadroons 6, 7
quinine 68
quintroons 6

Raglan, Lord 118–19, 142
raki 122, 126
rats 120, 145
Reeves, John Sims 178
Reform Club 115, 161
Reid, Dr Douglas 107, 121
religious nursing orders 71, 86,
 125, 139, 140
Religious Tract Society 198
Renkioi 101
Rokeby, Lord 168
 Mary Seacole's bequest to 32,
  196
 and the Seacole
  Testimonial 162, 163, 175,
  177, 179, 185–6
Roman Catholicism 174, 181,
 182–3
Roots in Britain (exhibition)
 199
Royal American Regiment (60th
 Rifles) 10–11, 35
Royal Surrey Gardens
 Company 176, 179,
 180, 186
Rudersdorff, Erminia 178
Russell, W.H. (Billy) 66, 67,
 124, 139, 142, 150, 193
 Crimean War
  correspondent 82, 114,
  136–7
 friendship with Mary
  Seacole 121, 142, 158, 160,
  162, 168, 170, 183
 on Sevastopol 136–7
Russia see Crimean War
Russian Orthodox Church 78

St Mary's Catholic
 cemetery 181, 188

Saint-Domingue (Haiti) 6, 27–8
 Christmas Rebellion
  (1831) 27–8, 29
Salmon, Elizabeth 195
Salmon, Hon. John 195
sambos 6
Sancho, Ignatius 17
Sanitary Commission 114
Scutari 82–3, 84, 85, 100–4,
 148–9
Scutari teapot 116
Seacole, Ann 30
Seacole, Christopher
 Henricks 182, 183
Seacole, C.W. 30, 145,
 205n 14
Seacole, Edwin Horatio
 Hamilton (husband) 29,
 30, 31–2, 155
 death 33
 Nelson connection 30–1
Seacole, Mary
 African heritage, attitude
  towards 7, 29, 173–4, 200
 anglophile 13, 77, 145
 autobiography see Mrs Seacole's
  Wonderful Adventures in Many
  Lands
 bankruptcy 160–1, 165–6
 birth 7
 business partner see Day,
  Thomas
 characteristics xi-xii, 18, 22,
  40, 141, 200
 cholera epidemic
  experiences 36, 50–5, 68
 commercial enterprises
  17–19, 26, 32, 126, 154, 157
 contemporary accounts
  of 121–2, 142, 143, 144,
  156–7, 159–60, 162–3, 177,
  178, 187
 Crimean War
  experiences 75–154

death and burial   197, 198
doctress in Jamaica   24–6,
   70–2
dress style   46, 87, 101, 131,
   153, 194
early interest in
   medicine   11–12
family background   6–7, 8–9,
   10–11
first visits England   14–15
hand injury   114
hotel-keeping see Blundell
   Hall; British Hotel, Cruces;
   British Hotel, Spring Hill
and Lola Montez   65–8
marriage   29–30, 32
medals and decorations   167,
   200
meets Florence
   Nightingale   103–4
moral character   124–5
New Granadian
   adventure   41–70, 72–4
obituaries   198
Order of Merit   200
performs autopsy   52–3
photograph   194–5
portraits and busts   36, 142,
   167, 171, 192–3
posthumous reputation   xii,
   199–200
prejudice, experience of   16,
   45, 62–3, 69, 90, 173
public acclaim   156–7,
   178–9, 192
Roman Catholicism   174,
   181–3
royal friendships   192–4
Seacole Testimonial
   (subscription fund)   161–3,
   165–6, 168–9, 170, 175–9,
   185–7, 193
self-belief   200
snobbery   118–19, 128, 159

social position   13, 28–9
voyages   14, 19–20, 26–7,
   43–4, 92–6, 99–100, 104, 156
Will   7, 10, 32, 167, 195–6,
   197–8
Seacole, Sarah   145, 154–6, 196
Seacole, Thomas   30, 31
Seacole and Miller   30
Sellon, Miss (administrator of
   nursing order)   71, 86
Sevastopol   82, 113, 131, 143
   fall of   114, 132–3
   Mary Seacole's visit to   135–8
   race meeting   147–8
   Russian hospital   136–7, 139
Sharpe, Sam   27
Shaw Stewart, Mrs (Crimean
   nurse)   126
shipboard life   14
Sillery, Major   83
Simmett, Matilda   21, 195,
   205n 1
Simpson, William   121, 142
Sinope   76, 139
Sisters of Charity   86, 139
Sisters of Mercy   71
slave trade   4–6, 13, 22
   abolition   6, 27, 28
   slave religions   22–3
   slave revolts   6, 27–8
Smith, Elizabeth   71
Smyrna   101
Snell, Hannah   81
soldiers' wives   96–7, 138–9,
   140–1
Soyer, Alexis   115–16, 120, 122,
   130, 143, 145, 153, 154
   army catering reforms   116
   death   181
   friendship with Mary
      Seacole   110–11, 118–19,
      161, 172, 178, 181, 198
   philanthropy   115
Soyer, Philippe   115

Spring Hill 109, 152, 195
   see also British Hotel, Spring
      Hill
Stanley, Mary 88, 100, 208
Stewart, Mrs (Kingston
      acquaintance) 187–8
Stewart, W.J. 168
'A Stir for Seacole' 163–5
Strickland, Susanna 213n 2
Surrey Gardens, London 156–7
sutlers 126
Swinburne, Henry 94–5

The Times 76–7, 82, 83, 114,
      154, 156–7, 159, 161, 177,
      189–90, 196
Toussaint L'Ouverture, Francois-
      Dominique 204n 10
Trafalgar 94
Trollope, Anthony 10, 183–4
Turkey see Crimean War

Up-Park Camp 22, 23, 35, 71,
      89, 172

Valletta 96
Varna 82, 85
Verney, Sir Harry 190, 192
Vicars, Hedley 108, 182
Victoria, Crown Princess 190,
      193
Victoria, Queen 158, 186,
      192, 193

vivandieres 124, 139, 146, 147
Volusia 19–20, 21

Wallachia 79
War Office 87–8
Washington, George 71
Waterloo 14
Weekes, Henry 192–3
West Granada Mining
      Company 87
West India Dock 15
Wilberforce, William 4
Williams, Cynric 29
women
   camp-followers 96, 101
   Jamaican doctresses 7–8, 11,
      22–3, 24–5
   officers' wives 97
   prostitution 101, 124
   soldiers 81
   soldiers' wives 96–7, 138–9,
      140–1
   travellers 45–6, 49, 95, 137
   vivandieres 124, 139, 146,
      147
   women-only hotels 64
   see also nurses
Wortley, Lady Emmeline
      Stuart 58

yellow fever 8, 25, 35, 70–1, 72

Zebra Vicarage 109

A Brief History of The Crimean War
Alexis Troubetzkoy

'Theirs not to reason why,
Theirs but to do or die.'
.   **Alfred, Lord Tennyson**

In September 1854, the armies of Britain, France and Turkey invaded Russia, ostensibly over disputed access to the holy sites of Jerusalem. But few wars in history reveal greater confusion of purpose than this 'notoriously incompetent international butchery' (Hobsbawm). In the months that followed over half a million soldiers died from wounds, disease, starvation and sheer cold. We all know of the heroic folly of the Charge of the Light Brigade.

The Crimean War was a medieval conflict fought in a modern age. This new account by a Russian historian shows that the extraordinary struggle was fought not only in the Crimea, but also along the Danube, in the Arctic Ocean, in the Baltic and Pacific.

Much has been written about the war itself and Troubetzkoy does not aim to cover old ground, but traces its true causes and sketches a vivid picture of the age that made it possible.

Robinson paperback original
ISBN-13: 978-1-84529-420-5
ISBN-10: 1-84529-420-3
£8.99

A Brief History of Mysogyny
Jack Holland

Humanity's oldest prejudice?
A history of the war against women

In this powerful book, the highly respected writer and commentator Jack Holland sets out to answer a daunting question: how do you explain the oppression and brutalization of half the world's population by the other half, throughout history?

The result takes the reader on an eye-opening journey through centuries, continents and civilizations as it looks at both historical and contemporary attitudes to women. Holland's spotlight falls impartially on the Church, witch-hunts, sexual theory, Nazism and pro-life campaigners and on today's developing world, where women are increasingly and disproportionately at risk because of radicalized religious belief, famine, war and disease. Well-informed and researched, highly readable and often entertaining, this is no outmoded feminist polemic, but a refreshingly straightforward investigation into an ancient, pervasive and enduring injustice. It deals with the fundamentals of human existence – sex, love, violence – that have always shaped out lives. This important and timely book will make a long-lasting contribution.

'An invaluable addition . . . meticulously researched and briskly related.' *Sunday Times*

Robinson paperback original
ISBN-13: 978-1-84529-371-0
ISBN-10: 1-84529-371-1
£8.99